THE ESSENTIAL CORPORATION HANDBOOK

BY CARL R.J. SNIFFEN

The Oasis Press® / PSI Research
Grants Pass, Oregon

012197

Published by The Oasis Press
The Essential Corporation Handbook
© 1992, 1995 by Carl R.J. Sniffen

This publication is designed to provide accurate and authoritative information in regard to the subject matter covered. It is sold with the understanding that the publisher is not engaged in rendering legal, accounting, or other professional service. If legal advice or other expert assistance is required, the services of a competent professional person should be sought.
    — from a declaration of principles jointly adopted by a committee of the American Bar Association and a committee of publishers

Editor: Vickie Reierson
Editorial Assistance & Formatting, First Edition: Scott Crawford
Editorial Assistance & Formatting, Second Edition: Erin Wait
Formatting: Melody Joachims

Please direct any comments, questions, or suggestions regarding this book to The Oasis Press, Editorial Department, at the address below.

The Oasis Press offers PSI Successful Business Software for sale.
For information, contact:

    PSI Research
    P.O. Box 3727
    Central Point, OR 97502
    (541) 479-9464
    info@psi-research.com *email*

The Oasis Press is a Registered Trademark of Publishing Services, Inc., an Oregon corporation doing business as PSI Research.

Sniffen, Carl R. J.
    The essential corporation handbook / by Carl R.J. Sniffen. -- 2nd ed.
        p.   cm. -- (PSI successful business library)
    Includes index.
    ISBN 1-55571-342-4 (pbk.) : $21.95
    1. Corporation law--United States. 2. Small business--Law and legislation--United States.   I. Title. II. Series.
KF1414.3.S65 1995
346.73'066--dc20
[347.30666]   94-41150
                                                                      CIP

Printed in the United States of America
Second edition 10 9

 Printed on recycled paper when available.

About the Author

Carl R.J. Sniffen

Carl R.J. Sniffen, a partner with the law firm of Foster, Purdy, Allan, Peterson & Dahlin in Medford, Oregon, has more than 17 years business law experience. He is a member of the Oregon and Missouri bar associations and is admitted to practice law in those states.

Mr. Sniffen holds a B.S. in journalism from the University of Kansas, and a J.D., with distinction, from the University of Missouri-Kansas City School of Law. While at UMKC, he served as editor-in-chief of the UMKC Law Review and was a member of the Order of the Bench and Robe.

He is a co-author of a number of books by The Oasis Press, including *A Company Policy and Personnel Workbook, Developing Company Policies,* and the Oregon state chapter of the *Starting and Operating a Business* series.

An avid runner, he is a frequent lecturer and writer on subjects pertaining to road racing, including club organization and structure, how to conduct a road race, and children's running. Mr. Sniffen currently serves as president of the Road Runners Club of America and is a member of the board of directors of USA Track and Field.

Mr. Sniffen resides in Grants Pass, Oregon with his wife, Barb, and two sons, Neil and Brian.

Acknowledgments

Writing a book is hard work. This is especially true for a business lawyer trying to overcome more than 15 years of legalese and attempting to write in plain, common-sense English.

I would like to thank a number of people who have helped me with this task:

- All of the employees of PSI Research, and especially Rosanno Alejandro, Scott Crawford, Constance Dickinson, Melody Joachims, and Vickie Reierson whose skill, judgment, and good humor contributed immensely to this effort; and

- Ardella Ramey, Emmett Ramey, and Francie Marks, principals of PSI Research, whose commitment to small business is evident in each publication they produce.

Although their contributions to this book were less direct and immediate, I would also like to thank the following:

- Bob Mann and Don Stubbs, Kansas City lawyers, who taught me that there's more to life than the billable hour;

- Dorothy and Ted Sniffen, my parents, who taught me respect for and tolerance of others; and

- The West 79th Street Striders, a rag-tag bunch of runners and ne'er-do-wells who can always put me in my place.

- Last, but certainly not least, I want to thank and acknowledge Barb Sniffen, my wife and favorite pediatrician, and sons, Neil and Brian, who provide a constant source of joy, love, and inspiration.

Carl R.J. Sniffen

Table of Contents

Sample Documents, Checklists, and Forms

Introduction

The Essential Corporation Handbook is built on this simple proposition: To devote more time and energy to running your corporation successfully and to avoid potential financial risk, you need to know your state's business corporation act and have efficient, well-organized procedures for dealing with the extensive amount of required paperwork.

To accomplish this, you need to first learn about corporate formalities and mechanics. This knowledge will help you:

- Avoid personal liability for corporate actions;
- Save money by preplanning corporate goals, avoiding common mistakes, and handling corporate maintenance in-house;
- Have a better understanding of issues when consulting with your attorney and accountant; and
- Realize corporations are flexible entities that can be tailor-made to fit your needs.

The Essential Corporation Handbook strives to emphasize the areas of corporate formalities and mechanics you need to handle and maintain to gain the benefits and avoid the risks of owning and operating a corporation. For example, good recordkeeping, compliance with state law, knowledge of your articles of incorporation and bylaws, and shareholder and director meetings are among the many topics this handbook covers within its six sections.

Quickly Find What You Need to Know

Corporations are complicated by nature and have numerous requirements and issues surrounding them. By breaking the issues into focused sections, this book tries to make it as easy as possible for you to quickly locate the information you are interested in.

Section I, Sources of Authority, explains and defines business corporation acts, articles of incorporation, and bylaws. Devoting a chapter to each topic, this section details:

- How state business corporation acts provide the legal basis for forming and operating your corporation while allowing for flexibility;

- What information the articles of incorporation must or may contain and why this is important to you personally and to your corporation; and

- Why you need to know what your bylaws require and how you can structure them to give you what you want in your corporation.

Section II, The Corporate Players, a one-chapter section, identifies the many participants involved in the corporate world. By clearly defining corporate roles — such as promoter, director, shareholder, and agent — you gain a better understanding of knowing who is responsible for what in your corporation, and you can reduce your potential personal liability.

Section III, The Paper Trail, consists of chapters 5, 6, and 7 and covers the various types of paperwork you must complete to maintain your corporate status. Chapter 5 deals with corporate stock, its characteristics, issuance, and classes, while Chapter 6 guides you in creating a shareholders' agreement that will provide for your needs in future situations. Chapter 7 helps you preserve your corporate status by discussing the importance of other documents and records, such as a corporate minute book and corporate resolutions.

Section IV, Meetings, focuses on meetings which your corporation's board of directors and shareholders are required by statute and corporate bylaws to have. Both chapters in this section tell you how and when to call specific types of meetings; what procedures to follow at the meetings; and why consent resolutions are important.

Section V, Why You Should Care, gives you the reasons behind why you need to know about corporate formalities and paperwork. Chapter 10 discusses basic information about suing and being sued as a corporation, while Chapter 11 brings the point home by relating real life cases where corporations were judged liable for injuries or debts because of such things as their poor recordkeeping, inadequate capital, absence of resolutions and stock records, and personal use of corporate funds.

Section VI, Related Concepts, expands on some related concepts that are mentioned in the text. Learn more about professional corporations, not-for-profit corporations, close corporations, limited liability companies, and professional teams in chapters 12–16.

Use the Book's Features as Handy References

Sample Documents, Checklists, and Forms. Throughout this book, you will find sample documents, checklists, and forms. These items are included to help you better understand the issues discussed and to demystify the corporate process. For a complete list of these resources, refer to the Table of Contents. If you would like to use any of these forms in your corporation, consult your lawyer or accountant for input and advice.

Margin Notes. As you read the text, notice the boldface comments and tips located in the pages' margins, such as that shown at right. These margin notes are provided to emphasize important aspects of a discussion or to highlight additional information. They are particularly helpful when reviewing a chapter or when studying one of the larger sample documents, such as the stock purchase agreement.

Margin notes emphasize important aspects of a discussion or highlight additional information. They are particularly helpful when reviewing a chapter or when studying one of the larger sample documents.

Footnotes. If you are interested in doing further research on some of the material included in the text, footnotes are noted throughout several chapters. Appropriate resources are cited at the end of the text.

Glossary. Because of the legal and structured nature of corporate formality and procedures, there may be a term or phrase within the book's discussions that you may not quite understand. To help you quickly find easy definitions to such terms as "piercing the corporate veil," "tort," and "indemnification," you can refer to the Glossary, which is located near the back of the book.

Appendix. Since the secretary of state's office (or its equivalent) will be an initial as well as follow-up resource for your corporation, a complete list of these offices' addresses and telephone numbers for all 50 states, plus the District of Columbia, is included in this section.

A Final Thought

It would be impossible to cover all the corporate bases in one volume. As a law professor once said: "This course will focus on the peaks." Likewise, this book focuses on the peaks of corporate formalities and law. If you are interested in exploring some the valleys, your local law library is a good source of information.

The Essential Corporation Handbook is not intended to be a substitute for competent legal and professional advice. Laws change; the business environment changes. Don't try to do it all. As a business person, you must develop good working relationships with a lawyer, an accountant, and an insurance agent. Be aware that laws vary from state to state, and the issues presented in this book are general in nature. Use your own professionals to help you make this book work for you.

Sources of Authority

Chapter 1

Business Corporation Acts

The good news is that every state has a business corporation act, and there are many similarities from state to state. The bad news is that despite the similarities, there is no uniform law in effect in all states. When you incorporate in a particular state, you agree to comply with its business corporation act, and it is presumed you know its requirements. If there is a conflict between the state statute and your articles or bylaws, the statute will prevail.

The Revised Model Business Corporation Act (RMBCA),[1] drafted by the Committee on Corporate Laws of the Section of Corporation, Banking and Business Law of the American Bar Association, has been adopted as law by 15 states.[2] The RMBCA reflects the modern trend in corporate business laws, and it represents the subjects commonly found in all state corporation statutes.

Therefore, to help you better understand business corporation act requirements and to provide a helpful guide to this chapter's discussion, the RMBCA will serve as a model of a typical business corporation act.

Before jumping into this discussion, two concepts should be explained. The first is the concept of sources of authority. A corporation is a creature of statute and can only do what state laws permit it to do. Most state corporation laws provide a general outline of what corporations can and cannot do. Corporation laws often defer to a corporation's articles of incorporation or bylaws to fill in the gaps. As a result, the corporation laws, articles of incorporation, and bylaws provide the sources of authority which control what a corporation can do and how it must act.

The second concept is the distinction between a statute and an act. Both terms reflect laws duly adopted by Congress or by the state legislature. All

This chapter will focus on the Revised Model Business Corporation Act. The law in your state may vary slightly.

of the laws adopted by Congress or a state legislature are statutes. Some of these statutes may empower an administrative agency like the Internal Revenue Service to pass rules to implement the statute. A specific body of statutes is an act. For example, in most states, all of the statutes which pertain to corporations are found together in the business corporation act. Acts are sometimes referred to as codes, including the Internal Revenue Code, Uniform Commercial Code, or a criminal code.

Filing Mechanics

A number of corporation documents must be filed with the secretary of state.

The RMBCA and all business corporations acts set forth technical requirements for filing articles of incorporation.[3] For example, the statute requires that articles be submitted on a form prescribed by the secretary of state. In most states, the secretary of state will provide you with a pre-printed form of articles of incorporation. If you choose, you may fill in the blanks and submit the articles along with the required filing fee, and you have created a corporation. Bear in mind, however, that filling in blanks on a form without more information could prove costly in the future.

When you file your articles, provide your name and telephone number in your cover letter. Let the secretary of state's office know that they can contact you if they have any questions concerning your filing. In some states, minor errors in the articles can be corrected over the telephone without the need to resubmit the articles. For your convenience, a list of addresses and telephone numbers for the various secretaries of state is found in the Appendix.

Articles must by typed or handwritten and signed by an authorized corporate officer or incorporator. One signed and one photocopied version of the articles must be submitted to the secretary of state. If approved by the secretary of state, your corporation's existence begins on the date of filing with the secretary of state.[4] The secretary will file stamp the photocopy of the articles and return it to you. In some states, this file stamped copy must also be sent to the local recorder of deeds for filing. When returned by the secretary of state or local recorder's office, keep the articles in your corporation's minute book.

It is a crime to make a false statement in articles of incorporation.[5] Read them carefully before filing. In addition, contact the secretary of state's office before filing to determine the required filing fee. In some states, a flat fee is assessed for filing articles of incorporation. In others, the fee is based on the number of shares of stock which the corporation is authorized to issue.

Articles of Incorporation and Bylaws

What must you include in the articles of incorporation? As you will see, very little information is required.[6] However, in most instances, you will want to include more information than is actually required. Corporation statutes provide that any other lawful information may be included. Chapter 2 discusses in more detail what you must include in your articles of incorporation.

Business corporations acts also require that the corporation adopt bylaws for the purpose of managing and regulating the affairs of the corporation.[7] More specific information pertaining to bylaws and amendments is provided in Chapter 3.

Purposes and Powers

For what purposes can a corporation be formed? A purpose is a statement of why the corporation was formed. Once formed, what powers may a corporation exercise? Powers tell us what a corporation can do to carry out its purpose. Because corporations are creatures of statute, the answers to these questions are found in the business corporations acts.

Early corporation statutes were quite restrictive. Corporations could only engage in those activities or purposes which were carefully defined in the articles of incorporation. Similarly, corporate powers had to be stated in great detail in the articles of incorporation. Corporations could not exceed their stated purposes or powers.

For example, a corporation might describe in its articles that its purpose is to operate a retail clothing store. Alternatively, the corporation could broaden its purpose to include the purchase, sale, lease, barter, or exchange of goods and merchandise at wholesale or retail. Plainly, the second purpose clause is broader than the first.

Historically, the corporation's articles would list a detailed list of powers which the corporation could engage in to carry out its purposes. The list of purposes and powers could extend for many pages.

Today, however, under the RMBCA, a corporation is presumed to be formed to engage in any lawful purpose unless a more limited purpose is stated in the articles.[8] You could state in your articles that the corporation is formed to operate a retail clothing store and for no other purpose; however, it would be foolish, to limit your purposes. Without any limitation in the articles, the corporation may engage in any lawful act, subject, of course, to any other statutes or laws which might impact the corporation's activities or business.

With respect to corporate powers, the RMBCA and other business corporation acts include the power:

- To sue and be sued in the corporate name;
- To have a corporate seal (no longer required in most states);
- To make and amend bylaws;
- To acquire and own real or personal property, whether by lease, purchase or otherwise, and to use or improve that property;
- To sell, mortgage, lease and otherwise dispose of all or any part of its property;
- To acquire stocks, bonds, or notes of other corporations, partnerships or other businesses;
- To make contracts and guarantees, borrow money, issue its notes, bonds, and other obligations and secure any of its obligations by mortgage of any of its property;
- To lend money, invest and reinvest its funds, and receive and hold real and personal property as security for repayment;
- To be a promoter, partner, member, associate or manager of any partnership, joint venture, trust or other entity;

As a practical matter, banks, suppliers, and others with whom you may need to establish a credit or working relationship with may request to see copies of your articles and bylaws and may be more apt to establish a relationship if some specific description of purposes and powers is included in the articles.

- To conduct its business anywhere, subject, of course, to the foreign corporation statutes of other states;
- To elect board of directors and appoint officers, employees and agents of the corporation, define their duties, fix their compensation and lend them money and credit;
- To establish benefit plans;
- To make donations for the public welfare or for charitable, scientific, or educational purposes;
- To transact any lawful business; and
- To do anything else which isn't illegal and which furthers the business and affairs of the corporation.[9]

Unlike earlier statutes, modern business corporation acts permit corporations to do anything legal. If you wish to limit the powers which your corporation can exercise, you will need to limit the powers in the articles of incorporation or bylaws. As a result, the description of the corporation's purposes and powers now occupy only a few lines in the articles and not several pages.

Corporate Name

Every corporation must have a name; however, you may be surprised to learn how often your first or second choices for a corporate name are not available for one reason or another.

Before you submit your articles of incorporation, make certain that the name which you have chosen is available. When selecting a name, have two or three choices ready in the event that your first choice is not available.

The RMBCA requires that each corporate name contain the word, "corporation," "incorporated," "company," "limited," or "association." Abbreviations are also permitted.[10] Corporate names can not imply that the corporation is formed for an unlawful purpose; for instance, "Contract Killers, Inc." would probably not be accepted in most states.

Your corporation's name must not be confusingly similar to the name of any existing corporation or fictitious name registered to a corporation or any other business entity. A fictitious name is a trade name. For example, Publishing Services, Inc., an Oregon corporation, does business as PSI Research. The name PSI Research has been registered as a fictitious name with the Oregon Secretary of State.

States differ in their interpretations of what is confusingly similar. For some states, the phrase is synonymous with identical. In other states, even minor deviations are not permitted. For example, the names, "AAA Body Shop" and "AAA Body Repair" would be considered confusingly similar in some states and not in others.

All states allow you to reserve a corporation name for 60 to 90 days upon completion of a name reservation form and payment of a fee to the secretary of state.[11] Most states will advise you by telephone as to name availability, and many lawyers will use this approach to determine availability prior to submitting articles. The risk of using the telephone is that the person providing the information could make a mistake (state computers are often down), or someone else could file articles using that name before you do.

Name availability is also a concern for foreign corporations. Contrary to what you might think, a foreign corporation is generally not a corporation from a foreign country. Rather, it is a corporation from another state. Corporations formed and organized pursuant to the laws of your state are considered domestic corporations. All other corporations are foreign corporations.

Foreign corporations may have established name recognition in one state, but when the corporation seeks authority to do business in another state, it may find that the name it has been using is unavailable because someone else is already using it.

There are ways to protect a name, including:

- Register your corporate name or logo as a trademark or service mark pursuant to federal laws and acquire the right to use your name anywhere in the country (subject to the right of persons using the name prior to your registration of the trademark or service mark);
- Use state trademark or service mark registration laws to protect your name within the state where you register; or
- Reserve the corporate name in all states where the corporation will do business, remembering that the reservations are generally available for no more than 60 to 90 days. Some states do not permit renewal of name reservation.

For more information about name availability, fictitious name registration, or corporate name reservation, contact your secretary of state's office before you file your articles of incorporation. (Addresses and telephone numbers are found in the Appendix). Although state registration of trademarks or service marks is a simple process of completing a form, you may wish to consider using a trademark attorney to assist you with any federal registration of names or logos.

Registered Office and Registered Agent

These terms sound like something from the manuals of the Central Intelligence Agency. Unfortunately, they are not nearly so glamorous or exciting. Every corporation must designate a registered office and a registered agent who can be found at that office.[12] The purpose of the registered agent is to have someone available who can receive service of process in the event of a lawsuit or other official notices from the state. The registered office is simply the location where the registered agent can be found.

In many instances, the attorney who forms the corporation will also serve as registered agent. Because the primary role of the agent is to receive service of lawsuits, the attorney is a good person to receive such information. Many corporations simply name the president of the corporation as agent and list the corporation's headquarters as resident office.

Some states use the term "resident agent" in lieu of "registered agent." Terminology is often different from state to state. For example, in Kansas, you have stockholders. In neighboring Missouri, you have shareholders.

The concept of registered office and registered agent is important. Your articles must name a registered agent and list a registered office. If the agent or office should change for any reason, you must promptly notify the secretary of state in writing. Failure to designate a new office or agent within 60 days of any change can result in an automatic forfeiture of the corporate charter.

Your registered agent should be someone who can be easily found and is reliable. Lawsuits must be responded to promptly or you will lose by default. Your registered agent should appreciate the responsibility to forward materials served on him or her without delay. Consider using your corporate attorney or company president for this purpose.

State laws also restrict the manner in which a registered agent may resign. For example, in some states, the resigning agent must provide prior written notice to the corporation and the secretary of state before the resignation is effective.

Corporate Stock

Corporate stock may refer to the ownership of a corporation, evidenced by stock certificates, or it may refer to the amount of capital (cash or other property) contributed to the corporation. Business corporation acts devote much attention to corporate stock, including such concepts as stock issuance, dividends, preemptive rights, stock certificates, and more. Each of these concepts is discussed in detail in Chapter 5.

For now, two commonly used terms should be distinguished. The term "authorized shares" refers to the maximum number of shares which a corporation can lawfully issue to shareholders. This number is usually stated in the articles. The term "issued and outstanding" refers to the number of shares of stock which a corporation has actually issued at any point in time.

A related term, "treasury stock," refers to shares of stock which had been issued by the corporation to a shareholder but which were later reacquired by the corporation.

To illustrate these terms, consider the following example: John Doe, Inc. is an Oregon corporation. Under its articles, it is authorized to issue up to 30,000 shares of common stock. John Doe, Inc. has three shareholders, John, Jane, and Joan, each of whom own 1,000 shares of common stock. John Doe, Inc. has 30,000 shares of authorized common stock. John Doe, Inc. has 3,000 shares of issued and outstanding stock.

Shareholders/Stockholders – Directors and Officers

Shareholders, directors, and officers are vital parts of any corporation. Who these players are, what they can and can't do, how they do the things they do are all important elements of business corporation acts, articles, and bylaws. Meetings, record dates, proxies, voting requirements, quorum, voting trusts, qualifications and duties of directors and officers, loans to officers and directors are all subject matters considered in later chapters.

Fundamental Changes

All business corporation acts provide technical and mechanical rules for fundamental changes. As the name implies, a fundamental change is one which impacts on the corporation in a significant way. For example, merger or consolidation, dissolution or liquidation, reorganization, sale of most of a corporation's assets, or amending the articles of incorporation are considered fundamental changes.

With the exception of amendments to your corporate articles, fundamental changes are beyond the scope of this book. Mergers, dissolutions, and sale of a business are complicated transactions with diverse legal implications. Tax, securities, and antitrust are only a few of the legal issues which may be involved. Because your focus is on running your business, consider using the services of a competent business attorney in these areas.

A brief discussion of the more common fundamental changes follows.

Merger or Consolidation

A merger involves the combining of two corporations. One, referred to as the disappearing corporation, is absorbed into the other, known as the surviving corporation. The disappearing corporation ceases to exist for all purposes, with only the surviving corporation continuing. In general, the surviving corporation stands in the shoes of the disappearing corporation, taking over all rights, liabilities, debts, and obligations of the disappearing corporation.

A consolidation is quite similar, involving an agreement of two or more corporations to unite as a single corporation. Often, a consolidation involves the formation of a third corporation into which the assets and liabilities of the other or constituent corporations are transferred. For most business corporation acts, the concepts of merger and consolidation are treated in the same fashion.

To merge, the board of directors causes a plan of merger to be prepared. The board votes to approve the plan and recommends that the plan be submitted to the shareholders for approval. Specifics regarding board and shareholder meetings and voting are found in later chapters.

A plan of merger includes:

- The corporations participating in the merger;
- Which corporation will be the survivor and which will disappear;
- When the merger will take effect;
- How many shares of stock of the surviving corporation will shareholders of the disappearing corporation receive; and
- Any other information which the corporations wish to include (for example, whether the name of the surviving corporation will change when the merger is effective, whether a new registered agent or office will be appointed, whether there are any contingencies which must occur before the merger is effective).[13]

A sample plan of merger providing for a one-for-one stock exchange is located on pages 9 and 10. The companies involved, ABC, Inc. and DEF, Inc. are fictitious companies.

Once the plan of merger has been approved by the board of directors and shareholders of both corporations, articles of merger must be prepared and submitted to the secretary of state. Like articles of incorporation, many secretary of state offices will provide form articles of merger for your use. You must attach a plan of merger to the articles of merger. If the merger involves

When you contact the secretary of state's office to obtain articles of merger, specify whether or not a parent/subsidiary merger is involved. Different forms of articles of merger are used depending on the type of merger. The secretary of state will also tell you what the fee is for filing articles of merger. Don't forget to consult with your business attorney as well.

a foreign corporation, articles of merger must be sent to the secretary of state in both states.[14] Two separate forms used in the state of Oregon as of this writing are provided on pages 11 and 12 for your reference.

Articles of merger should include:

- A copy of the plan of merger;
- The total number of shares outstanding and entitled to vote on the merger issue for each corporation, designated by class, if any (a discussion of classes of stock is contained in Chapter 5);
- The number of shares voted for and against the plan of merger;
- An undertaking on the part of the surviving corporation to assume the debts and liabilities of the disappearing corporation, if not already included in the plan of merger; and
- The signature of authorized officers of each corporation.[15]

If the merger involves parent and subsidiary corporations no shareholder approval is required. This procedure, known as a short form merger, is available only where one corporation owns at least 90% of the outstanding stock of the other corporation.[16]

Sale of Assets

A corporation has the power to buy, sell, and dispose of its property by virtue of powers granted in the business corporation act. Without this power, the corporation would be hard pressed to conduct business. No shareholder or director approval is required to approve purchases or sales of corporate property in the ordinary conduct of the corporation's business.[17]

If a business proposes to sell all or most of its assets or make an unusual sale outside of its ordinary course of business, board approval is required. Shareholder approval may be required as well.[18]

The sale of all or most of a corporation's assets will usually trigger the bulk sales laws of the Uniform Commercial Code, if still in effect in your state. For a brief but accurate description of bulk sales laws, see the Starting and Operating a Business *series which is published by The Oasis Press. The purchase or sale of a business is a complicated process. Include your business attorney and accountant as a part of any purchase or sale.*

If approval is required, the board adopts a resolution authorizing the sale and requesting that the sale be submitted to the shareholders for approval. Meeting and notice requirements are discussed later in the book, and these must be strictly followed. Unless the articles or bylaws require a higher percentage approval or super majority, the sale would require only majority shareholder approval. Unlike merger or dissolution, no articles respecting the sale need to be filed with the secretary of state.

Dissolution and Liquidation

Dissolution is the decision to stop the active conduct of a business. A dissolution can be voluntary by the actions of the directors or shareholders, or involuntary, imposed by a court. Dissolution can also occur administratively as where a corporate charter is forfeited or revoked for failure to file required annual reports, pay franchise taxes, or maintain a registered office or agent.

During the dissolution process, all activities of the corporation are geared to an orderly winding up of the corporation's business and liquidating of its assets. The focus of this discussion will be on voluntary dissolution.

SAMPLE: Plan of Merger

Agreement and Plan of Merger

This Agreement and Plan of Merger is made this February 14, 1992 between ABC, Inc., a Washington corporation ("ABC") and DEF, Inc., an Oregon corporation ("DEF").

Recitals

ABC is a Washington corporation with its principal place of business located in Anytown, Washington. ABC is authorized to issue 30,000 shares of common stock, no par value, of which, 1,000 shares are issued and outstanding as of the date of this Agreement.

DEF is an Oregon corporation with its principal place of business located in Anytown, Oregon. DEF is authorized to issue 100,000 shares of common stock, of which 10,000 shares are presently issued and outstanding as of the date of this Agreement.

The first two paragraphs identify the merging corporations.

The boards of directors of ABC and DEF agree that it is in the best business interests of the corporations and their shareholders that DEF be merged into ABC, in accordance with the terms and conditions of this Agreement and Plan of Merger, in such manner that this transaction qualify as a reorganization within the meaning of Section 368(a)(1)(A) of the Internal Revenue Code of 1954, as amended.

The merger is intended to qualify as a tax-free reorganization.

Therefore, in consideration of the mutual covenants set forth in this Agreement and subject to the terms and conditions of this Agreement, the parties agree as follows:

1. DEF shall merge with and into ABC, which shall be the surviving corporation.
2. On the effective date of the merger, the separate existence of DEF shall cease, and ABC shall succeed to all the rights, privileges, immunities, and franchises, and all the property, real, personal or mixed of DEF without the necessity for any separate transfer. ABC shall thereafter be responsible and liable for all liabilities and obligations of DEF, and neither the rights of creditors nor any liens on the property of the absorbed corporation shall be impaired by the merger.

ABC will be the survivor, assuming all of the rights, properties, and liabilities of DEF.

3. Each share of the common stock of DEF issued and outstanding as of the effective date of merger shall be converted into an equal number of shares of common stock of ABE on a one-for-one basis. Upon the effective date of the merger, holders of outstanding stock of DEF shall surrender their shares to ABC and shall thereafter be issued new shares of ABC stock in exchange.
4. The Articles of Incorporation of ABC shall continue to be its articles of incorporation following the effective date of the merger, subject to the

Stock will be exchanged on a one share for one share basis.

SAMPLE: Plan of Merger (continued)

ABC's articles will govern, as amended, to change the name of the corporation to ABC/DEF, Inc.

ABC officers and directors will continue.

Both ABC and DEF will continue to operate in their ordinary course of business until the merger.

The shareholders of both corporations must approve the plan.

following amendment:

Article I of the Articles of Incorporation shall be amended to read as follows:

The name of the corporation is ABC/DEF, Inc.

5. The bylaws of ABC shall continue to be its bylaws following the effective date of merger.

6. The directors and officers of ABC on the effective date of the merger shall continue as the directors and officers of ABC for the full unexpired terms of their offices and until their successors have been elected or appointed and qualified.

7. Neither ABC nor DEF shall, prior to the effective date of the merger, engage in any activity or transaction other than in the ordinary course of business, except that each corporation may take all action necessary or appropriate under federal or state law to consummate this merger.

8. This Agreement and Plan of Merger shall be submitted for the approval of the shareholders of ABC and DEF, such approval to be obtained on or before December 31, 1992.

9. The effective date of this merger shall be the date when a certificate of merger is issued by the Secretary of State of the State of Washington.

In witness whereof, the parties have executed this Agreement and Plan of Merger as of the date set forth above.

ABC, Inc.   DEF, Inc.

by_____   by_____
President   President

Attest:

_____   _____
Secretary   Secretary

SAMPLE: Articles of Merger by Business and/or Nonprofit Corporations

Phone: (503) 986-2200
Fax: (503) 378-4381

Articles of Merger

Secretary of State
Corporation Division
255 Capitol St. NE, Suite 151
Salem, OR 97310-1327

For office use only

Check the appropriate box below:

☐ BUSINESS/PROFESSIONAL/NONPROFIT CORPORATION
(Complete only 1, 2, 3, 4, 10, 11)

☐ FOR PARENT AND 90% OWNED SUBSIDIARY
WITHOUT SHAREHOLDER APPROVAL
(Complete only 5, 6, 7, 8, 9, 10, 11)

Registry Number: _____

Attach Additional Sheet if Necessary
Please Type or Print Legibly in **Black** Ink

BUSINESS/PROFESSIONAL/NONPROFIT CORPORATION ONLY

1) **NAMES OF THE CORPORATIONS PROPOSING TO MERGE**

   A. _____

   B. _____

2) **NAME OF THE SURVIVING CORPORATION** _____

   ☐ Check here if there is a name change in this plan of merger.

3) **A COPY OF THE MERGER PLAN IS ATTACHED.**

4) **CHECK THE APPROPRIATE STATEMENTS FOR CORPORATION A AND CORPORATION B BELOW.**

Corporation A	Corporation B
☐ Shareholder/membership approval was not required. The plan was approved by a sufficient vote of the board of directors.	☐ Shareholder/membership approval was not required. The plan was approved by a sufficient vote of the board of directors.
☐ Shareholder/membership approval was required. The vote was as follows:	☐ Shareholder/membership approval was required. The membership vote was as follows:

If Corporation A is a business/professional corporation:

Class or series of shares	Number of votes entitled to be cast	Number of votes cast FOR	Number of votes cast AGAINST

If Corporation B is a business/professional corporation:

Class or series of shares	Number of votes entitled to be cast	Number of votes cast FOR	Number of votes cast AGAINST

If Corporation A is a nonprofit corporation:

Class(es) entitled to vote	Number of members entitled to vote	Number of votes entitled to be cast	Number of votes cast FOR	Number of votes cast AGAINST

If Corporation B is a nonprofit corporation:

Class(es) entitled to vote	Number of members entitled to vote	Number of votes entitled to be cast	Number of votes cast FOR	Number of votes cast AGAINST

FOR PARENT AND 90% OWNED SUBSIDIARY WITHOUT SHAREHOLDER APPROVAL

5) **NAME OF PARENT CORPORATION** _____

   Oregon Registry Number _____

6) **NAME OF SUBSIDIARY CORPORATION** _____

   Oregon Registry Number _____

7) **NAME OF SURVIVING CORPORATION** _____

8) **COPY OF PLAN**

   A copy of the plan of merger setting forth the manner and basis of converting shares of the subsidiary into shares, obligations, or other securities of the parent corporation or any other corporation or into cash or other property is attached.

9) **CHECK THE APPROPRIATE BOX**

   ☐ A copy of the plan of merger or summary was mailed to each shareholder of record of the subsidiary corporation on or before _____,
   19 ___ .

   ☐ The mailing of a copy of the plan or summary was waived by all outstanding shares.

10) **EXECUTION**

Printed Name	Signature	Title
_____	_____	_____

11) **CONTACT NAME**   **DAYTIME PHONE NUMBER**

_____   _____

CR117 (Rev. 8/96)

FEES

Make check for $10 payable to "Corporation Division."

NOTE: Filing fees may be paid with VISA or MasterCard. The card number and expiration date should be submitted on a separate sheet for your protection.

SAMPLE: Articles of Merger without Shareholder Approval

Submit the original
and one true copy
$10.00

Survivor's Registry Number:

THIS SPACE FOR OFFICE USE ONLY

Corporation Division - Business Registry
Public Service Building
255 Capitol Street NE, Suite 151
Salem, OR 97310-1327
(503) 986-2200 Facsimile (503) 378-4381

ARTICLES OF MERGER
For Parent and 90% Owned Subsidiary
Without Shareholder Approval

PLEASE TYPE OR PRINT LEGIBLY IN BLACK INK

1.　　Name of parent corporation:　_____

　　　　Oregon registry #:　_____

2.　　Name of subsidiary corporation:　_____

　　　　Oregon registry #:　_____

3.　　Name of surviving corporation:　_____

4.　　A copy of the plan of merger setting forth the manner and basis of converting shares of the subsidiary into shares, obligations, or other securities of the parent corporation or any other corporation or into cash or other property is attached.

5.　　Check the appropriate box:

☐　　A copy of the plan of merger or summary was mailed to each shareholder of record of the subsidiary corporation on or before _____, 19 ___.

☐　　The mailing of a copy of the plan or summary was waived by all outstanding shares.

Execution: _____
　　　　　　　　Signature　　　　　　　　　　　　Printed name　　　　　　　　　Title

Person to contact about this filing: _____
　　　　　　　　　　　　　　　　　　　Name　　　　　　　　　　　　　Daytime phone number

MAKE CHECKS PAYABLE TO THE CORPORATION DIVISION **OR** INCLUDE YOUR *VISA OR MASTERCARD* NUMBER AND
EXPIRATION DATE _____-_____-_____-_____ ___/___ . SUBMIT THE COMPLETED FORM AND FEE TO
THE ABOVE ADDRESS **OR** FAX TO (503) 378-4381.

116 (11/93)

Like merger and consolidation, dissolution usually requires director and shareholder approval.[19] Dissolution also requires the filing of articles of dissolution with the secretary of state.

The board of directors initiates the process by recommending dissolution and further recommending that the plan be presented to the shareholders for approval. Certain states permit shareholders alone to authorize a dissolution without any prior board action. Unless articles or bylaws provide otherwise, a majority of the holders of shares can approve this action.

Articles of dissolution provide:

- The name of the corporation to be dissolved;
- The date the dissolution was authorized by the board of directors and shareholders;
- The number of votes entitled to be cast for and against the dissolution (broken down by class of shares) and the number voting for and against the dissolution; and
- The signature of an authorized officer of the corporation.[20]

Because of the serious consequences of dissolution, the board of directors should notify each shareholder of the proposed dissolution plan and the time, place, and date of the shareholders' meeting to vote on the plan. Even the holders of nonvoting shares may be eligible to vote on a plan to dissolve.

The dissolution is effective on the date the articles of dissolution are filed with the secretary of state unless a different date is set forth in the articles. There is a fee charged for filing articles of dissolution.

Activities During Dissolution

What can a corporation do after it has filed articles of dissolution? The corporation may:

- Continue to exist as a corporation to wind up and liquidate its business and affairs;
- Collect its assets;
- Dispose of properties that will not be distributed to its shareholders;
- Discharge or make provision for discharging its liabilities; and
- Distribute its remaining properties among its shareholders according to their interests.[21]

What can't the corporation do after articles of dissolution have been filed? It can't do anything not reasonably calculated to conclude its business. For example, signing a long-term contract to supply goods to another business or obligating the dissolving corporation to purchase goods over a long term would not be consistent with an intent to dissolve the corporation.

How Do You Handle Claims Against a Dissolving Corporation?

The RMBCA provides a mechanism for handling claims against the dissolved corporation. The RMBCA divides claims into two kinds: those which the corporation knows about and those which it does not.

For claims which the corporation knows about (contract, government obligations, etc.), the corporation must notify each creditor in writing of the dissolution and the need for the creditor to submit its claim. The notice should

If your corporation has more than one place of business, you can publish the required notice to creditors in a newspaper of general circulation in each county where the corporation has a business location.

specify a deadline for submitting claims, but in no event can the deadline be sooner than 120 days following the written notice. Creditors who fail to file their claims before the deadline will find their claims are barred.[22]

An unknown claim is one that the corporation doesn't know about. For example, the product which your corporation manufactures contains a defect which you don't know about. Sooner or later, the defect will be discovered, resulting in the possibility that claims will be filed against the corporation. Common areas where unknown claims exist are products liability, negligence, and environmental disputes.

For unknown claims, the dissolving corporation should publish a notice of dissolution in a newspaper which is circulated generally in the county where the corporation is located. The notice should describe the corporation and its business and provide that claims against the corporation must be filed within five years.[23] The notice will specify when and how claims are to be filed. Claims not filed within five years of publication will be barred.

Enforcing Claims Against Dissolved Corporations

Under the RMBCA, claims of those who respond within the claim period may be enforced against the corporation. Recovery is limited to those corporate assets which the corporation has not already distributed to its shareholders or other creditors. If the assets have been distributed, claims may be enforced against the shareholders but recovery is limited to the value of assets distributed to the shareholders. In the absence of fraud or other unusual circumstance, no shareholder shall be personally liable for claims in an amount greater than the value of assets distributed to the shareholder.[24] Courts will not permit a corporation or its shareholders to transfer corporate assets where the purpose of the transfer is to defraud the claimant. In certain circumstances, corporate transfers to one claimant may be attacked by another claimant if the corporation unfairly preferred the first claimant over the second.

Because dissolution involves the potential that a creditor could knock on your door to recover the value of assets you receive in a corporate dissolution, it is important that any statutory claims procedure be followed. Because of tax and other aspects of a dissolution, you would be well served to work closely with a good business attorney.

Dissenters Rights/Shareholders Appraisal Rights

Shareholders don't always agree with each other. While one shareholder believes that a merger is the best thing for a corporation, another may feel just the opposite. In addition, not all shareholders are equal. Some own voting shares, others may own nonvoting shares. One shareholder may own more than 50% of the outstanding voting shares of a corporation, and thus be considered a controlling shareholder (at least for matters which require majority approval). Shareholders who don't own a controlling interest in stock are considered minority shareholders.

Statutory Protection for Minority Shareholders

Because shareholders don't always agree and because minority shareholders can be directly impacted by decisions of the controlling shareholders, most state statutes now provide for dissenters rights or shareholder appraisal rights.[25] These rights are intended to protect a minority shareholder who does not believe that a proposed fundamental change is in the best interests of the corporation. A shareholder exercising his or her dissenters or appraisal rights can compel the corporation to purchase his or her shares.

When Do These Rights Apply?

Under the RMBCA, dissenters rights arise whenever:

- A plan of merger is submitted;
- Any exchange of shares is proposed if the shareholder has voting rights;
- The corporation proposes to sell all or most of its assets outside of the ordinary conduct of its business;
- Amendments to the articles are proposed which would affect any preferential stock right, redemption or preemptive right; and
- Any other corporate action to which the articles or bylaws attach dissenters or appraisal rights.[26]

How Do These Rights Work?

If a corporation proposes any action to which dissenters or appraisal rights apply, the notice to shareholders noting the meeting's time, date, and place must also indicate that dissenters rights are available.[27] Upon receipt of this notice, a shareholder must notify the corporation of his or her election to exercise dissenters rights.

If the proposed corporate action is later approved, a corporation must renotify all shareholders who indicated their intent to exercise dissenters rights. This notice must include a form of demand for payment and a time table by which the shareholders must make their demand. In addition, a corporation must include financial information and a statement indicating its estimate of the per share value of the corporation's stock and how it arrived at its estimate.

The shareholder can accept the corporation's estimate and make demand for payment. If the shareholder does not agree with the estimate, he or she should submit a demand for payment which indicates the shareholder's estimate of value.[28] If the corporation does not agree with the estimate, the parties can petition the local court for its determination of value.[29]

Shareholders who wish to take advantage of dissenters rights can't vote their shares in favor of the proposed corporate action. If they do, the rights are not available to them. In addition, both shareholders and the corporation would be well served to come to an agreement concerning the value of shares without resort to the courts. Legal action in the courts is uncertain and expensive.

Corporate Records

Corporations are required to keep the following records:

- Minutes of all board of directors and shareholder meetings;
- A record of all actions taken by the board of directors or shareholders without a meeting;

It's easy to develop bad recordkeeping habits. Obtain a corporate minute book and keep your corporate minutes in it. Develop a file folder for each type of record you are required to maintain, and keep the information inside the folder current. Although your focus is on running your business, good recordkeeping is an important part of maintaining your corporate status.

- A record of all action taken by a committee of the board in place of board action;
- Any currently effective board of directors' resolutions creating one or more classes or series of shares and fixing their relative rights, preferences, and limitations;
- A list of the names and addresses of current officers and directors;
- All written communication by the corporation to the shareholders within the last five years; and
- The most recent annual report of the corporation submitted to the secretary of state.[30]

The RMBCA also requires that the corporation furnish each shareholder with annual financial information consisting of:

- A balance sheet
- An income statement
- A statement of changes in shareholders equity[31]

The financial statements should contain the report of the public accountant who prepared the statements, or if prepared by the corporation without the use of a public accountant, a statement of the person preparing the report indicating whether or not the report was prepared in accordance with generally accepted accounting principles.[32]

Finally, the corporation must provide a written summary to shareholders of any indemnification or loans or advances to corporate officers and directors and of any board decision to issue corporate shares in exchange for promissory notes or future services. This notice must be provided with or before any notice of shareholders meetings.[33]

Records must be available for inspection by shareholders upon five business days prior written notice. The notice must be submitted in good faith for a proper business purpose.[34] For example, it would be a legitimate purpose to acquire a list of shareholders' names and addresses to raise issues about the corporation's management. It would not be a valid business purpose to obtain such a list with a view to selling the list to a junk mail distributor.

To help you determine whether or not you are doing business in a particular state, ask yourself these questions:

- Is the corporation physically present in the state either in the form of an office or through employees or independent contractors?
- If the corporation uses independent sales representatives or contractors, are they truly independent? The answer to this question is complicated and requires specific reference to state law. The determining factor is usually the level of control which the corporation imposes on the representative or contractor.
- How much revenue does the corporation generate from sales or services attributable to the other state?

- How much expense or cost incurred by the corporation is attributable to activities of that corporation in that state?

The greater the level of activity, either through physical presence or volume of business, the greater the likelihood that you are doing business.

Foreign Corporations

A foreign corporation is any corporation which was incorporated in another state. For example, John Doe, Inc., was incorporated in the state of Oregon. As business grew, John Doe, Inc. found itself doing business in Idaho, Washington, and California. John Doe, Inc. is a domestic corporation in Oregon, the place of its incorporation. It is a foreign corporation in Idaho, Washington, and California.

Unlike sole proprietors and most partnerships, corporations must obtain permission from each state in which the corporation does business. To gain permission to conduct business in the state, the corporation submits an application for certificate of authority with the appropriate secretary of state.

The Concept of Doing Business

What constitutes doing business in a particular state? Like the shifting sands, that question is hard to answer. The RMBCA and many business corporation acts define "doing business" by what it is not rather than by what it is. One might wonder, if the legislators don't know what it is, how is a business person to know? The answer lies in the amount of activity a corporation engages in and the level of control it imposes on those who purport to act on behalf of the corporation in the foreign state.

The RMBCA provides a partial list of acts which do not constitute doing business. It includes:

- Maintaining, defending, or settling any proceeding;
- Holding meetings of the board of directors or shareholders within the state or carrying on other activities involving internal corporate matters, such as committee meetings;
- Maintaining bank accounts;
- Maintaining stock transfer offices;
- Selling through independent contractors;
- Soliciting or obtaining orders, whether by mail or through employees or agents or otherwise, if the orders require acceptance outside their state before they become contracts;
- Creating or acquiring indebtedness, mortgages, and security interests in property securing the debt;
- Owning, without more, real or personal property;
- Conducting an isolated transaction that is completed within 30 days and is not one in the course of repeated transactions of a like nature; and
- Transacting business in interstate commerce.[35]

As noted, the list on the previous page is partial, and states are seeking to expand the types of activities and level of business which constitute doing business. For example, businesses which rely heavily on mail order sales are under attack by several states which seek to impose sales tax on mail order sales despite a U.S. Supreme Court case to the contrary.[36] In addition, the commonwealth of Massachusetts now seeks to impose its sales tax laws on vendors who come into the state to appear at trade shows.[37] Previously, such an action would have been considered to be an isolated transaction.

Any significant physical presence or large volume of income or expense attributable to a particular state is a good indication that the corporation is doing business in that state. If in doubt, consult your business attorney.

The Certificate of Authority

If a corporation is determined to be doing business in a state, it should seek a certificate of authority from the secretary of state of that state. This procedure is similar to filing articles of incorporation. To obtain a certificate of authority, contact the appropriate secretary of state for the necessary forms. You will need to include:

To do business in a state, contact the appropriate secretary of state's office to obtain required forms, to find out what filing fee must be paid, and what supporting documents must be provided.

- The name of the corporation, and, if different, the name under which the corporation intends to engage in business in the state;
- The state and date of incorporation;
- The purpose(s) (see the discussion above under the Purposes and Powers heading);
- The principal office address in the state of incorporation;
- The address of the registered office and the name of the registered agent in the state in which you are seeking to do business;
- The names and respective addresses of its officers and directors;
- The aggregate number of shares the corporation has authority to issue, itemized by class and series;
- The aggregate number of issued shares itemized by class and series; and
- The date on which the business will begin operations in the state.[38]

If you don't have an attorney or corporate officer in the state, contact a commercial registered agent, such as Corporate Agents (800) 877-4224.

In addition, the application for certificate of authority should include a certificate of good standing from the secretary of state of the state of incorporation. This certificate states that the corporation is in good standing and that its charter has not been forfeited by the secretary of state. Some states require a copy of the corporation's articles of incorporation certified by the secretary of state of the state of incorporation.

What if You Fail to Get Permission?

Corporations that engage in business without obtaining the necessary certificate of authority from the secretary of state are subject to the following potential sanctions:

- The corporation can not sue in the foreign state, and it may not be able to defend claims against it until it qualifies; and
- A daily penalty can be assessed by the state for each day the corporation does not qualify to do business up to a stated maximum. These penalties are sometimes waived where excusable neglect can be shown.

If a corporation which has qualified to do business in a state no longer engages in the business, it can formally apply to withdraw by filing an application for certificate of withdrawal with the secretary of state. In the application, the corporation will designate the secretary of state for the foreign state as its agent for service of process.

Where Do You Incorporate?

For most small businesses, the answer to this question is easy. Incorporate in the state where you do business. If your business is conducted solely in the state of Kansas, incorporate in Kansas. You don't have to, but if you incorporate elsewhere, you will have to qualify to do business in Kansas anyway, and you end up paying fees and taxes in both states.

Historically, some states had business corporation acts which were more permissive than others. Today, state statutes tend to be liberal and up to date eliminating the need to shop for a favorable state law. Of course, there are still differences in state laws, and some states are still more progressive than others. For example, not all states permit corporations to elect to be treated as close corporations. Other states have provisions which make it more difficult for other corporations to acquire them.

If you are considering where to incorporate, first determine where your principal place of business is to be located. Then look at a particular state's tax structure to see if you can save money on taxes. Consider calling business development offices located in each state to find out what benefits may be awaiting your business.

Close Corporation Statutes

A number of states have adopted close corporation statutes,[39] which supplement a state's business corporation act. If a close corporation statute exists, corporations must elect to be governed by it. The election is made in the articles of incorporation.

You should distinguish between a closely held corporation and a close corporation. A closely held corporation's stock is not publicly traded on any national stock exchange. As a general rule, closely held corporations have a small number of shareholders, but there is no absolute limit on this number. Close corporations are formed pursuant to a specific statute permitting close corporations. Not all states have close corporation statutes. Where close corporation statutes exist, a corporation must affirmatively elect to be a close corporation in its articles. Close corporations must have no more than 50 shareholders.[40]

While most close corporations are closely held, not all closely held corporations are close corporations. Close corporations require that a corporation affirmatively state in its articles of incorporation its intention to be treated as a close corporation.

Why Are You Required to File Documents?

When corporate documents are filed, they provide a public notice. For example, articles of incorporation notify the public that a corporation has been formed and identifies the person to contact in the event of a claim. Articles of dissolution inform the public that a corporation is discontinuing its business. Articles of merger inform the public that two corporations are now one.

The concept of notice is important because it identifies a corporation which in turn makes it easier for government agencies to assess a corporation for its share of taxes and other fees. Public notice also lets creditors know who and where to serve lawsuits in the event of a dispute.

On the opposite page, you will find a sample letter on how to request information regarding another corporation from your secretary of state's office. Because of the notice requirements, requesting this type of information is made convenient. If you ever need to find out more about a particular corporation, feel free to use the sample letter as a guide.

Final Thoughts on Business Corporation Acts

To help you remember what's in a business corporation act, a statutory checklist on pages 22–24 lists the items which are usually found in these acts. A second list describing the most common documents which are filed with the secretary of state follows on page 25. Most of these documents are required or permitted to be filed by a business corporation act.

More importantly, remember that most sections of business corporation acts are prefaced with the language: "Unless otherwise provided in the articles of incorporation or bylaws ...."

You have the flexibility to customize your corporation to fit your needs. The statutes are important, but your articles and bylaws will more often than not tell you what your corporation is required to do.

SAMPLE: Request for Information Letter

Secretary of State

Street

City, State, Zip

Attn: Corporations Division

If you want to learn more about another corporation, contact the appropriate secretary of state, using a form letter similar to the one shown at left.

Re: John Doe, Inc.

Dear Sir or Madam:

Please furnish the following information concerning John Doe, Inc.:

1. The complete name of the organization and the date of incorporation;

2. Whether or not the organization is incorporated in the state, and the name and address of its registered agent and office;

3. Names of officers and directors as shown on the last annual report;

4. Is this corporation registered as a foreign corporation authorized to do business in the state, and if so, list the name and address of its registered agent and office;

5. If the corporation is authorized to do business in the state, list the date it was first authorized to do so; and

6. If the captioned name is registered as a fictitious name, please list the name and address of the person(s) shown as the owner(s) of the business.

A fee in the amount of $_____ is enclosed. Thank you for your prompt and courteous attention to this matter.

Yours truly,

Arnold Murphy

XYZ Company

Anytown, USA 00012

Statutory Checklist

Use this checklist to help you recognize areas where you may need to refer to your state's statute to determine the proper course of action. Many of these concepts are described in later chapters.

- ☐ Filing requirements
- ☐ Incorporators
- ☐ Articles of incorporation
- ☐ Liability for preincorporation transactions
- ☐ Bylaws
- ☐ Emergency bylaws
- ☐ Corporate purposes and powers
- ☐ Corporate name
- ☐ Name reservation
- ☐ Registered office and registered agent
- ☐ Changing registered office or agent
- ☐ Resignation of registered agent
- ☐ Service of process on corporations
- ☐ Authorized shares of stock
- ☐ Terms of classes or series of stock
- ☐ Issued and outstanding shares
- ☐ Subscription for shares before incorporation
- ☐ Issuance of shares
- ☐ Liability of shareholders
- ☐ Form and content of stock certificates
- ☐ Restriction on transfer of shares
- ☐ Preemptive rights of shareholders
- ☐ Corporation's ability to acquire its own shares
- ☐ Distributions to shareholders
- ☐ Shareholder annual and special meetings
- ☐ Court ordered shareholder meetings
- ☐ Consent resolutions by shareholders without meeting
- ☐ Notice of shareholder meetings
- ☐ Waiver of notice of shareholders meetings
- ☐ Record date

Statutory Checklist (continued)

- ☐ Shareholders list for meeting
- ☐ Voting entitlement for shares
- ☐ Proxies
- ☐ Corporations' acceptance of shareholder votes
- ☐ Quorum and voting requirements for voting groups
- ☐ Modification of quorum or voting requirements
- ☐ Voting for directors/cumulative voting
- ☐ Voting trusts
- ☐ Voting agreements
- ☐ Derivative lawsuits
- ☐ Requirements and duties of board of directors
- ☐ Qualifications of directors
- ☐ Number and election of directors
- ☐ Election of directors by certain classes of shareholders
- ☐ Terms of directors
- ☐ Staggered terms for directors
- ☐ Resignation of directors
- ☐ Removal of directors by shareholders
- ☐ Removal of directors by judicial proceeding
- ☐ Vacancies on the board
- ☐ Compensation of directors
- ☐ Board meetings
- ☐ Action by board without meeting/consent resolutions
- ☐ Notice of board meetings
- ☐ Waiver of notice of board meetings
- ☐ Quorum and voting
- ☐ Committees of the board
- ☐ General standards of conduct for board members
- ☐ Conflicts of interest
- ☐ Loans to directors
- ☐ Required officers for corporation
- ☐ Duties of officers

Statutory Checklist (continued)

☐ Standard of conduct for officers

☐ Resignation and removal of officers from office

☐ Authority to indemnify directors

☐ Advances to directors for expenses

☐ Court ordered indemnification

☐ Determination and authorization of indemnification

☐ Indemnification of officers, employees, and agents

☐ Amending the articles of incorporation

☐ Merger

☐ Sale of assets

☐ Dissenting shareholders rights

☐ Dissolution

☐ Authority of foreign corporations to transact business

☐ Consequences of transacting business without authority

☐ Application for authority to transact business

☐ Amendment to application for authority

☐ Corporate name of foreign corporation

☐ Registered office and agent of foreign corporation

☐ Change of registered office or agent of foreign corporation

☐ Resignation of registered agent of foreign corporation

☐ Service of process on foreign corporation

☐ Withdrawal of a foreign corporation

☐ Corporate records required

☐ Inspection rights of shareholders

☐ Scope of shareholders' inspection rights

☐ Reports to shareholders about indemnification

☐ Corporation annual report

☐ Penalty for signing a false document

Frequently Filed Documents Checklist

Your secretary of state requires you to file certain corporate documents. These documents will usually include:

- ☐ Request to reserve corporate name
- ☐ Fictitious name reservation
- ☐ Articles of incorporation
- ☐ Amendment to articles of incorporation
- ☐ Annual report
- ☐ Change of registered office or registered agent
- ☐ Request for certificate of good standing or certificate of fact
- ☐ Application for certificate of authority
- ☐ Articles of merger
- ☐ Articles of dissolution
- ☐ Application for withdrawal of certificate of authority
- ☐ Appointment of secretary of state for certificate of service
- ☐ Application to reinstate corporate charter

Chapter 2

Articles of Incorporation

In terms of importance, the state's business corporation act has first priority; your articles of incorporation are second; and your bylaws are considered third. In the event of a conflict between the articles of incorporation and your state's act, the act will control. If a conflict exists between the articles and the bylaws, the provision in the articles will prevail.

All business corporation acts require that certain items of information be included in the articles of incorporation and that the articles, when completed, be filed with your secretary of state.

The required items are:

- The name of the corporation;
- The number of shares of stock the corporation is authorized to issue;
- The name of the registered agent and the registered office;
- The name and address of each incorporator; and
- The signature of the incorporator(s).[1]

Articles of incorporation may also include:

- The names and addresses of the initial board of directors;
- A list of the corporation's purposes;
- Any provisions which define, limit, or regulate the powers of a corporation, its board of directors or shareholders (These provisions would include any requirement for greater than majority approval for board or shareholder action, a provision prohibiting a corporation from engaging

in a particular activity, or a provision eliminating a board of directors under a close corporation statute.);

- A par value for authorized shares;
- Classes of stock with different rights and attributes; for example, preferred stock, voting and nonvoting shares, redeemable shares, convertible shares;
- Any provision imposing personal liability on shareholders for corporate debts (this would be rare); and
- Any provision required or permitted to be set forth in the bylaws.[2]

Other common provisions in the articles of incorporation include:

- Whether or not preemptive rights exist;
- Whether or not cumulative voting is available in the election of board members;
- The number and qualifications, if any, of the board;
- Whether the term of board members will be staggered;
- Whether corporate stock is intended to qualify under Section 1244 of the Internal Revenue Code, as amended;
- Whether or not the corporation elects to be a close corporation under any applicable close corporation statute — this is a mandatory requirement for corporations wishing to make this election; and
- Any provisions authorizing the indemnification of corporate officers and directors.

What Information Should You Include in Your Articles?

Your articles of incorporation should include all the required items outlined above as well as any of the other optional items listed, which are required by your state. Next, determine how much information you wish to make public. Articles of incorporation are a public record and available for inspection. As a result, many business owners wish to reveal as little information as possible about the makeup of their corporations, relying instead on bylaws and corporate minutes to provide this information.

It is virtually impossible to hide the identity of your corporate officers and directors, however. Even if the articles do not name your directors, most annual reports to the secretary of state will require the disclosure of this information. Annual reports are also public records.

Keep in mind that articles of incorporation are just one piece of the puzzle that makes up your corporation. There are risks involved in merely completing blank forms of articles which you receive from the secretary of state. Blank forms do not indicate the range of optional provisions which you can include in the articles.

For example, fill-in-the-blank forms will not tell you whether preemptive rights or cumulative voting exist nor will they explain what these things are.

The forms don't reveal whether a close corporation statute exists in your state and if it is advisable for you to use. Form articles of incorporation, therefore, limit your flexibility.

How Do You Amend Your Articles?

Most changes to the articles of incorporation require that an amendment to the articles be prepared and that the amendment process satisfy certain formalities required by your state's statutes. Shareholders have no vested right resulting from any provision in the articles of incorporation, including the articles' provisions pertaining to the management, control, capital structure, dividend entitlement, purpose, or duration of the corporation. So long as proper procedures are followed, your articles may be amended.

For certain changes, the board may amend the articles of incorporation on its own. These changes include:

- Extending the duration of a corporation formed for a limited, nonperpetual duration;
- To delete the names and addresses of the initial board of directors;
- To change the address or name of the registered office or registered agent;
- To change each issued and unissued authorized share of an outstanding class to a greater number of whole shares, if the corporation only has shares of that class outstanding; or
- To change the name to substitute the term "corporation," "incorporated," "company," "limited," or any abbreviation of the term.

Once a corporation has accepted subscriptions to purchase shares of stock, all other changes except the ones noted above require the approval of the board of directors and shareholders. Unless a greater majority is required by the articles or bylaws, a simple majority of any quorum is sufficient to authorize an amendment. A quorum is the minimum number of directors or shareholders which must be present to transact business.

Any amendment which would affect a particular class or series of shares will generally require that shareholders affected by the change have the right to vote on the change. This is true regardless of whether or not the shares are otherwise nonvoting. Examples of where this right would arise are:

The holders of nonvoting shares may have a right to vote on matters which directly impact those shares.

- Increasing or decreasing the number of authorized shares of the class;
- Reclassifying the shares into different classes or series;
- Changing rights or preferences; or
- Limiting or denying existing preemptive rights.

To be effective, articles of amendment must be filed with the appropriate secretary of state in the same manner as the articles of incorporation were originally filed. Articles of amendment should include:

- The name of the corporation;
- The full text of each amendment adopted;

- Procedures to be followed to implement the change, if the amendment provides for the exchange, reclassification, or cancellation of issued shares;
- Date each proposed amendment was adopted;
- A statement that no shareholder action was required, if amendments were adopted by the incorporator or the board; and
- A statement of the number and class of shares entitled to vote, the number actually present or represented at the meeting, and either the total number of shares voted for or against, or a statement the number of votes cast in favor was sufficient for approval, if the amendment was required to be approved by the shareholders.

Amendments to articles can also be made part of a reorganization plan. For example, articles of merger may indicate that the name of the surviving corporation shall be changed after the merger from "ABC, Inc." to "John Doe, Inc." This change takes effect on the date the articles of merger are approved by shareholders and directors. No further approval or filing is required.

In addition, if you are qualified to do business in more than one state, you will likely be required to amend your application for certificate of authority in each state where you are qualified every time you amend your articles.

The secretary of state's office charges a fee for filing articles of amendment. Contact the appropriate office to learn the fee and any peculiar filing requirements in your state.

Final Thoughts on Articles of Incorporation

Articles of incorporation are of critical importance. Once filed, your corporation springs into existence, at least in the eyes of the state. Your articles are a public document, available to anyone who might request a copy from the secretary of state. At a minimum, the articles tell the public who you are and how you may be contacted; who the directors are and their addresses; the business which the corporation will engage in; and any restrictions which may be imposed upon the voting rights of directors and shareholders.

Unlike bylaws which can often be amended by a vote of directors with no public declaration, most amendments to the articles require shareholders' approval utilizing statutory articles and bylaws procedures and requirements, and the filing of articles of amendment with the secretary of state.

What you don't say in your articles can have important consequences. Failure to provide for preemptive rights or cumulative voting in your articles will mean that your corporation won't have them in certain states or that your corporation will have them in others.

It's important to know what your state law is before you file your articles. Beware of fill-in-the-blank-form articles. What you don't know could hurt you. Forewarned is forearmed.

For your review, a sample form of articles of incorporation follows this chapter. The sample has been annotated to explain briefly its contents, and it demonstrates the types of provisions which are required or considered optional in the articles. It would be rare indeed to find a set of articles filed recently which contain all of the sample provisions. Working with your business lawyer, see what works best for you.

SAMPLE: Articles of Incorporation

ARTICLES OF INCORPORATION OF JOHN DOE, INC.

The undersigned, a natural person of the age of 18 or more, for the purpose of forming a corporation under the General Business Corporation Act of the State of Oz, hereby adopt the following Articles of Incorporation:

ARTICLE I. Name

The name of the corporation is John Doe, Inc.

ARTICLE II. Stock

The aggregate number of shares of stock which the corporation shall have authority to issue is 30,000 shares, each of which shall have no par value, and all of which shall be of one classification.

ARTICLE III. Registered Agent/Office

The address of the corporation's initial registered office in the state of Oz is 1600 Pennsylvania Ave., Anytown, OZ 11111, and the name of its initial registered agent at such address is Jane Doe.

ARTICLE IV. Incorporator

The name and address of the incorporator is as follows: Ima Lawyer, Esq., 123 Main St., Anytown, OZ 11111

The undersigned incorporator declares under penalty of perjury that he or she has examined the foregoing Articles of Incorporation and that to the best of his/her knowledge, information and belief, the information contained therein is true, correct, and complete.

_____

Signature(s) of incorporator(s)

The person to contact with any questions concerning this filing is: Ima Lawyer, Esq., 123 Main St., Anytown, OZ 11111, (503) 555-1234.

OPTIONAL PROVISIONS UNDER RMBCA

ARTICLE V. Initial Board of Directors

The number of directors to constitute the board of directors shall be three, as determined by the bylaws of the corporation. The names and addresses of the initial board of directors are as follows:

Name	Address
Jane Doe	1600 Pennsylvania Ave., Anytown, OZ 11111
John Doe	1600 Pennsylvania Ave., Anytown, OZ 11111
Joan Doe	1600 Pennsylvania Ave., Anytown, OZ 11111

State the maximum number of shares the corporation may issue and if you had more than one class of stock.

Use your lawyer or CEO as registered agent.

Using your lawyer as incorporator can protect the identities of your directors and officers and facilitate the processing of any lawsuits against the corporation.

If required, you will need to have your articles notarized. Check with the secretary of state.

SAMPLE: Articles of Incorporation (continued)

ARTICLE VI. Perpetual Duration

The duration of the corporation is perpetual.

ARTICLE VII. Purpose

This corporation is organized and formed to [add specific purpose] and to engage in any lawful act or activity for which corporations may be organized under the Oz General Business Corporation Act.

ARTICLE VIII. Grant of Preemptive Rights

Alternate Article I

The preemptive rights of shareholders to acquire additional shares of capital stock of the corporation are as follows: each shareholder shall be entitled as a matter of right to subscribe for, purchase or otherwise acquire any additional shares of the specific class of stock of the corporation held by the respective shareholder including, but not limited to, shares which are authorized herein but issues on or hereafter the date of incorporation, shares which are subsequently authorized and issued and shares which are acquired and reissued by the corporation.

Alternate Article II

There shall be no preemptive rights.

ARTICLE IX. Close Corporation Election, Elimination of Board

This corporation elects to be treated as a statutory close corporation, and as such determines to eliminate its board of directors.

ARTICLE X. Bylaw Amendments

The board of directors may repeal or amend the bylaws of the corporation and may adopt new or additional bylaws, and the articles of incorporation shall be amended as provided in the Oz General Business Corporation Act.

ARTICLE XI. Cumulative Voting for Directors

Alternate Article I

At each election of directors, each shareholder entitled to vote shall be entitled to cast cumulative votes in accordance with the terms and conditions of the bylaws of the corporation. In such event, each shareholder may vote either by giving one candidate as many votes as equals the number of directors to be elected multiplied by the number of the shareholder's shares or by distributing such cumulative votes among any number of such candidates.

Alternate Article II

There shall be no cumulative voting for directors.

Lenders and suppliers like to see a list of purposes in your articles.

In some states, preemptive rights exist unless your articles exclude them. Other states are just the opposite.

If you wish to have a close corporation, your articles must say so. Then you must delete or modify any other mentions of the board of directors.

Like preemptive rights, cumulative voting for directors exists automatically in some states. In others, your articles must provide for it.

SAMPLE: Articles of Incorporation (continued)

ARTICLE XII. Board Vacancies

Any vacancy of the board of directors may be filled by the affirmative vote of majority of the remaining directors. Any director so elected shall serve until the director's successor has been elected and qualified.

ARTICLE XIII. Indemnification

The corporation shall have the power to indemnify to the fullest extent permitted by law any person who is made, or threatened to be made, a party to any action, suit or proceeding, whether civil, criminal, administrative, investigative or otherwise (including an action, suit or proceeding by or in the right of the corporation) by reason of the fact that the person is or was a director, officer, employee or agent of the corporation, or a fiduciary within the meaning of the Employee Retirement Security Act of 1974, as amended, with respect to any employee benefit plans of the corporation, or serves at the request of the corporation as a director, officer, employee, or agent, or as a partnership, joint venture, trust or other enterprise, and their respective heirs, administrators, personal representatives, successors and assigns. Indemnification specifically provided by the Oz General Business Corporation Act shall not be deemed exclusive of any other rights to which such director, officer, employee or agent may be entitled under any bylaw, agreement, vote of shareholders or disinterested directors or otherwise. The corporation, its officers, directors, employees or agents shall be fully protected in taking any action or making any payment under this Article or in refusing to do so upon the advice of independent counsel.

ARTICLE XIV. No Personal Liability

No director of the corporation shall be personally liable to the corporation or its shareholders for monetary damages for conduct as a director, except that this provision shall not apply to: (a) Any breach of the director's duty of loyalty to the corporation or its shareholders; (b) Any acts or omissions not in good faith or which involve intentional misconduct or a knowing violation of law; (c) Any distribution which is unlawful; (d) Any transaction from which the director derived an improper personal benefit; or (e) Any act or omission occurring prior to the date on which these Articles of Incorporation are filed with the Secretary of State.

ARTICLE XV. Corporation Purchase of Its Own Shares

The corporation shall have the right to purchase, directly or indirectly, its own shares to the extent of unreserved and unrestricted capital surplus available therefore.

Your ability to attract outside directors will be enhanced if your corporation authorizes the indemnification and no personal liability provisions in Articles XIII and XIV. Note, however, that there is no relief from personal liability where the claim is based on breach of duty, intentional misconduct, unlawful distribution, any transaction where a director improperly receives a personal benefit, or for any act occurring prior to the filing of the articles.

Chapter 3

Corporate Bylaws

The third part of the sources of authority trilogy is bylaws. Bylaws are rules and procedures and deal with such things as meetings of shareholders and directors, officers, quorum, and more. While there is no magic number of pages or provisions which bylaws must contain, a good set of bylaws should be comprehensive. This chapter describes such a set.

As long as shareholders, officers, and directors are in accord, little attention is paid to the formal requirements and procedures found in the bylaws; however, the more shareholders, officers, or directors which a corporation has, the greater likelihood of disagreement and the need to resort to the bylaws.

For example, assume that your corporation has three shareholders. Historically, each shareholder has worked well with the others. Now, however, one of the shareholders has rebelled. For whatever reason, the shareholder no longer agrees with the other two and refuses to sign consent resolutions. The board has no choice but to have formal meetings for itself and its shareholders. The bylaws will tell you how to call a meeting and how to transact business at it.

Issues commonly addressed in bylaws are:

- Authority of the board to fix the location of the corporation's principal executive office;
- The place for shareholder's meetings (either the corporation's principal place of business or wherever the board may choose);
- The time and place for annual shareholder meetings, usually designated by the "second Monday of December" or similar language;

- The manner of calling special meetings of the shareholders:
  - Can be called by the board, the president, or the holders of at least 10% of outstanding shares — the 10% requirement is intended to prevent the calling of meeting to discuss insubstantial or nuisance matters;
  - Require a written notice mailed or personally delivered to all shareholders not more than 60 nor less than 10 days before the meeting;
  - Require a quorum to act, usually more than 50% of the outstanding shares of voting stock required unless the bylaws or articles require a higher percentage; and
  - Whether or not a meeting can be adjourned and reconvened without requiring a new notice to shareholders — normally acceptable if meeting is reconvened within 45 days and the new date and time are announced prior to adjournment;
- Voting at shareholder meetings, including such issues as cumulative voting, record date, proxies, and election inspectors, all of which are discussed in Chapter 9;
- Issues pertaining to the board of directors, including:
  - The powers of the board;
  - The number and qualification of directors;
  - How directors are elected;
  - The term of office;
  - How board vacancies are filled;
  - Procedures for calling regularly scheduled or special meetings of the board;
  - How the board can act without meeting;
  - Whether or not the board can designate committees, and if so, the make up and powers of the committee;
  - The standard of care which directors must exercise;
  - Provisions relating to indemnification of board members or corporate officers, including a list of each office a description of the duties of each officer (discussed in Chapter 4); and
- Other maintenance matters, including:
  - Restrictions regarding loans to or guarantees of director or officer debts;
  - Who can sign corporate checks;
  - Restrictive language limiting stock transfers;
  - Required records and reports;
  - Maintenance and inspection of corporate records; and
  - Procedures for amending the bylaws.

As you can see, bylaws cover a lot of territory. By their nature, bylaws provide technical rules of procedure. Bylaws should be tailored to fit your corporation. Because so many provisions of the business corporation acts can be modified by the bylaws, you should actively participate in their creation. If you don't, you could lose flexibility and may find yourself with procedural safeguards that you don't want.

For example, you own more than 50% of John Doe, Inc. Jane and Joan together own 49% of the corporation. You wish to sell John Doe, Inc., but Jane and Joan don't agree. Over cocktails, you learn from a lawyer friend that your proposed sale only requires a majority vote of the shareholders under the state statute. As the lawyer drifts away, she suggests that you check the corporate bylaws to see if the requirement has been modified. So you dust off the corporate bylaws that you acquired when you bought your corporate minute book, and as you read through the bylaws, you are appalled to learn that a sale requires a two-thirds shareholder approval and not a mere majority. You think to yourself, "I would never have agreed to that." No sale.

Bylaws are the primary source of authority for procedures to be followed in calling and conducting board and shareholder meetings. You don't have to refer to the bylaws often, but when you do, it's comforting to know that they will work as you intended when you prepared them.

How Do You Amend Bylaws?

Generally, the board of directors retains the right to amend or repeal corporate bylaws. However, articles of incorporation or bylaws often require shareholder approval to amend all or certain portions of the bylaws. Whether director or shareholder approval is required, a majority vote is usually sufficient unless a higher percentage is required by the articles or bylaws. The amendment process would be handled in the manner described in chapters 8 and 9 pertaining to director and shareholder meetings. Even if the articles and bylaws don't require shareholder approval in order to amend the bylaws, shareholders can also amend or repeal bylaws.

Final Thoughts on Bylaws

Remember those words which preface most portions of business corporation acts: "Unless otherwise provided in the articles of incorporation or bylaws ...?" These words provide the opportunity to modify your corporation to fit your needs. This is especially true for bylaws.

Bylaws provide rules and procedures that deal with the internal governance of your corporation. How many officers will you have? How are directors elected? Are there to be any super majority voting requirements? Issues of vital importance to corporate health and well-being are defined in the bylaws.

To illustrate the importance of bylaws, a sample set of bylaws follows this chapter. It is annotated to help you identify key areas which may be important for your business. It is only a sample; there are many different forms of bylaws which can be used. Following the sample bylaws, there is a checklist to assist you in preparing your own bylaws.

SAMPLE: Bylaws

Bylaws of John Doe, Inc.

ARTICLE I. Offices

Section 1.1 Principal Office. The board of directors shall fix the location of the Corporation's principal place of business within or outside the state of Oz. The Corporation may have such other offices, either within or without the state of Oz, as the board of directors may designate or as the business of the Corporation may require.

Section 1.2. Registered Office; Registered Agent. The registered office of the Corporation required by the Oz Business Corporation Act to be maintained in the state of Oz may be, but need not be, identical with the principal office in the state of Oz, and the address of the registered office may be changed from time to time by the board of directors. The board of directors shall also designate and maintain a registered agent within the state of Oz in accordance with the Oz Business Corporation Act.

ARTICLE II. Shareholders

State the date and time for annual meetings. No further notice may be required for the annual meeting.

Section 2.1. Annual Meetings. The annual shareholders' meeting shall be held on the first Monday of December of each year at 10:00 A.M. for the purpose of electing directors and for the transaction of such other business as may come before the meeting. If the day fixed for the annual meeting shall be a legal holiday in the state of Oz, such meeting shall be held on the next succeeding business day. Failure to hold the annual meeting at the designated time shall not work a forfeiture or dissolution on the Corporation.

Section 2.2. Failure to Hold the Annual Meeting. If the annual meeting is not held at the designated time, the president or the board of directors may call the annual meeting at a time fixed by them not more than 60 days after such designated time by proper notice designating the meeting as the annual meeting. If the annual meeting is not held at the designated time or during the 60-day period thereafter, the annual meeting may be called by the holders of not less than 10 percent of all the shares entitled to vote at the meeting. In such event, notice shall be given not more than 15 days after the expiration of such 60-day period. Such notice shall fix the time of the meeting at the earliest date permissible under the applicable notice requirements.

Shareholders' meetings, other than annual meetings, are called special meetings. Determine who can call a special meeting and how.

Section 2.3. Special Meetings. Special meetings of the shareholders, for any purpose or purposes, unless otherwise prescribed by statute, may be called by the president or by the board of directors, and shall be called by the president at the request of the holders of not less than 10 percent of all the outstanding shares of the Corporation entitled to vote at the meeting. If a special meeting is called by any person or persons other than the board of directors, the request shall be in writing specifying the time of such meeting and the general nature of the business proposed to be transacted. The request shall be delivered personally or sent by registered mail or by telegraphic or other fac-simile transmission to the president or vice-president and the secretary of the Corporation. Upon receiving the request, the secretary shall cause notice of the meeting to be provided to the shareholders entitled to vote in accordance with Section 2.5.

Section 2.4. Place of Meeting. The board of directors may designate any place, either within or without the state of Oz, as the place of meeting for any annual meeting or special meeting called by the board of directors. A waiver of notice signed by all shareholders entitled to vote at a meeting may desig-nate any place, either within or without the state of Oz, as the place for hold-ing the meeting. If no designation is made, or if a special meeting is other-wise called, the place of meeting shall be at the principal office of the Corpo-ration in the state of Oz.

Section 2.5. Notice of Meeting. Written notice stating the place, day and hour of the meeting and, in the case of a special meeting, the purpose or pur-poses for which the meeting is called, shall be delivered not fewer than 10 nor more than 50 days before the date of the meeting, either personally or by mail, by or at the direction of the president, the secretary, or the persons call-ing the meeting, to each shareholder of record entitled to vote at such meet-ing. If mailed, such notice shall be deemed to be delivered when deposited in the United States mail, addressed to the shareholder's address as it appears on the stock transfer books of the Corporation, postage prepaid. An affidavit of the mailing or other means of giving any notice of any shareholders meet-ing shall be executed by the secretary, assistant secretary, or any other person providing the notice on behalf of the Corporation. Shareholders may waive notice of any meeting by a signed writing. Attendance by the shareholder at any meeting shall also constitute a waiver of notice of that meeting.

Section 2.6. Closing of Transfer Books; Record Date. For the purpose of determining the shareholders entitled to notice of, or to vote at, any meeting of shareholders or any adjournment of the meeting, or to determine the share-holders entitled to receive payment of any dividend, or in order to make a determination of shareholders for any other proper purpose, the board of directors may provide that the stock transfer books shall be closed for a stat-ed period not to exceed, in any case, 50 days. If the stock transfer books shall be closed for the purpose of determining shareholders entitled to notice of, or to vote at, a meeting of shareholders, such books shall be closed for at least 10 days immediately preceding such meeting. In lieu of closing the stock transfer books, the board of directors may fix in advance a date as the record date for any such determination of shareholders, such date in any case to be not more than 50 days and, in case of a meeting of shareholders, not fewer than 10 days prior to the date on which the particular action requiring such

It is a good idea to provide notice of every meeting. This facilitates establishing a quo-rum. For special meetings, the pur-pose of the meet-ing must be stated.

Who receives notice, who is entitled to vote, or who receives any declared dividend? The board should declare a record date.

SAMPLE: Bylaws (continued)

determination of shareholders is to be taken. If the stock transfer books are not closed, and no record date is fixed for the determination of shareholders entitled to notice of, or to vote at, a meeting of shareholders, or shareholders entitled to receive payment of a dividend, the date on which notice of the meeting is mailed or the date on which the resolution of the board of directors declaring such dividend is adopted, as the case may be, shall be the record date for such determination of shareholders. When a determination of shareholders entitled to vote at any meeting of shareholders has been made as provided in this section, such determination shall apply to any adjournment of such meeting.

Section 2.7. Voting Record. The officer or agent having charge of the stock transfer books for the shares of the Corporation shall make, at least 10 days before each shareholders' meeting, a complete record of the shareholders entitled to vote at such meeting, or any adjournment of such meeting, arranged in alphabetical order, with the address of and the number of shares held by each, which record, for a period of 10 days prior to the meeting, shall be kept on file at the the registered office of the Corporation, and shall be subject to inspection by any shareholder at any time during usual business hours. Such record shall also be produced and kept open at the time and place of the meeting, and shall be subject to the inspection of any shareholder during the whole time of the meeting. The original stock transfer books shall be *prima facie* evidence as to who are the shareholders entitled to examine such record or transfer books, or to vote at any shareholders' meeting.

Section 2.8. Quorum. A majority of the outstanding shares of the Corporation entitled to vote, represented in person or by proxy, shall constitute a quorum at a shareholders' meeting. If less than a majority of the outstanding shares are represented at a meeting, a majority of the shares so represented may adjourn the meeting in accordance with Section 2.13. The shareholders present at a duly organized meeting may continue to transact business until adjournment, notwithstanding the withdrawal of enough shareholders to leave fewer than a quorum.

Section 2.9. Proxies. At all meetings of shareholders, a shareholder may vote in person, by proxy executed in writing by the shareholder, or by the shareholder's duly authorized attorney-in-fact. Such proxy shall be filed with the secretary of the Corporation before, or at the time of, the meeting. No proxy shall be valid after 11 months from the date of its execution, unless otherwise provided in the proxy. A validly executed proxy, which does not state that it is irrevocable, shall continue in full force and effect unless (i) revoked by the person executing it prior to the vote by a writing signed by the shareholder and delivered to the Corporation stating that it is revoked or by a subsequent proxy executed by the person executing the earlier proxy or by

Before each meeting, the corporate secretary will compile an alphabetical list of shareholders entitled to vote.

Unless otherwise stated, a quorum occurs when a majority of shares cast (not shareholders) is present.

A proxy is a written authorization to vote another's shares. They are generally easily revoked.

SAMPLE: Bylaws (continued)

the shareholder's attendance at the meeting and voting in person; or (ii) written notice of the death or incapacity of the maker of the proxy is received by the Corporation prior to the vote.

Section 2.10. Voting. Each outstanding share entitled to vote shall be entitled to one vote upon each matter submitted to a vote at a meeting of shareholders, except as otherwise provided in the articles of incorporation. The vote of the holders of a majority of the shares present and entitled to vote at any duly organized meeting shall decide any question unless the vote of a greater number shall be required by law or the articles of incorporation.

Section 2.11. Consent Resolutions. Any action required to be taken at a meeting of the shareholders, or any other action which may be taken at a meeting of the shareholders, may be taken without a meeting if a consent in writing, setting forth the action so taken, shall be signed by all shareholders entitled to vote with respect to the subject matter of the action.

Section 2.12. Cumulative Voting. At each election for directors, each shareholder entitled to vote shall be entitled to cast cumulative votes, either by giving one candidate as many votes as equals the number of directors to be elected multiplied by the number of the shareholder's shares, or by distributing such cumulative votes among any number of such candidates.

Section 2.13. Adjourned Meeting. Any shareholders' meeting, annual or special, whether or not a quorum is present, may be adjourned from time to time by the vote of a majority of shares represented at the meeting, either in person or by proxy, but in the absence of a quorum, no further business may be transacted. If a meeting is adjourned, notice need not be given of the adjourned meeting if the time, date and place are announced at the meeting at which the adjournment is taken, unless a new record date for the adjourned meeting is fixed or unless the adjournment is for more than forty-five (45) days from the date set for the original meeting, in which case the board of directors shall set a new record date, and shareholders shall be notified in accordance with Section 2.5.

Section 2.14. Election Inspectors. Before any meeting of shareholders, the board of directors may appoint any persons other than the nominees for office to act as inspectors of election at the meeting or its adjournment. The number of inspectors shall be either one or three. Inspectors shall (i) determine the number of shares outstanding and the voting power of each, the shares represented at the meeting, the existence of a quorum, and the authenticity, validity and effect of proxies; (ii) receive ballots, votes or consents; (iii) hear and determine all challenges in any way arising in connection with the right to vote; (iv) count and tabulate all votes and consents; (v) determine when polls should close; (vi) determine the result of the election; and (vii) do any other acts that may be required to properly and fairly conduct the election.

Here, there is one vote per share. If you desire greater voting rights, your articles and bylaws would have to provide for it.

You can avoid face-to-face meetings. See Chapter 9.

Cumulative voting is provided in section 2.12. This provision should be consistent with your articles.

If you lack a quorum, you can adjourn to a later date. Whether or not new notice is required depends on how much time elapses between the scheduled and the reconvened meetings.

SAMPLE: Bylaws (continued)

ARTICLE III. Board of Directors

Section 3.1. General Powers. The business and affairs of the Corporation shall be managed by its board of directors. Without limiting this general power, the board shall have the power and authority to (i) select and remove all officers, agents, and employees, prescribe their duties and fix their compensation; (ii) change the principal executive office or the principal business office of the Corporation, cause the Corporation to qualify to do business in all jurisdictions where it is doing business, and designate locations within and without the state of Oz for shareholders' meetings; (iii) authorize the issuance of shares of stock, upon such terms and conditions as the board may deem lawful and proper; and (iv) borrow and incur indebtedness for corporate purposes, execute and deliver notes, bonds, evidences of indebtedness, mortgages, or other security for any such indebtedness.

Section 3.2. Number; Tenure. The number of directors shall be set forth in the articles of incorporation, as amended from time to time. Each director shall hold office until the next annual meeting of shareholders and until the director's successor has been duly elected and qualified. Directors need not be residents of the state of Oz to serve.

Section 3.3. Regular Meetings. A regular meeting of the board of directors shall be held without further notice other than this bylaw immediately after, and at the same place as, the annual meeting of shareholders. The board of directors may provide by resolution the time and place, either within or without the state of Oz, for the holding of additional regular meetings without other notice than such resolution.

Section 3.4. Special Meetings. Special meetings of the board of directors may be called by, or at the request of, the president or any director. The person or persons authorized to call a special meeting of the board may fix any place, either within or without the state of Oz, as the place for holding any special meeting of the board of directors called by him, her, or them.

Section 3.5. Conference Call. Any regular or special meeting of the board of directors may be by means of conference telephone or similar communications equipment allowing all persons participating in the meeting to hear each other. Participation in such a meeting shall constitute presence in person at the meeting.

Section 3.6. Notice. Notice of any special meeting shall be given at least 10 days prior to such meeting by written notice delivered personally or mailed to each director at the director's business address, or by telegram. If mailed, such notice shall be deemed to be delivered when deposited in the United States mail, properly addressed with postage prepaid. If notice is given by telegram, such notice shall be deemed to be delivered when the telegram is delivered to the telegraph company. Any director may waive notice of any

---

The board receives a broad grant of power to act.

Section 3.2 should be consistent with the articles.

Boards have regularly scheduled meetings and special meetings, including a meeting immediately after the annual shareholders' meeting.

You should recognize the availability of a wide range of transmission services.

As with shareholders, special meetings of directors must be properly noticed and called. Failure to comply could invalidate any action taken.

SAMPLE: Bylaws (continued)

meeting. The attendance of a director at a meeting shall constitute a waiver of notice of such meeting, except where a director attends a meeting for the express purpose of objecting to the transaction of any business because the meeting is not lawfully called or convened. Neither the business to be transacted at, nor the purposes of, any regular or special meeting of the board need be specified in the notice or waiver of notice of such meeting.

Section 3.7. Quorum. A majority of the number of directors shall constitute a quorum for the transaction of business at any meeting of the board of directors. If less than a majority is present at a meeting, the director or directors present may adjourn the meeting from time to time in accordance with Section 3.14.

Majority rules unless you provide otherwise.

Section 3.8. Manner of Acting. The act of the directors present at a meeting at which a quorum is present shall be the act of the board of directors.

Section 3.9. Removal. All or any number of the directors may be removed, with or without cause, at a special meeting of the shareholders called for that purpose, by a vote of the majority of the shares then entitled to vote at an election of directors. If fewer than all of the directors are removed, no one director may be removed if the votes cast against such director's removal would be sufficient to elect such director if then cumulatively voted at an election for the entire board of directors.

Directors can be removed by shareholders at any time with or without cause.

Section 3.10. Vacancies. Any vacancy occurring in the board of directors may be filled by the affirmative vote of a majority of the remaining directors, event though less than a quorum of the board of directors, or by a sole remaining director. A director elected to fill a vacancy shall be elected for the unexpired term of the director's predecessor in office. Any directorship to be filled by reason of an increase in the number of directors shall be filled by election at an annual meeting or at a special meeting of shareholders called for that purpose, unless otherwise provided in the articles of incorporation.

The board retains the right to fill vacancies. Appointed board members fill the unexpired term of a director's predecessor.

Section 3.11. Compensation. By resolution of the board, each director may be paid the director's expenses, if any, of attendance at each meeting of the board of directors, and may be paid a stated salary as director, or a fixed sum for attendance at each meeting of the board of directors, or both. No such payment shall preclude any director from serving the Corporation in any other capacity and receiving compensation for such service.

Director's fees are acceptable and should be reasonable in amount.

Section 3.12. Presumption of Assent. A director who is present at a meeting of the board at which action on any corporate matter is taken is presumed to have assented to the action taken, unless the director's dissent shall be entered in the minutes of the meeting, or unless the director shall file his or her written dissent to the action with the person acting as the secretary of the meeting before the adjournment of the meeting, or unless the director shall

If a director attends a meeting but doesn't speak, he or she is presumed to agree with any action authorized.

forward such dissent by registered mail to the secretary of the Corporation immediately after the adjournment of the meeting. Such right to dissent shall not apply to a director who voted in favor of such action.

See Chapter 8 for more on consent meetings.

Like shareholders, a director's meeting can also be adjourned and reconvened when no quorum exists.

Section 3.13. Action by Consent. Any action that may be taken at a meeting of the directors may be taken without a meeting is a consent in writing, setting forth the action so taken, shall be signed by all the directors.

Section 3.14. Adjournment. A majority of the directors present, whether or not constituting a quorum, may adjourn any meeting to another time and place. Notice of the time and place for holding an adjourned meeting need not be given unless the meeting is adjourned for more than 24 hours, in which case notice of such time and place shall be given prior to the time of the adjourned meeting to the directors who were not present at the time of adjournment.

A director's standard of care is important. See Chapter 4.

Section 3.15. Standard of Care; Liability. Each director shall exercise such powers and otherwise perform such duties in good faith, in the matter which the director believes to be in the best interests of the Corporation and with such care, including reasonable inquiry using ordinary care and prudence as a person in a like position would use under similar circumstances. In performing his or her duties, each director shall be entitled to rely on information, opinions, reports or statements, including financial statements or data prepared or presented by (i) one or more officers or employees of the Corporation which the director believes to be reliable and competent; (ii) counsel, independent accountants or similar outside experts; or (iii) a committee of the board on which the director is not a member unless the director has reason to believe after reasonable inquiry that reliance on the report is not warranted.

Common committees include executive, finance, compensation, and long-range planning committees.

Section 3.16. Committees. The board by resolution adopted by a majority of the directors may designate one or more committees, each consisting of one or more directors, to serve at the pleasure of the board. Any such committee shall have the authority of the board, except with respect to (i) the approval of any action which by law, articles of incorporation or these bylaws requires shareholder approval; (ii) the filling of vacancies on the board or any committee; (iii) the fixing of compensation for board members; (iv) the amendment or repeal of bylaws or the adoption of new bylaws; (v) the amendment or repeal of any board of directors' resolution; or (vi) the creation of other committees of the board.

ARTICLE IV. Officers

Section 4.1. Number. The officers of the Corporation shall include a president, one or more vice-presidents (number to be determined by the board), a secretary, and a treasurer, each of whom shall be appointed by the board. Such other officers and assistant officers and agents as may be deemed necessary may be appointed by the board. Any two or more offices may be held by the same person.

SAMPLE: Bylaws (continued)

Section 4.2. Appointment; Term of Office. The officers of the Corporation to be appointed by the board shall be appointed annually at the first meeting of the board held after each annual shareholders' meeting. If the appointment of officers shall not be held at such meeting, the officers shall be appointed as soon thereafter as may be convenient. Each officer shall hold office until a successor is appointed, or until the officer's death, or until the officer resigns, or is removed in the manner provided in Section 4.3.

Section 4.3. Removal. Any officer or agent may be removed by the board whenever in its judgment the best interests of the Corporation will be served by such removal, but such removal shall be without prejudice to the contract rights, if any, of the person so removed. Appointment of an officer or agent shall not, in itself, create contract rights.

Section 4.4. Vacancies. A vacancy in any office because of death, resignation, removal, disqualification, or otherwise may be filled by the board for the unexpired portion of the term.

Section 4.5. President. The president shall be the principal executive officer of the Corporation and subject to the control of the board. The president shall supervise and control all the business and affairs of the Corporation. Without limitation, the president shall preside at all meetings of shareholders and directors, perform all duties incident to the office of president, and such other duties as may be prescribed by the board from time to time.

Section 4.6. Vice-President. In the absence of the president or in the event of the president's death, or inability or refusal to act, the vice-president shall perform the duties of the president, and when so acting, shall have all the powers of, and be subject to all the restrictions upon the president. In addition, the vice-president shall perform such other duties as may be assigned to him or her from time to time by the board.

Section 4.7. Secretary. The secretary shall (i) keep the minutes of the shareholder and the board of directors' meetings in one or more books maintained for that purpose; (ii) provide for the giving of notices required by these bylaws or by law; (iii) be custodian of the corporate records and of the Corporate seal; (iv) keep a register of the mailing address of each shareholder, which shall be furnished to the secretary by each shareholder; (v) sign with the president or vice-president certificates of the Corporation's shares of stock, the issuance of which shall have been authorized by resolution of the board of directors; (vi) have general charge of the stock transfer books of the Corporation; and (vii) perform all duties incident to the office of secretary and such other duties as from time to time may be assigned to him or her by the president or the board.

Section 4.8. Treasurer. The treasurer shall (i) have charge and custody of, and be responsible for, all funds and securities of the Corporation; (ii)

You name the offices, and directors appoint the individuals to fill the role. Officers are usually removable at any time, with or without cause. If an officer has an employment agreement, he or she can still be removed, but the corporation may be liable to the officer for breach of contract.

Statutes generally require only a president and a secretary.

SAMPLE: Bylaws (continued)

receive, and give receipts for, moneys due and payable to the Corporation from any source, and deposit all such moneys in the name of the Corporation in such depositories as may be designated by the board from time to time; and (iii) perform all other duties incident to the office of treasurer and such other duties as may be assigned to him or her by the president or the board.

Section 4.9. Salaries. The salaries of officers shall be fixed from time to time by the board. No officer shall be prevented from receiving a salary by reason of the fact that the officer is also a director of the Corporation.

ARTICLE V. Certificates for Shares and Transfer

Section 5.1. Certificates for Shares. Certificates representing shares of the corporation shall be in the form determined by the board. Certificates shall be signed by the president or vice president and the secretary or any assistant secretary. All certificates shall be consecutively numbered or otherwise identified. The name and address of each person to whom shares are issued, together with the number of shares and date of issue shall be entered on the stock transfer books of the Corporation. All certificates surrendered to the Corporation shall be cancelled. No new certificate shall be issued until the former certificate for a like number of shares shall have been surrendered and cancelled, except that in the case of a lost, destroyed or mutilated certificate, a new one may be issued for it upon such terms and indemnity to the Corporation as the board may require.

The board approves the stock certificate. As noted in Chapter 5, there is no magic to this form.

Section 5.2. Transfer. Shares of the Corporation's stock may be transferred only on the stock transfer books of the Corporation by the holder of record of such shares or by his or her legal representative. The person in whose name the shares are issued on the books of the Corporation shall be deemed by the Corporation to be the owner of such shares for all purposes.

ARTICLE VI. Contracts, Loans, Checks, and Deposits

Section 6.1. Contracts. The board may authorize any officer, employee, or agent to enter into any contract, or execute and deliver any instrument, in the name of and on behalf of the Corporation, and such authority may be general or confined to specific instances.

Section 6.2. Loans. No loans shall be contracted on behalf of the Corporation, and no evidences of indebtedness shall be issued in its name, unless authorized by a resolution of the board. Such authority may be general or confined to specific instances.

Section 6.3. Checks, Drafts. All checks, drafts, or other orders for the payment of money, notes or other evidences of indebtedness issued in the name of the Corporation, shall be signed by such officer, officers, agent or agents of the Corporation and in such manner as shall from time to time be determined by board resolution.

SAMPLE: Bylaws (continued)

Section 6.4. Deposits. All funds of the Corporation not otherwise employed shall be deposited from time to time to the credit of the Corporation in such banks, trust companies, or other depositories as the board selects from time to time.

ARTICLE VII. Indemnification; Interested Parties; Insurance

Section 7.1. Indemnification. The Corporation shall indemnify to the fullest extent permitted by the Oz Business Corporation Act any director, officer, employee, agent, or any other person who has been made, or is threatened to be made, a party to an action, suit, or proceeding, whether civil, criminal, administrative, investigative, or otherwise (including an action, suit, or proceeding by or in the right of the Corporation) by reason of the fact that the person is or was a director, officer, employee or agent of the Corporation, or a fiduciary within the meaning of any federal, state or local law or regulation. The right to and the amount of indemnification shall be determined in accordance with the provisions of the Oz Business Corporation Act in effect at the time of the determination.

These provisions should be consistent with your articles and applicable state law.

Section 7.2. Interested Parties. A director of the Corporation shall not be disqualified by the director's office from contracting with the corporation as vendor, purchaser, or otherwise; nor shall any contract or arrangement entered into by or on behalf of the Corporation in which any director is in any way interested be avoided on that account, provided that such contract or arrangement shall have been approved or ratified by a majority of the board without counting in such majority the interested director, although such director may be counted toward a quorum, or shall have been approved or ratified by the affirmative action of the holders of a majority of the outstanding shares of the Corporation, and the interest shall have been disclosed or known to the approving or ratifying directors or shareholders.

This provision relates to the duty of loyalty that is described in Chapter 4.

Section 7.3. Insurance. The Corporation may upon a determination by the board purchase and maintain insurance on behalf of any agent of the Corporation, including its directors, officers and employees, against any liability which might be asserted against or incurred by the agent in such capacity, or which might arise out of the agent's status as such, whether or not the Corporation would have the power to indemnify the agent under Section 7.1.

ARTICLE VIII. Corporate Loans and Guarantees

Section 8.1. Corporate Loans and Guarantees to Agents. Except as provided below, the Corporation shall not make any loan of money or property to, or guarantee any obligations of, any director, officer, employee or agent of the Corporation unless the loan or guarantee is otherwise adequately secured, except by the vote of the holders of a majority of the shares of all classes of stock, regardless of whether or not such classes of stock otherwise provide for voting rights.

SAMPLE: Bylaws (continued)

ARTICLE IX. Amendments

Section 9.1. Amendments. These bylaws may be altered, amended, or repealed, and new bylaws may be adopted by a majority vote of the board at any regular or special meeting, subject to repeal or change by action of the shareholders.

Corporate Secretary

Approved by the Board of Directors
of John Doe, Inc.

Date

Key Matters for Bylaws Checklist

- ☐ Does the Board of Directors have the power to fix the principal office location of the corporation?
- ☐ What is the time, date, and place of annual shareholders' meetings?
- ☐ Are there procedures for calling a special shareholders' meeting?
- ☐ Is notice required for shareholders' meetings and are there provisions for waiving notice?
- ☐ What are quorum requirements for shareholders' meetings?
- ☐ Is there a procedure for adjourning shareholders' meetings?
- ☐ How do you vote at shareholders' meetings?
- ☐ Are there any requirements for proxies?
- ☐ How do you determine record date and eligibility to vote?
- ☐ Are consent resolutions permitted for shareholders?
- ☐ Who designates election inspectors?
- ☐ What are the directors' powers?
- ☐ How many directors are there?
- ☐ Who can be a director?
- ☐ How are directors elected? What are there terms of office? How do you fill vacancies on the board?
- ☐ Who sets the time, place, and date of annual or regularly scheduled meetings?
- ☐ Who can call special meetings?
- ☐ What constitutes a quorum for directors' meetings?
- ☐ Who can adjourn a directors' meeting?
- ☐ Are consent resolutions for directors permitted?
- ☐ What are directors' standards of care?
- ☐ Can directors appoint committees?
- ☐ Which officers must the corporation have and which ones are optional?
- ☐ What are the officers' duties?
- ☐ How are officers removed and who fills officer vacancies?
- ☐ Can officers, directors, employees, and agents of the corporation be indemnified by the corporation?
- ☐ May corporate loans to, and loan guarantees of of directors, officers, and employees be permitted?
- ☐ Are there any restrictions on transfers of shares?
- ☐ What reports are required?
- ☐ Are there any shareholder inspection rights?
- ☐ How do you amend the bylaws?
- ☐ Are there any super majority voting requirements on significant corporate actions?
- ☐ Are there preemptive rights or cumulative voting?

The Corporate Players

Chapter 4:
Promoters, Incorporators, Directors,
Officers, Shareholders, and Agents

Chapter 4

Promoters, Incorporators, Directors, Officers, Shareholders, and Agents

It has been said that you can't tell the players without a scorecard. This chapter will serve as a scorecard of sorts, identifying the various roles that are played in a corporate setting. In addition to the roles, this chapter will look at the responsibilities and duties of each player.

For many corporations, the same individuals wear different hats. One person may serve as director, officer, and shareholder as well as promoter and incorporator. Which hat you wear at any point in time could be significant in determining whether or not you could have personal liability for corporate actions.

This chapter will expand on concepts introduced in the preceding chapter concerning directors, officers, and shareholders. Additional materials explaining director and shareholder meetings are found in chapters 8 and 9.

Promoters

Although the term "promoter" conjures up images of a slick salesperson in an expensive looking suit, a promoter is anyone who claims to act for or on behalf of a corporation prior to incorporation. For example, you want to start your own business, and you plan on incorporating it. Prior to incorporating, you talk with potential investors — hopefully, in compliance with securities law requirements — suppliers, and customers.

During these preincorporation activities, you are a promoter. As a promoter, you are personally liable to any third party for preincorporation activities, such as contracting with suppliers or others. You will also be personally

Because promoters are personally liable for their preincorporation activities, ask for a written acknowledgment from potential suppliers, customers, or investors that clearly states you are acting on behalf of the corporation and only the corporation is liable in the event of a dispute.

liable for your torts, such as fraud, misrepresentation, or negligence. Although the corporation, once formed, can agree to indemnify (reimburse your cost, expenses, and liability) you from this preincorporation liability, the third person can still look directly to you and your personal assets for any recovery unless the third party agrees, in writing, to look only to the corporation for recovery. In contract terms, this written release from the third party is called a novation.

As a promoter, you must deal fairly with the corporation. This requires full and fair disclosure of all aspects of a transaction between you and the corporation. For example, you own a piece of real estate. You have owned it for five years. Recently, you and John Doe decide to form a corporation and start a business together. Your real estate would be perfect for the corporation. After full and fair disclosure to John Doe, you may sell the real estate to the corporation for its fair market value.

Assume, however, that you did not own any real estate. After you and John Doe decided to go into business, you locate a piece of property which would be perfect for your corporation. You recognize that the real estate is grossly undervalued. You purchase the real estate for $100, even though it is worth at least $10,000. You must sell the real estate to the corporation for $100. Otherwise, you would have made a secret profit and not dealt fairly with the corporation.

When do you become a promoter? As lawyers say, that is a question of fact based on all the facts and circumstances of a particular case. If you are uncertain, consider these questions:

- When was the idea to form the corporation conceived?
- When did you begin any action related to the proposed corporation's business?

If you engage in an act or acquire property prior to deciding to form a corporation, you are not a promoter. However, it is not always easy to tell when an idea was conceived. If your activities or acquisitions relate directly to the business of the later-formed corporation, there is a stronger possibility that your actions will be considered those of a promoter.

Incorporators

An incorporator is the person who actually signs the articles of incorporation. Generally, the only requirement is that the incorporator be at least 18 years of age.[1] Any number of people can serve as incorporator.

To make false statements in the articles is a crime.[2] Therefore, if you sign off as incorporator, read the articles carefully to make certain that the information in them is accurate.

If you use an attorney to form your corporation, let the attorney sign off on the articles as incorporator. This step will save you a return trip to the attorney's office, and it can preserve your anonymity. Articles are public records, and using an attorney or third person as incorporator can keep others from knowing that you are forming a corporation; however, this anonymity will eventually be lost when annual reports are filed with the secretary of state. The sample articles of incorporation located in Chapter 2 use this approach.

Board of Directors

The board of directors is responsible for the general supervision and control of the corporation. The board paints with a broad brush, delegating specific tasks regarding day-to-day operations to the corporations' officers; overseeing the activities of management; and conducting much of its activities in board meetings.

How Many Directors Do You Need?

Most states require that there be at least one director;[3] although the actual number varies from business to business. Close corporations may eliminate the board altogether.[4] For closely held corporations with five or fewer shareholders, each shareholder can serve as a director.

Common sense tells you that the size of the board must be workable. Too large a group may foster a board which is not able to respond quickly to the demands of the marketplace. An even number of board members could result in deadlock, a situation where no agreement can be reached on an issue.

Where Do Directors Come From?

Often, directors are the officers and shareholders of the corporation. If a director is also an officer or employee of the corporation, he or she is described as an inside director. If the director has no other role with the corporation, he or she is described as an outside director. Outside directors often consist of attorneys, accountants, insurance agents, prominent business or civic leaders, or business educators.

How Does the Board Act?

The board of directors conducts meetings at regularly scheduled intervals or at special meetings called by a board member, the president, or shareholders. At these meetings, the chairperson or president of the corporation normally presides. For more information on directors' meetings, refer to Chapter 8.

Unless the articles or bylaws require a higher percentage, a majority of directors present at a meeting constitutes a quorum,[5] and a majority of the quorum is sufficient to authorize the corporation or particular officers or agents to act on behalf of the corporation. These authorizations or directives usually appear in the form of a corporate resolution.

How Long Do Board Members Serve?

The articles or bylaws should provide the answer to this question. While there is no magic number, board members commonly serve a one-year term, subject to reelection by the shareholders or removal by the board or shareholders. Board member terms are sometimes staggered to promote continuity on the board and to minimize the impact of cumulative voting. For example, John Doe, Inc. has a nine-member board. If it chooses, the shareholders could select nine members each year. As an alternative, the shareholders could select three board members each year, resulting in three-year terms for each board member. This technique insures that at least some of the board members will have prior experience.

Can the Board Delegate Authority?

Boards can and do delegate authority to corporate officers, employees, and others. Boards sometimes create committees consisting of board and non-board members to focus on specific issues for the corporation. A board member can't delegate all of the board members' power and authority. Board members are required to bring their independent business judgment to the board, and this judgment can't be delegated. For example, the board can authorize an officer or committee to study the feasibility of selling the business or merging with another. The board can't delegate the ultimate decision of whether or not to sell or merge.

Duties of Due Care and Loyalty

Board members and corporate officers owe several duties to the corporation and its shareholders. If a board member fails to satisfy these duties, he or she may be personally liable to the corporation or the shareholders. There are several duties which exist: the duty of due care, the duty of loyalty, the duty of fair dealing, and a duty to act in good faith. The duties of due care and loyalty are the most significant.

Duty of Due Care

As a director, you need to exercise ordinary care.[6] This means you must act as any ordinary prudent person would under the same circumstances and use your best business judgment in reaching a decision. Some independent investigation of the matters being considered is required, because if you merely rubber stamp the recommendations and actions of management without further investigation and follow up, you may later be liable for failing to exercise your proper duty of care.

Passive board members can find themselves involved in a claim for breach of the duty of care. If you accept the responsibility to serve on a board, be prepared to become active and involved.

For example, John, Jane, and Joan are the only directors of John Doe, Inc. The corporation has more than a dozen shareholders located in several states. John and Jane have formed several other corporations on the side. These corporations supply John Doe, Inc. with the raw materials it needs to make its widgets. Joan has no interest in these other corporations. The contracts between these corporations and John Doe, Inc. bind John Doe, Inc. for a long term to purchase materials at an exorbitant rate. Joan attends board meetings and is aware that John and Jane have an interest in these other corporations. Joan does not investigate the fairness of these contracts. She simply goes along with John and Jane. Without question, John and Jane have breached their duty of loyalty to the corporation (described below). Joan, on the other hand, has breached her duty of due care to John Doe, Inc.

To satisfy the duty of care, you must:

- Act in good faith and in the best interests of the corporation;
- Exercise good business judgment;
- Use ordinary care; and
- Make an independent investigation and determination of matters presented to the board.[7]

Can Directors Rely on Information Provided by Others?

Directors may rely on reports of company officers or outside experts where it would be reasonable to do so. For example, if the board received a recommendation from outside attorneys or accountants to take certain action to avoid a major tax liability, it would probably be reasonable for the director to rely on such a report. However, if the report was prepared by the company president who stands to profit from the proposed transaction, it would not be reasonable for the director to rely on the president's report without further investigation.

Duty of Loyalty

As a director, you are also required to give your undivided loyalty to the corporation.[8] To satisfy this duty, you must fully and fairly disclose all material facts in any proposed transaction with the corporation in which you have a potential conflict of interest. You should not profit personally from inside information.

Conflicts of interest involving officers and directors and the corporation are common. For example:

- An officer or director owns an interest in a competitor or a supplier;
- The officer or director owns real estate which the corporation is seeking to lease or buy; or
- The officer or director's family member has an interest in a supplier, competitor, or real estate the company is interested in.

In these situations, full disclosure of the relationship should be made. Although as the interested director, you may wish to participate in the discussion, you should abstain from voting on whether or not to approve the transaction.

Corporate Opportunity Doctrine

Another aspect of the duty of loyalty is known as the corporate opportunity doctrine. Under this theory, a director or officer may not independently pursue a business opportunity related to the corporation's business without first offering the corporation the chance to pursue it.

A three-part test to determine whether or not a corporate opportunity has been presented is listed below.

- Is the corporation financially able to undertake the opportunity?

- Is the opportunity in the corporation's line of business (either actual or reasonably foreseeable)?
- Is the corporation interested in the opportunity?[9]

To avoid personal liability, board members should:
- *Be independent;*
- *Monitor the quality of management;*
- *Demand and study relevant company data;*
- *Avoid self-dealing and conflicts of interest;*
- *Assist in good audit and legal procedures; and*
- *Be willing to vote against the majority of the board or even resign if a suggested course of conduct is unlawful or ill advised.[10]*

If the answer to these questions is yes, you need to disclose the opportunity to the board and give the corporation the first opportunity to pursue it. If in doubt, always disclose.

To illustrate, John, Jane, and Joan are the officers and directors of John Doe, Inc. The corporation sells widgets at retail. It has explored the possibility of manufacturing widgets for resale in the past but has not acted on the idea. John learns that Widget, Inc., a widget manufacturer, is for sale. Unbeknownst to Jane and Joan, John forms a separate corporation and buys the assets of Widget, Inc. Did John breach his duty of loyalty to the corporation? If John Doe, Inc. was financially able to pursue the purchase of Widget, Inc., the answer is probably yes. To be safe, John should have presented the information about Widget, Inc. to the John Doe, Inc. board of directors and let the board decide whether or not to pursue the opportunity.

Statutory Sources of Liability for Directors

In addition to the duties described above, several statutes also impose personal liability on directors or officers in certain circumstances, such as:

- The failure to file articles of incorporation or an application for certificate of authority;
- Wrongful declarations or payment of dividends or unlawful distribution of corporate property;
- False statements made in articles, annual reports, or similar items; and
- The failure to pay required taxes.[11]

Advisory Board of Directors

Some corporations utilize an advisory board of directors as well as a regular board of directors. Advisory board members are selected by the corporation's board of directors. They are not elected by shareholders, and the actions of the advisory board are not binding on the corporation.

An advisory board can and does provide useful advice and information for the elected board. One advantage to the advisory board is that its members are not subject to the same standards and conduct ordinarily imposed upon elected directors. Business leaders may be unwilling to serve on your elected board because of liability concerns. These concerns disappear for advisory directors.

An advisory board can include any number of people. Good candidates include your corporation's banker, lawyer, accountant, and insurance agent. Other possibilities include representatives of a key supplier or customer group.

Corporate Officers

Since a corporation can not act on its own, it is dependent upon the actions of others. Most often, those others are the board of directors and corporate officers. Corporate officers are most often charged with the task of carrying out the directives of the board of directors and managing the daily affairs of the corporation.

Who Are the Officers?

Once again, the specific offices to be filled and the role of the corporate officers are largely left to the control of the board and shareholders. Most business corporation acts specify which officers a corporation must have — usually a president and a secretary — and describe those officers which a corporation may elect to have.[12] The bylaws generally contain a brief description of the officers' responsibilities.

Becoming an Officer

Corporate officers are appointed by the board of directors and serve at the pleasure of the board. Officers can be terminated at any time by the board, with or without cause. If termination is in breach of an existing employment agreement between the corporation and the officer, the corporation may be liable for damages, but the officer may still be removed.

Which Offices Do You Need?

The following discussion illustrates the types of offices which commonly exist for corporations and includes a brief description of each office. Remember, however, that your corporation may only need a president and a secretary, and that you can create any officer's job description to fit your corporation's needs.

A good set of bylaws will require that a corporation have a president, secretary, and treasurer. The bylaws may authorize the board of directors to appoint a chairperson of the board, one or more vice-presidents, and one or more assistant secretaries or assistant treasurers. This flexibility may prove useful in later years. For example, a long standing president who no longer wishes to devote full-time energies to the corporation but who still has value to the corporation could be designated chairperson of the board. Similarly, valued employees could be named as a vice-president or assistant secretary without significantly changing their job responsibilities. This form of recognition to your employees could be invaluable in promoting goodwill among your key employees.

Officer Job Descriptions

Chairperson of the Board

If there is a chairperson of the board, he or she ordinarily presides over board of director meetings. Like all officers, the chairperson can perform any other duties assigned to him or her by the board or bylaws.

The sample bylaws found at the end of Chapter 3 provide a bylaw description for these offices.

President

The president is usually the chief executive officer of the company, responsible for managing the day-to-day operations of the corporation. With no chairperson, the president presides over board of director and shareholder meetings. Occasionally, this position is described as president and chief executive officer. In other corporations, these are considered separate offices which are occupied by different individuals.

Vice-President

The vice-president, if any, does what most vice-presidents do — fill in when the president is unavailable. Unlike the president of the United States, corporate vice-presidents do not automatically become president upon the president's death or removal from office.

Secretary

A corporate secretary is not a clerical position. The secretary is responsible for maintaining required corporate records, such as minutes, shareholder lists, and financial records. Many corporate secretaries record minutes of board and shareholder meetings. Secretaries also send out notices of such meetings when required by the bylaws. Corporate secretaries conduct elections at shareholder meetings and track such things as voter eligibility, proxies, and vote tabulations.

Treasurer

The treasurer keeps and maintains corporate books of account, including records of its assets, liabilities, gains, losses, and other financial and tax information. The treasurer, sometimes referred to as the chief financial officer, may or may not be involved with the daily recording of financial entries for the corporation. Bookkeepers or company-employed accountants usually perform these tasks, but the treasurer would oversee them.

Assistant Secretaries or Treasurers

If assistant secretary or treasurer offices exist for a particular corporation, it is probably because the corporation has grown to such a size that one person cannot perform all the required tasks. For example, many documents require the signature of the company president or vice-president and a secretary or assistant secretary. If a corporation has offices in a number of locations, it is time consuming to ship documents around to find people who can sign them. As a result, each location may employ persons who are named as vice-presidents or assistant secretaries. Modern transmission services, such as telecopy machines, and overnight delivery, reduce the need to have corporate officers at each business location.

Indemnification and Insurance for Directors and Officers

The RMBCA and other modern business corporation acts permit a corporation to indemnify its directors, officers, employees, and agents under certain circumstances. This is an important concept. Without it, your corporation could have a difficult time attracting competent and qualified officers and directors. This is especially true for outside directors whose only connection with the corporation is that they serve on the board of directors.

Indemnification is a promise to reimburse. Assume that an officer or director is sued, and as a result of the lawsuit has a judgment entered against him or her which he or she pays. If the officer or director is eligible for indemnification, the corporation would repay the officer or director his or her costs, expenses (possibly including legal fees), and judgment paid. Articles and bylaws may limit the type of expenses or costs which can be reimbursed or put a limit on the aggregate amount of the reimbursement.

Indemnification is optional, and except in rare instances, corporations need not provide for it. If indemnification is available, as a director, you must:

- Act in good faith; and
- Reasonably believe your conduct is in the best interest of the corporation.[13]

If indemnification is permitted, it includes all your cost, expense, or liability, including the cost of any attorneys fees.

Your corporation is required to indemnify its officers and directors under the RMBCA whenever an officer or director is brought into a claim solely because he or she is an officer or director and not because of any active wrongdoing on the part of the officer or director. To be eligible, an officer or director must be successful in his or her defense of the claim.

No indemnification is permitted an officer or director if:

- The claim proceeding determines that the officer or director is liable to the corporation; or
- The director or officer is charged with receiving an improper personal benefit.[14]

To further protect your corporation and its directors, officers, and employees, the corporation should acquire insurance. There are many different types of insurance available to meet most risks which modern businesses face. A good insurance agent, like an accountant and lawyer, is a valuable and necessary part of your business team.

Insurance can help you meet the needs of your business through liability insurance (coverage for claims against the corporation resulting from corporate acts); fire insurance; health insurance for employees; errors or omissions insurance (to protect against employee theft or dishonesty); and officers and directors insurance. Various forms of life and disability insurance are also available to fund stock redemptions or to provide a fund of money to recruit and hire a new employee to replace a deceased key employee.

Shareholders

Shareholders are the owners of the corporation. They vote to elect directors, and they vote on other fundamental matters presented to them. In certain situations, such as merger or sale of assets, shareholders may be able to demand that a corporation purchase their shares.

As a general rule, shareholders are not liable for the debts and responsibilities of a corporation; however, this rule is not absolute. As you will learn in Chapter 11, shareholders who dominate and control corporate activities increase their exposure to personal liability for corporate acts.

Unlike officers and directors, shareholders ordinarily owe no duty to the corporation or fellow shareholders. Increasingly, however, large shareholders owning a controlling interest of corporate stock are required to avoid activities designed to oppress the voting rights of minority share interests.

Although personal liability may be avoided by shareholders, it remains important to distinguish the capacity in which one acts. Because the same individual is often a shareholder, officer, and director in small closely held corporations, know which hat you are wearing when you act for or on behalf of your corporation.

Agency Principles

If you do business in a corporate form, you and the persons with whom you do business need to know who can act on behalf of the corporation. This is vitally important to your corporation because a corporation can only act through its agents. To understand the importance, you need to know some basic principles of agency law.

An agent is a person or entity who performs an act for or on behalf of another person or entity known as the principal. The real estate broker who sold your house acted as your agent. You were the principal. Sports and entertainment figures hire agents to negotiate lucrative contracts for them. Your business lawyer and accountant act as your agent for all matters in which you retain their services.

Agents don't need to be individuals. They can be partnerships or corporations. In most instances, agents have the authority to act, and this authority comes from the principal. In the case of a corporation, the authorization usually comes from the board of directors or the president. As you will see, not all acts are authorized, yet some unauthorized acts may still be binding on the corporation.

Express or Implied Authority

Without question, anyone authorized by name or office to perform an act on behalf of the corporation has authority. This is known as express authority. When the corporation seeks to borrow from a bank, the board of directors will pass a corporate resolution customarily authorizing the president to negotiate the loan within certain board-defined parameters and to sign off on the loan documents. The corporate resolution should use language such as "John Doe, company president," rather than authorizing merely "John Doe" or the "company president."

When express authority exists, the person or agent with the authority normally has the implied authority to perform all acts necessary to carry out the express authority.

Apparent Authority

A more dangerous type of authority for corporations and others is known as apparent authority. Apparent authority is based on perception. For example, a corporation's president is presumed to have authority to perform acts which are related to the corporation's ordinary business. A salesperson for that same corporation would not ordinarily have any apparent authority to perform any act on behalf of the corporation.

Apparent authority can also exist when express authority has been withdrawn. For example, John Doe was employed as purchasing agent for your corporation. John switches jobs within the corporation and is no longer involved in purchasing. The corporation should notify its suppliers that John Doe is no longer authorized to purchase items for the corporation. Without this notice, John Doe still retains apparent authority to purchase on behalf of the corporation and bind the corporation.

Apparent authority may also exist as the result of prior dealings or a course of business. For example, if your warehouse clerk has always ordered shipping services which your company has paid for, it is reasonable for the shipper to conclude that the shipping clerk is authorized to perform this task. If this should change, you should notify the shipper.

Similarly, when your corporation does business with others, determine whether the individuals you are dealing with are, in fact, authorized to act. You may request a copy of a board resolution authorizing the specific action or a letter from the company president indicating that a particular agent has authority to bind the business.

To avoid unwanted corporate liability, your board resolutions or directives should clearly state who is authorized to act on behalf of the corporation. In addition, language in your business contracts stating that the agreement is not binding on the corporation until executed by the corporation's president will eliminate many problems so long as the president is in fact authorized to execute that particular contract.

Ratification Authority

The final type of authority is called ratification or estoppel authority. Technically, this is not a form of authority since this type of authority is the result of events which occur after the agreement has been reached. For example, your corporation's board of directors could approve the unauthorized purchases made by John Doe in the preceding example, thereby ratifying the purchases. For ratification authority to apply, the board must be made aware of all of the terms and conditions of the transaction. The corporation could also use the goods and be precluded or stopped from later challenging the purchases on grounds that the purchases were unauthorized.

Final Thoughts on the Players

There are many different hats worn in the corporate world, and many different roles to be played. For small businesses, it isn't uncommon for a person to serve as incorporator, promoter, director, officer, and shareholder.

Which hat you're wearing at any point in time may determine your exposure to personal liability. Promoters are generally personally liable for all of their activities whereas shareholders are usually not liable to outsiders for claims against the corporation. For your convenience, an overview of the corporate players' roles, duties and responsibilities, and liabilities is located on the opposite page.

Blending your corporate roles together is a factor which courts and administrative agencies will consider when deciding whether to impose personal liability on corporate directors, officers, and shareholders.

It is important that in whatever role you are filling, you hold yourself out to others as acting on behalf of the corporation. Equally important, make certain that those with whom you do business know who has authority to obligate your corporation. If that authority should change, notify these businesses of the change to avoid disputes down the road.

Corporate Player Overview

	Duties and Responsibilities	**Personal or Corporate Liability**
Promoter	Conducts preincorporation activities. Must deal fairly with the corporation that is being formed.	Personally liable unless third party agrees to look solely to the corporation for payment. Corporation may agree to indemnify.
Incorporator	Signs and files articles of incorporation.	Personal liability for making false statements in the articles of incorporation; otherwise, corporate liability.
Directors	General supervision and control of the corporation. Duty of due care. Duty to act in good faith. Duty of loyalty to the corporation. Elected by the shareholders.	Corporate liability so long as no breach of duty; director exercises sound business judgment; or statute does not impose personal liability on directors. Personal liability if factors exist to permit piercing of corporate veil* or director involved in intentional misconduct or criminal act. Corporation may indemnify directors under certain situations.
Officers	Daily supervision and control of the corporation. Carry out directives of the board. Appointed or elected by the board. Serve at the pleasure of the board. Duty of due care. Duty to act in good faith. Duty of loyalty to the corporation.	Same as directors' liabilities listed above.
Shareholders	Elect board of directors. Duty to act in good faith, especially with regard to the holders of minority interests.	Generally, no liability; only risk is the loss of value of shares held. Personal liability if factors allow piercing of corporate veil or if majority shareholders conspire to oppress interests of minority shareholders.

* *Definition in Glossary.*

The Paper Trail

Chapter 5

Corporate Stock

Ask three people what corporate stock is and you're likely to get three different answers. It's not an easy question to answer, because several definitions can apply to corporate stock.

This chapter will focus on different characteristics that corporate stock can possess. For example, stock can be common, preferred, convertible, redeemable, and so on. The differences between these characteristics and why you would use one or more of them is explained.

The characteristics and mechanics of corporate dividends are explored, plus the free transferability aspect of corporate stock. Finally, a thumbnail sketch of securities laws is provided; these issues hang like a dark cloud on the horizon of any discussion of corporate stock.

As you read this chapter, think flexibility. Stock affords a significant opportunity to preserve control and attract investors. You have room to be creative, subject to the practical realities of the market place.

What Is Stock?

In one sense, stock is the value of money or other property invested in the corporation. Stock ownership represents ownership in the corporation. The shareholders of stock are referred to as stockholders in some states and shareholders in others. Amounts paid for stock are considered to be the equity of the corporation and are at risk. If the corporation does not succeed, amounts paid for stock may be lost for good.

For example, John Doe, Inc. is authorized to issue 1,000 shares of corporate stock. John Doe, Inc. has issued 100 of those shares to John Doe in exchange for $100. John Doe owns all of the issued and outstanding stock of John Doe, Inc., and the corporation's balance sheet will show a capital stock line item of $100. John Doe's stock ownership would ordinarily be evidenced by the issuance of stock certificates, but not always. Stock certificates are not stock, they merely serve as evidence that stock has been issued.

Stock has an accounting aspect as well. As noted in the previous example, the balance sheet contained a line item for capital stock of $100. This is what has been paid for the stock. Some financial statements refer to capital stock, while others will contain line items for stated capital and additional paid in capital or capital surplus. The terms may differ, but the concept is the same. Each of these items relate to amounts paid for stock.

What gets allocated to a stated capital account and what goes into an additional paid in capital account or capital surplus account is largely left to the discretion of the board of directors. One factor to consider in making the allocation is whether or not the stock has a par value.

Stock can have a stated par value ($1 per share is common), or it can be no par value. The articles of incorporation will tell you whether or not the shares have a par value. When stock has a par value, it can't be sold for anything less than the par value and is often sold for more than its par value. If the stock has no par value, the board is free — subject to the restrictions described below under diluted stock — to fix a value.

In the example above, assume John Doe, Inc.'s articles indicated that its shares were $1 par value. In that example, John Doe, Inc. issued 100 shares of its stock. As a result, its stated capital account would be $100, the same as its capital stock account. If the shares had no par value, the board could set a value. For example, the board could determine that for every $1 received, $0.10 (10 cents) would be allocated to stated capital (100 x 0.10, for a total of $10) and $0.90 (90 cents) to additional paid in capital or capital surplus (100 x 0.90, for a total of $90).

Take heart in knowing that the RMBCA and other modern business corporation acts have eliminated the concept of par value.

Under the RMBCA and modern business corporation statutes, the concepts of par, no par, and stated capital have been eliminated. Check with the business corporation act in your state to find out if these concepts still exist.

Stock Characteristics

Stock is personal property. It is freely transferable, and unless its transfer is restricted, it can be bought, sold, mortgaged, given away, or disposed of the same way as any other personal property.

Remember that business corporation acts provide ample opportunity for flexibility in tailoring a corporation to fit your needs. This is especially true with respect to stock. You can create as many different classes of stock as you wish with many different characteristics.

In most corporations, the articles of incorporation authorize the issuance of one class of stock: common stock with voting rights. Each share permits one vote on corporate matters. Although that may be the most common form of stock authorization, it is by no means the only form.

Stock can be nonvoting as well as voting. Stock can have preferences, as is usually the case with preferred stock. Nonvoting shares can be used to preserve control of the corporation within a certain group. They can also be used for retiring employees or children and other family members of officers and directors.

Stock can be convertible, either at the option of the shareholder or the corporation, to another class of stock. Stock can be redeemable, at the option of either the shareholder or the corporation, at a stated time or upon the occurrence of a stated event.

If you own corporate stock, you own the right to participate in the corporation's activities as a shareholder. Participation is usually limited to the right to vote for directors and to approve fundamental corporate changes. Ownership of stock also includes the right to participate on a pro rata basis in dividend distributions or distributions made pursuant to a corporate dissolution. This right to participate, however, may vary among shareholders owning different classes of stock.

Unless a close corporation has elected to eliminate its board of directors, stock ownership provides no right to participate in the management or control of the corporation. That authority is vested in the board of directors and the corporate officers. Ownership of corporate stock does not give you any ownership interest or right to specific corporate property, since the corporation is a distinct legal entity, and the corporation — not its directors, officers, or shareholders — owns its property.

What Characteristics Do You Give Your Corporate Stock?

The answer to this question depends largely on your current and future needs; how badly the corporation needs the cash or other property to be invested; and the bargaining strength of your prospective investor. For example, if you need an equity investor, you may wish not to surrender control of the corporation. Similarly, your investor may be more interested in an immediate return on his or her investment. In such a case, you would want to limit the voting rights of the stock. Your corporation could authorize the issuance of common stock, some of which would be voting, some nonvoting. Your investor might desire preferred stock which would pay him or her a fixed dividend over time and perhaps offer a preference on liquidation.

To preserve your control over your corporation, you might wish to issue stock, voting or nonvoting, which the corporation has the right to redeem after a period of time. Your investor, on the other hand, might wish to have his or her preferred stock converted to common stock after a period of time or upon the occurrence of a particular event. If your investor loans money to your corporation rather than acquiring stock, he or she may wish to have the right to convert his or her loan to stock at some later time.

Where Are Stock Characteristics Described?

If you wish to create different classes of stock with different rights or preferences, you must describe the classes in your articles of incorporation. If the classifications change, an amendment to the articles of incorporation must be made. The articles must describe the different classes to be created and the rights, preferences, and limitations of each class. In addition, the number of shares of each class must be specified. For example, your corporation authorizes the issuance of 30,000 shares as follows: 10,000 shares of common stock with voting rights; 10,000 shares of common stock with no voting rights; and 10,000 shares of cumulative preferred shares with an 8% return payable quarterly and no voting rights.

Don't create classes of stock for the sake of having classes of stock. Put yourself in the shoes of a prospective investor. What will he or she require to put money at risk in your corporation? The answer may involve some combination of a fixed return in the form of preferred stock, some voting rights — certain classes of stock can vote on some corporate issues, but not all — and some ability to compel redemption or conversion from one class of stock to another.

Without a rich or passive investor, one class of voting, common shares is probably all that is necessary. You can amend your articles later to accommodate investors who wish to have additional rights or preferences.

Contract Law Applies

The issuance of stock by your corporation creates a contractual relationship between the corporation and its shareholders. Your corporation is bound by its articles of incorporation to act consistently with the articles. If the articles provide certain rights or preferences for its shareholders, the holders of those classes of shares are entitled to receive those benefits. While the board of directors usually retains discretion as to whether or not to declare a dividend, the articles can eliminate or limit this discretion.

How Does Your Corporation Issue Stock?

For corporations which have not yet been formed, promoters often locate prospective investors. If these investors wish to purchase stock, they sign a subscription agreement similar to the sample stock subscription agreement which is located at the end of this chapter. Keep in mind that the offer to sell shares of stock is subject to state and federal securities laws. Exemptions from these laws are available, but the exemptions tend to be technical; you need a business lawyer. The stock subscription agreement is an irrevocable offer to purchase shares, and it is not effective until the corporation is formed, and its board accepts the subscription.

The board fixes a price for the shares. By resolution, the corporation authorizes the appropriate officers, usually the president and secretary, to issue a certain number of shares to a named individual in exchange for the payment of a stated sum of money. Stock can also be issued for property, and the board must set the value being assigned to the property. Absent fraud or other unusual circumstance, the board's determination of value is conclusive.

For example, a board couldn't sell board members stock at an unreasonably low value while selling stock to others at a higher price. In such a case, the board's determination of value could be challenged.

When the board has passed the authorizing resolution, the secretary will prepare the stock certificate and deliver it to the purchasing shareholder in exchange for the money or property. The name and address of the shareholder are entered on the corporate stock records together with a description of the number and class of shares acquired.

What Can Be Accepted in Payment for Stock?

Money or property are always acceptable forms of payment for stock. If the corporation is willing to accept your prize bull, it may do so. Past services are usually acceptable as well. John Doe, Inc. can issue 100 shares of its stock to you in exchange for your computer programming services. You will have to recognize income on your personal tax return, however, equal to the value of the shares received.

Under the RMBCA, any form of consideration is acceptable.[1] Promissory notes, the promise of future services or any other form of property will work. Most states probably don't go this far yet, and you should check with your attorney if your corporation will receive anything other than cash, property, or past services.

Are Stock Certificates Required?

In many states, there is no specific requirement for stock certificates; however, it is a good idea to issue stock certificates as proof of ownership of corporate shares. Stock certificates can and should contain any language restricting the right of the shareholder to transfer the shares.

There is no particular secret to what a stock certificate should look like, and many business stationary stores can provide blank forms of certificates. A certificate should contain:

- The name of the issuing corporation;
- The state of incorporation;
- The name of the person to whom the stock is issued;
- The number of shares issued;
- A description of the class of shares issued, including a brief description of any rights, preferences, or limitations; and
- Any restrictive transfer language.

Usually the corporation's president and secretary sign and date the share certificates. If a corporate seal exists, it can be used, though most states no longer require that corporate documents contain the corporate seal.

Your corporation should maintain a separate stock ledger which lists the names and addresses of each current shareholder; a description of the class of shares held by the shareholder; and the number of shares held. This ledger should be updated as often as possible.

In many smaller corporations, stock certificates are kept in the corporate minute book. This is probably as good a place as any, so long as the corporate minute book is retained in a safe and secure place. Some shareholders wish to retain their stock certificates. If this is the case, shareholders should be advised to keep the certificate in a safe deposit box or similar place of safe keeping. Two sample forms of stock certificate are provided on the following pages, and are equally effective. One is more ornate than the other, you can simply choose the style you prefer.

What if You Lose Your Stock Certificate?

If you lose a certificate, you need to sign a lost stock affidavit. This document represents that your shares of stock have been lost and that efforts to locate the shares have been unsuccessful. You undertake to indemnify the corporation for any cost or expense in the event that the shares resurface in another's possession. A sample lost stock affidavit is provided on page 79.

Preferred Stock

Preferred stock is stock with a preference or priority. The most common preference is with respect to dividends, where preferred shareholders are entitled to receive dividends prior to any dividends payable to the holders of any common shares. Preferred shares often provide for a dividend payable at a fixed rate at stated intervals. For example, a preferred dividend could provide for an 8% return payable quarterly.

As explained below, dividends can't be paid if the corporation doesn't have the funds available. Because of this risk, preferred shares are often made cumulative. Cumulative preferred means that if a dividend is not paid for one or more stated intervals, amounts which should have been paid are accumulated. All accumulated amounts must be paid to the cumulative preferred shareholders prior to any payment of dividends to common shareholders or noncumulative preferred shareholders.

Preferred stock may be convertible to common stock, usually at the option of the shareholder, if the articles so provide. Whether convertibility is desirable depends upon the need of the corporation and its investors.

Dividends

A dividend is a distribution made to shareholders of a corporation in the form of cash or stock made out of the net earnings and profits of the corporation. Dividends are made on a pro rata basis to the holders of the shares entitled to the dividend.

Do All Classes of Shares Receive Dividends?

Generally, the board of directors has discretion to declare a dividend. Whether that discretion is limited depends, in part, on the contract nature of stock.

SAMPLE: Stock Certificate – Alternate A (front)

Certificate Number:

_____

For Number of Shares:

_____

Of Corporation:

_____

Issued to:

_____

Address:

_____

_____

Date:

_____

From Whom
Transferred:

_____

_____

Date:

_____

Number of Original
Shares:_____

Original Certificate
Number _____

Number of Shares
Transferred:

_____

Received Certificate No.

_____

For Number of Shares:

_____

Date:

_____

Stock Certificate

Certificate Number:

_____

Full Corporate Name of Issuing Corporation:

_____

State of Incorporation: _____

Shares Issued to: _____

Number of Shares: _____

Class of Shares Issued: _____

Witnessed by these authorized officers of the corporation:

_____

Secretary

_____

President

_____

Date

SAMPLE: Stock Certificate – Alternate A (back)

This side is completed only when shares are sold or transferred from one shareholder to another party.

In addition to this stock transfer language, any language restricting the transfer of shares should be set forth on this page.

Of my shares represented by this certificate, for value received I hereby transfer the number of shares identified below to the party named, and I instruct the corporation's secretary to record this transfer on the books of the corporation.

Shares transferred from:

_____   _____
Signature   Print Name

Number of Shares _____

Shares Transferred to: _____

_____

SAMPLE: Stock Certificate – Alternate B (front)

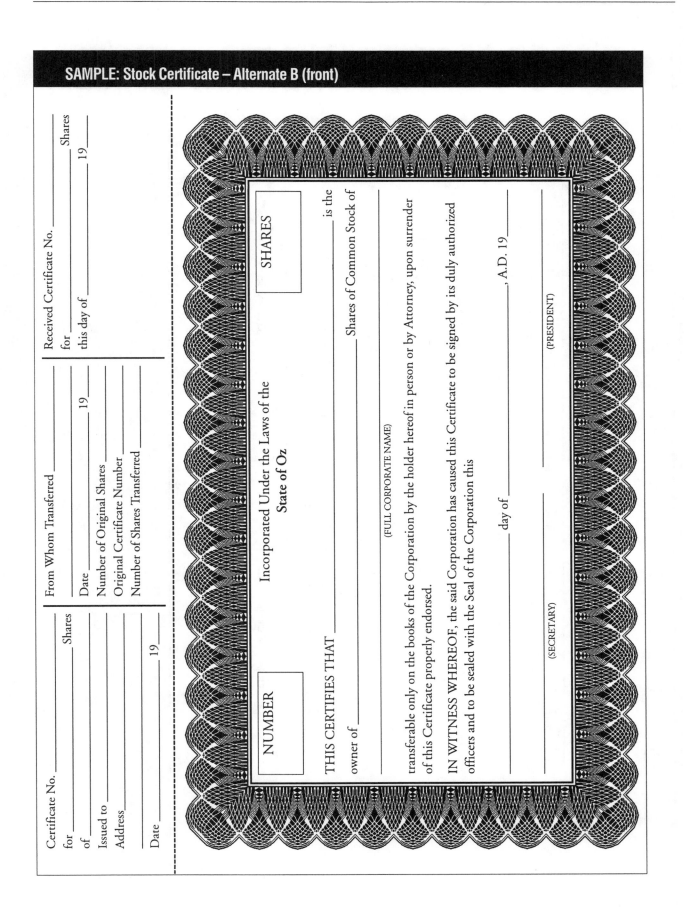

Certificate No. _____

for _____ Shares

of _____

Issued to _____

Address _____

Date _____ 19 ___

From Whom Transferred _____

Date _____ 19 ___

Number of Original Shares _____

Original Certificate Number _____

Number of Shares Transferred _____

Received Certificate No. _____

for _____ Shares

this day of _____ 19 ___

NUMBER

SHARES

Incorporated Under the Laws of the
State of Oz

THIS CERTIFIES THAT _____

owner of _____ Shares of Common Stock of

_____ is the

(FULL CORPORATE NAME)

transferable only on the books of the Corporation by the holder hereof in person or by Attorney, upon surrender of this Certificate properly endorsed.

IN WITNESS WHEREOF, the said Corporation has caused this Certificate to be signed by its duly authorized officers and to be sealed with the Seal of the Corporation this

_____ day of _____, A.D. 19 ___

_____
(SECRETARY)

_____
(PRESIDENT)

SAMPLE: Stock Certificate – Alternate B (back)

For Value Received, _____ hereby sell, assign and transfer

onto _____

_____ Shares

of the Capital Stock represented by the within Certificate, and do hereby irrevocably

constitute and appoint _____

to transfer the said Stock on the books of the within named Corporation with full power

of substitution in the premises.

Dated _____ 19 ____

In the presence of

_____

_____

Notice: The signature of this assignment must correspond with the name as written upon the face of the certificate,

in every particular, without alteration or enlargement, or any change whatever.

SAMPLE: Lost Stock Affidavit

Lost Stock Affidavit

State of Oz

County of Wishful

The undersigned, being first duly sworn upon his/her oath, states as follows:

1. The undersigned's name is John Doe. My address is 1600 Pennsylvania Ave., Anytown, Oz 11111.

2. The undersigned is the lawful owner of 100 shares of the issued and outstanding outstanding common stock of John Doe, Inc. (the "Shares").

3. The undersigned has not sold, transferred, exchanged, pledged or hypothecated the Shares in any manner whatsoever.

4. At all times since issuance, the Shares have been in the safekeeping, custody and possession of the undersigned at the undersigned's residence address.

5. To the undersigned's knowledge, no one else had access to the Shares.

6. Despite diligent effort, the undersigned has been unable to locate the Shares, and to the undersigned's knowledge and belief, the Shares have been lost, stolen or misplaced.

7. The purpose of this affidavit is to request John Doe, Inc. to issue a duplicate certificate evidencing the undersigned's ownership of the Shares without surrender or cancellation or transfer of the Shares.

8. The undersigned agrees to indemnify and hold harmless John Doe, Inc. for any cost, liability or expense, including reasonable attorneys fees, incurred by John Doe, Inc. resulting from any misstatement in this affidavit or from any reliance on this affidavit by John Doe, Inc.

_____

John Doe

_____

Date

Subscribed and sworn to before me this 14th day of February, 1992.

_____

Notary Public

Before a corporation issues a replacement certificate to a shareholder claiming to have lost or misplaced his or her stock certificate, the corporation should require that the shareholder submit a lost stock affidavit. The affidavit serves several important functions. First, it underscores to the shareholder that misplacing a corporate certificate is a serious act. Second, it requires the affirmative representation of the shareholder that the shares haven't been transferred or pledged by the shareholder. Finally, it contains an undertaking by the shareholder to pay all cost, liability, or expense incurred by the corporation because of the lost certificate.

For example, if a corporation has issued preferred shares, the board has no discretion but to declare and pay dividends in accordance with the stock preference; however, no declaration can be made if the corporation lacks sufficient net earnings and profits.[2]

The board of directors must treat all holders of the same class of shares equally. Dividends must be paid on a pro rata basis to all members of the same class and not just to a certain portion of members. The board, however, can treat holders of different classes of shares differently. For example, the board could declare a dividend for holders of a nonvoting class of common shares but not for a voting class of common shares.

What Are the Sources of Funds for Dividends?

Definitions vary slightly. Cash dividends are payable out of a corporation's earnings and profits. Stock dividends reduce a corporation's earnings and profits. The amount of the reduction is transferred to the corporation's capital stock account.

In essence, a corporation can't declare and pay a dividend if to do so would render the corporation insolvent. If the corporation lacks the ability to pay its debts as they fall due, the board can't declare and pay a dividend. Most business corporation acts make it illegal for the board to declare a dividend while the corporation is insolvent or a dividend which would render the corporation insolvent.[3] In addition, the RMBCA makes directors who vote in favor of an illegal dividend personally liable to the corporation for amounts distributed which exceed the amount for which earnings and profits existed.[4]

What Is a Stock Dividend?

A stock dividend is a distribution of a corporation's stock. A corporation must have a sufficient number of authorized but unissued shares in order to make a stock dividend. For example, John Doe, Inc. has 1,000 authorized shares. It has issued 500 shares which are currently outstanding. If the board of John Doe, Inc. declares a stock dividend of one share for each share outstanding, John Doe, Inc. will distribute 500 shares. Once the dividend has been declared and paid, John Doe, Inc. will have issued 1,000 shares. It will have no more authorized but unissued shares. For any future stock dividends to be made, John Doe, Inc.'s articles of incorporation will have to be amended to increase its authorized shares. For balance sheet purposes, whenever a stock dividend is made, an amount is transferred from the surplus account to the stated capital account.

How Are Dividends Declared?

To authorize the declaration of a dividend, the board of directors passes a corporate resolution. This resolution will set a record date, the date on which the corporate books and records are reviewed. Those persons or entities who are listed as shareholders as of the record date are entitled to receive a dividend.

For a cash dividend, the dividend is expressed either in terms of a certain amount of money per share ($1 per share) or by an aggregate sum which is then divided by all of the issued and outstanding shares ($1,000 to be distributed pro rata to the holders of 1,000 issued and outstanding shares).

Once declared by the board, a cash dividend can't be rescinded by the board without shareholder approval unless there are insufficient earnings and profits. Generally, a stock dividend can be rescinded by the board without shareholder approval prior to the issuance of the stock.

How Are Dividends Taxed?

Cash dividends are taxable upon receipt by the shareholder, and are not deductible by the corporation which pays the dividend. This creates a situation frequently described as "double taxation." Cash dividends are taxed at the corporate and shareholder level. Corporations receiving dividends are generally able to exclude a certain portion of dividends received for federal income tax purposes. Stock dividends are not taxed upon receipt. Any tax on stock dividend shares will occur upon sale or disposition of the shares by the shareholder.

If you purchase shares of stock from an individual, your purchase agreement should provide that you are entitled to any dividends which are declared or paid following the closing of the sale. There may be a gap between the time you acquire the shares and the corporate records are revised to show you as a record holder. If a record date is established during this gap, the seller would likely receive the dividend.

Preemptive Rights

Preemptive rights protect the interests of shareholders by giving them the right to maintain their percentage of stock ownership. Preemptive rights operate like a right of first refusal. If a corporation proposes to issue additional shares of stock, shareholders have a right to acquire their pro rata share of the new issue. For example, if you owned 10% of John Doe, Inc. and the corporation proposes to issue an additional 1,000 shares, you would have the right to acquire 10% of the new issue or 100 shares. Your percentage ownership of John Doe, Inc. would remain at 10%.

There is, however, a trick to preemptive rights. In some states, preemptive rights exist unless the articles expressly state that they do not exist. In other states, the result is just the opposite. No preemptive rights exist unless the articles expressly state that they do exist. If you simply fill in the blanks on articles of incorporation, you may never know for certain whether or not preemptive rights exist in your state. Under the RMBCA, preemptive rights do not exist unless the articles provide for them.

Preemptive rights generally apply only to the class of shares which the corporation proposes to issue. If your corporation has two classes of stock, Class A and Class B, and it proposes to issue additional Class B shares, only the Class B shareholders would have preemptive rights for this issue.

Even if preemptive rights exist, they do not apply to the following situations:

- Sale of treasury stock by the corporation;
- Sale by shareholders;
- Shares issued by the corporation for property contributed or services performed;

- Shares issued in cancellation or discharge of a debt;
- Shares issued pursuant to a plan of merger; or
- Any issuance of shares where the shareholders agree to waive their pre-emptive rights.

Stock Transfer Restrictions

One characteristic of corporate stock is that it is freely transferable. Shareholders can sell, mortgage, or give stock away. For smaller businesses, however, shares of stock are not freely transferable. There are several reasons for this.

- First, there is usually no public market for small closely held corporate stock.
- Second, securities laws restrict the offer for sale and sale of stock and other corporate securities. These restrictions severely limit a corporation shareholder's ability to communicate the desire to sell shares.
- Third, purchasers are hard to locate whenever less than a controlling interest of the corporation is offered for sale. No one wants to buy a minority interest.
- Fourth, even if a controlling interest is for sale, many purchases will purchase the assets of the corporation and not its stock. By acquiring the stock of a corporation, you automatically assume all corporate assets and liabilities, including ones you and your seller may not know about. By acquiring assets, you have some opportunity to pick and choose among the liabilities you wish to assume.
- Fifth, many shareholders voluntarily enter into agreements limiting their ability to transfer shares. This is especially true for smaller businesses where shareholders are active in the day-to-day operation of the business. When you and John Doe formed John Doe, Inc. to conduct your business, one factor in your decision was your willingness to work with John Doe, and he with you. You were compatible with each other. You aren't necessarily willing to work with anyone to whom John Doe might sell his shares or with his spouse or children if he should die. Because you want control over who you work with, shareholders will agree amongst themselves to restrict their ability to sell or dispose of their shares. More information about these types of agreements is found in Chapter 6.

What Types of Stock Transfer Restrictions Are Used?

Absolute prohibitions on the transfer of stock are not permitted. Any restriction must be reasonable. Common restrictions include:

- A right of first refusal giving the corporation or remaining shareholders the right to acquire your shares in the event you wish to sell to a third party; or
- A restriction on the types of persons who can acquire the shares. For example, only members of the profession can be shareholders in a professional corporation. Only licensed doctors can be shareholders of a medical

professional corporation. Another example would be a restriction which would permit transfers to your spouse or children, but not to others, without first providing for a right of first refusal.

How Do You Know if Shares You Are Acquiring Are Subject to Restrictions?

Share restrictions should be contained in a stock purchase agreement or buy-sell agreement entered into by the shareholders. Restrictions can also be found in the articles of incorporation and bylaws. Before acquiring any shares, ask to see these documents to verify the presence or absence of restrictions. The seller may have to obtain these items for you by making a shareholders request to the corporation. A discussion of stock purchase agreements and a form agreement are in Chapter 6.

Share transfer restrictions should be noted conspicuously on the stock certificate. You should request to examine the stock certificate before acquiring the stock to see if any language pertaining to transfer restrictions appears on the certificate.

If transfer restrictions apply to your corporation's shares, ensure that restrictive language appears on the stock certificate. A shareholder who acquires the stock without knowledge of the restrictions will not be bound by them.

Miscellaneous Stock Concepts

The discussion which follows is a potpourri of stock-related concepts, and it discusses definitions of terms which you are likely to encounter.

Basis

Basis is an important tax concept. Basis is the measuring rod by which gain or loss is determined when you sell an asset. In the case of stock, basis is generally what you pay for your stock, plus any additional capital contributions which you make to the corporation. Basis can also be decreased. For example, if a deduction or loss item passes through the corporation to you, individually, your basis will be decreased (but not below zero) by the amount of that deduction or loss. The concept can get painfully complicated, so consult with your personal tax adviser.

Watered or Diluted Stock

Stock which is sold for less than its par value is considered to be watered. The shareholder acquiring this stock remains personally liable for the water. The "water" is the difference between the par value and what is actually paid for the shares.

If no par stock is sold for different amounts over a short period of time, the shares held by those who pay the highest value for the shares are said to be diluted. Any value set by the board of directors must be reasonable and supported by legitimate business reasons. Board members who approve the issuance of diluted shares may face claims by shareholders for breach of the duty of due care or the duty to act in good faith. By and large, these concepts are rarely utilized under modern business corporation acts.

Treasury Stock

Treasury stock is stock which is reacquired by a corporation whether through redemption or repurchase. The corporation can sell its treasury stock for any price. Treasury stock is not considered to be originally issued stock, and does not qualify as Section 1244 stock. Preemptive rights do not apply to sales of treasury stock.

Subscription Agreement

A subscription agreement is any written agreement by which one subscribes or offers to purchase corporate shares. It represents an offer by the prospective shareholder to purchase shares. The offer does not become accepted unless and until the board agrees to accept it. Preincorporation subscription agreements are generally irrevocable for a six-month period.

Once a corporation has been formed, any post-incorporation subscription agreements can be revoked by the offering shareholder at any time prior to acceptance by the board of directors. Keep in mind that all efforts to offer or sell corporate securities should be preceded by a lengthy conversation with your business attorney.

Section 1244 stock

Section 1244 stock is a tax concept designed to encourage investment in small corporations. Section 1244 stock enables a shareholder to deduct as an ordinary loss amounts paid for stock issued to him or her by a small business corporation.[5] The ordinary loss may be claimed upon the sale, exchange, or worthlessness of stock. A loss is limited to $50,000 on separate returns and $100,000 on joint returns.

A small business corporation is one which receives $1 million or less in capital receipts (the amount of money and other property received by the corporation for stock, contributions to capital and paid-in surplus). The shares must be common stock, voting or nonvoting, originally issued by the corporation and not from treasury stock or from other shareholders. In addition, less than 50% of the corporation's gross receipts must come from royalties, rents, dividends, interest, annuities, and gains from the sale or exchange of securities.

S Corporations

An eligible corporation may elect to be taxed as an S corporation.[6] If this election is made, all shareholders as of the day of election must consent to it. An S corporation is taxed more as a partnership than as a corporation. Items of income, loss, deduction, and credit are taken into account on the shareholders personal tax returns. Rules for electing S corporation status and retaining this status are technical. Consult with your attorney or accountant to learn more.

To be eligible for S corporation status, a corporation must:

- Be a domestic corporation (created under the law of any state);
- Not be ineligible (financial institutions, insurance companies, Discs, etc.;
- Have no more than 75 shareholders (a husband and wife owning stock jointly are counted as one shareholder);
- Have shareholders which are individuals, decedent's estates, bankruptcy estates, certain trusts, or be wholly owned by an otherwise eligible S corporation;
- Have no nonresident alien shareholders; and
- Have only one class of stock issued and outstanding (one class of common which provided for voting and nonvoting rights would be permitted, however, common and preferred shares would make the corporation ineligible to make the election).[7]

For your reference, a copy of IRS *Form 2553, Election by a Small Business Corporation,* is shown on pages 87–90.

S Corporation Benefits

The principal benefit of S corporation status is that S corporations are taxed like partnerships. To the extent that a shareholder has basis, loss items pass through to the shareholder to offset other items of income. If the shareholder has no basis, loss items will carry over to other tax years when the shareholder has basis in his or her corporate stock. Because tax matters are handled at the shareholder level, taxation at the corporate level does not occur, thereby avoiding double taxation. Not all states provide this favorable treatment. Because state laws vary with respect to state income taxation of S corporations, talk with your business attorney or accountant.

These benefits are especially attractive for start-up corporations which are likely to experience losses in the early years. These losses could be used by shareholders to offset income from other personal sources. For existing corporations, the decision to elect S corporation status should be made only after consultation with their attorneys or accountants to avoid adverse and unintended tax consequences.

S Corporation Disadvantages

Because the S corporation rules are technical, care must be taken to make certain that the status is not inadvertently lost. For example, you must not have more than 75 shareholders or a nonqualifying shareholder. If you have too many or the wrong type of shareholders, you will lose S corporation status. Similarly, if you have made loans to your corporation which are not documented with promissory notes providing for a repayment schedule and a reasonable interest rate, the Internal Revenue Service (IRS) may characterize your loan as preferred stock resulting in a second and disqualifying class of stock.

Shareholders of S corporations are taxed on their pro rata share of corporate income whether or not that income is actually distributed to them. For example, you own 10% of the issued and outstanding stock of John Doe, Inc., an S corporation. John Doe, Inc. has $100,000 of net income. John Doe, Inc. doesn't want to distribute any of this $100,000 because it plans to acquire some real estate within the next several years. You will have to pay tax on your pro rata share of $10,000 even though you don't receive a distribution.

Terminating S Corporation Status

Why would you want to terminate S corporation status? In days gone by, shareholders would terminate S corporation status when the corporation became profitable. Because losses pass through, S corporations were used in the early years to pass loss through to the investors. Because individual income tax rates were higher than corporation rates, S corporation status would be terminated when profits were made.

Today, corporate rates are generally higher than individual rates. As a result, fewer S corporations are terminated when a corporation becomes profitable. Of course, if substantially all of a corporation's income is expensed out in the form of salaries, it may still be attractive to terminate the S corporation election.

More often than not, an S corporation election is terminated involuntarily and unintentionally. For example, if a corporation gains more than 35 shareholders or the wrong type of shareholder, the election terminates automatically. An S corporation can also be terminated if the corporation has too much passive investment income. These rules are technical, and your accountant should explain them to you.

The S corporation election can be terminated at any time if the holders of a majority of the stock agree. Whenever an election terminates, for whatever reason, the termination is effective upon the stated effective date, if voluntary, or upon the date of the occurrence of the event triggering the involuntary termination. If a termination occurs in the middle of the year, two tax returns are generally required, one for the portion of the year in which the election was in effect and another for the balance of the year.

After an election has been revoked or terminated, a corporation must wait five years before making another election. Although the IRS can consent to a shorter period, this is rare.

Securities Laws

Both federal and state governments regulate securities through a complex array of laws and regulations.[8] The offer to sell as well as the purchase and sale of securities is controlled. You should consult with an attorney who works extensively in the securities law area to help you with securities law questions. The following discussion highlights some areas you should know.

Why Are There Securities Laws?

Securities laws exist to protect investors from unscrupulous promoters. Most securities laws trace their origins to the post-Depression era. Entire fortunes were lost by people gambling on get rich schemes. Securities laws require that securities be registered prior to their offer or sale or that an exemption to registration be used. The rules are technical and require strict

IRS Form 2553 – Election by a Small Business Corporation

Form 2553
(Rev. September 1997)
Department of the Treasury
Internal Revenue Service

Election by a Small Business Corporation
(Under section 1362 of the Internal Revenue Code)
▶ For Paperwork Reduction Act Notice, see page 2 of instructions.
▶ See separate instructions.

OMB No. 1545-0146

Notes:
1. *This election to be an S corporation can be accepted only if all the tests are met under* **Who May Elect** *on page 1 of the instructions; all signatures in Parts I and III are originals (no photocopies); and the exact name and address of the corporation and other required form information are provided.*
2. *Do not file* **Form 1120S***, U.S. Income Tax Return for an S Corporation, for any tax year before the year the election takes effect.*
3. *If the corporation was in existence before the effective date of this election, see* **Taxes an S Corporation May Owe** *on page 1 of the instructions.*

Election Information

Please Type or Print

Name of corporation (see instructions)	**A** Employer identification number
Number, street, and room or suite no. (If a P.O. box, see instructions.)	**B** Date incorporated
City or town, state, and ZIP code	**C** State of incorporation

D Election is to be effective for tax year beginning (month, day, year) . . . . ▶ _____ / _____ / _____

E Name and title of officer or legal representative who the IRS may call for more information

F Telephone number of officer or legal representative ( )

G If the corporation changed its name or address after applying for the EIN shown in A above, check this box . . . . ▶ ☐

H If this election takes effect for the first tax year the corporation exists, enter month, day, and year of the **earliest** of the following: (1) date the corporation first had shareholders, (2) date the corporation first had assets, or (3) date the corporation began doing business . . . . ▶ _____ / _____ / _____

I Selected tax year: Annual return will be filed for tax year ending (month and day) ▶ _____

If the tax year ends on any date other than December 31, except for an automatic 52-53-week tax year ending with reference to the month of December, you **must** complete Part II on the back. If the date you enter is the ending date of an automatic 52-53-week tax year, write "52-53-week year" to the right of the date. See Temporary Regulations section 1.441-2T(e)(3).

J Name and address of each shareholder; shareholder's spouse having a community property interest in the corporation's stock; and each tenant in common, joint tenant, and tenant by the entirety. (A husband and wife (and their estates) are counted as one shareholder in determining the number of shareholders without regard to the manner in which the stock is owned.)	K Shareholders' Consent Statement. Under penalties of perjury, we declare that we consent to the election of the above-named corporation to be an S corporation under section 1362(a) and that we have examined this consent statement, including accompanying schedules and statements, and to the best of our knowledge and belief, it is true, correct, and complete. We understand our consent is binding and may not be withdrawn after the corporation has made a valid election. (Shareholders sign and date below.)		L Stock owned		M Social security number or employer identification number (see instructions)	N Share-holder's tax year ends (month and day)
	Signature	Date	Number of shares	Dates acquired		

Under penalties of perjury, I declare that I have examined this election, including accompanying schedules and statements, and to the best of my knowledge and belief, it is true, correct, and complete.

Signature of officer ▶ _____ Title ▶ _____ Date ▶ _____

See Parts II and III on back.   Cat. No. 18629R   Form **2553** (Rev. 9-97)

IRS Form 2553 – Election by a Small Business Corporation (continued)

Form 2553 (Rev. 9-97)   Page **2**

Selection of Fiscal Tax Year (All corporations using this part must complete item O and item P, Q, or R.)

O Check the applicable box to indicate whether the corporation is:
   1. ☐ A new corporation adopting the tax year entered in item I, Part I.
   2. ☐ An existing corporation retaining the tax year entered in item I, Part I.
   3. ☐ An existing corporation changing to the tax year entered in item I, Part I.

P Complete item P if the corporation is using the expeditious approval provisions of Rev. Proc. 87-32, 1987-2 C.B. 396, to request **(1)** a natural business year (as defined in section 4.01(1) of Rev. Proc. 87-32) or **(2)** a year that satisfies the ownership tax year test in section 4.01(2) of Rev. Proc. 87-32. Check the applicable box below to indicate the representation statement the corporation is making as required under section 4 of Rev. Proc. 87-32.

   1. Natural Business Year ▶ ☐ I represent that the corporation is retaining or changing to a tax year that coincides with its natural business year as defined in section 4.01(1) of Rev. Proc. 87-32 and as verified by its satisfaction of the requirements of section 4.02(1) of Rev. Proc. 87-32. In addition, if the corporation is changing to a natural business year as defined in section 4.01(1), I further represent that such tax year results in less deferral of income to the owners than the corporation's present tax year. I also represent that the corporation is not described in section 3.01(2) of Rev. Proc. 87-32. (See instructions for additional information that must be attached.)

   2. Ownership Tax Year ▶ ☐ I represent that shareholders holding more than half of the shares of the stock (as of the first day of the tax year to which the request relates) of the corporation have the same tax year or are concurrently changing to the tax year that the corporation adopts, retains, or changes to per item I, Part I. I also represent that the corporation is not described in section 3.01(2) of Rev. Proc. 87-32.

Note: *If you do not use item P and the corporation wants a fiscal tax year, complete either item Q or R below. Item Q is used to request a fiscal tax year based on a business purpose and to make a back-up section 444 election. Item R is used to make a regular section 444 election.*

Q Business Purpose—To request a fiscal tax year based on a business purpose, you must check box Q1 and pay a user fee. See instructions for details. You may also check box Q2 and/or box Q3.

   1. Check here ▶ ☐ if the fiscal year entered in item I, Part I, is requested under the provisions of section 6.03 of Rev. Proc. 87-32. Attach to Form 2553 a statement showing the business purpose for the requested fiscal year. See instructions for additional information that must be attached.

   2. Check here ▶ ☐ to show that the corporation intends to make a back-up section 444 election in the event the corporation's business purpose request is not approved by the IRS. (See instructions for more information.)

   3. Check here ▶ ☐ to show that the corporation agrees to adopt or change to a tax year ending December 31 if necessary for the IRS to accept this election for S corporation status in the event (1) the corporation's business purpose request is not approved and the corporation makes a back-up section 444 election, but is ultimately not qualified to make a section 444 election, or (2) the corporation's business purpose request is not approved and the corporation did not make a back-up section 444 election.

R Section 444 Election—To make a section 444 election, you must check box R1 and you may also check box R2.
   1. Check here ▶ ☐ to show the corporation will make, if qualified, a section 444 election to have the fiscal tax year shown in item I, Part I. To make the election, you must complete **Form 8716**, Election To Have a Tax Year Other Than a Required Tax Year, and either attach it to Form 2553 or file it separately.

   2. Check here ▶ ☐ to show that the corporation agrees to adopt or change to a tax year ending December 31 if necessary for the IRS to accept this election for S corporation status in the event the corporation is ultimately not qualified to make a section 444 election.

Qualified Subchapter S Trust (QSST) Election Under Section 1361(d)(2)*

Income beneficiary's name and address	Social security number
Trust's name and address	Employer identification number

Date on which stock of the corporation was transferred to the trust (month, day, year) . . . . **▶**   / /

In order for the trust named above to be a QSST and thus a qualifying shareholder of the S corporation for which this Form 2553 is filed, I hereby make the election under section 1361(d)(2). Under penalties of perjury, I certify that the trust meets the definitional requirements of section 1361(d)(3) and that all other information provided in Part III is true, correct, and complete.

_____   _____
Signature of income beneficiary or signature and title of legal representative or other qualified person making the election   Date

*Use Part III to make the QSST election only if stock of the corporation has been transferred to the trust on or before the date on which the corporation makes its election to be an S corporation. The QSST election must be made and filed separately if stock of the corporation is transferred to the trust after the date on which the corporation makes the S election.

Instructions for Form 2553

**Department of the Treasury
Internal Revenue Service**

(Revised September 1997)

Election by a Small Business Corporation

Section references are to the Internal Revenue Code unless otherwise noted.

General Instructions

Purpose.— To elect to be an S corporation, a corporation must file Form 2553. The election permits the income of the S corporation to be taxed to the shareholders of the corporation rather than to the corporation itself, except as noted below under **Taxes an S Corporation May Owe.**

Who May Elect.— A corporation may elect to be an S corporation only if it meets all of the following tests:

1. It is a domestic corporation.

2. It has no more than 75 shareholders. A husband and wife (and their estates) are treated as one shareholder for this requirement. All other persons are treated as separate shareholders.

3. Its only shareholders are individuals, estates, certain trusts described in section 1361(c)(2)(A), or, for tax years beginning after 1997, exempt organizations described in section 401(a) or 501(c)(3). Trustees of trusts that want to make the election under section 1361(e)(3) to be an electing small business trust should see Notice 97-12, 1997-3 I.R.B. 11.

Note: *See the instructions for Part III regarding qualified subchapter S trusts.*

4. It has no nonresident alien shareholders.

5. It has only one class of stock (disregarding differences in voting rights). Generally, a corporation is treated as having only one class of stock if all outstanding shares of the corporation's stock confer identical rights to distribution and liquidation proceeds. See Regulations section 1.1361-1(1) for more details.

6. It is not one of the following ineligible corporations:

a. A bank or thrift institution that uses the reserve method of accounting for bad debts under section 585;

b. An insurance company subject to tax under the rules of subchapter L of the Code;

c. A corporation that has elected to be treated as a possessions corporation under section 936; or

d. A domestic international sales corporation (DISC) or former DISC.

7. It has a permitted tax year as required by section 1378 or makes a section 444 election to have a tax year other than a permitted tax year. Section 1378 defines a permitted tax year as a tax year ending December 31, or any other tax year for which the corporation establishes a business purpose to the satisfaction of the IRS. See Part II for details on requesting a fiscal tax year based on a business purpose or on making a section 444 election.

8. Each shareholder consents as explained in the instructions for column K.

See sections 1361, 1362, and 1378 for additional information on the above tests.

An election can be made by a parent S corporation to treat the assets, liabilities, and items of income, deduction, and credit of an eligible wholly-owned subsidiary as those of the parent. For details, see Notice 97-4, 1997-2 I.R.B. 24.

Taxes an S Corporation May Owe.— An S corporation may owe income tax in the following instances:

1. If, at the end of any tax year, the corporation had accumulated earnings and profits, and its passive investment income under section 1362(d)(3) is more than 25% of its gross receipts, the corporation may owe tax on its excess net passive income.

2. A corporation with net recognized built-in gain (as defined in section 1374(d)(2)) may owe tax on its built-in gains.

3. A corporation that claimed investment credit before its first year as an S corporation will be liable for any investment credit recapture tax.

4. A corporation that used the LIFO inventory method for the year immediately preceding its first year as an S corporation may owe an additional tax due to LIFO recapture.

For more details on these taxes, see the Instructions for Form 1120S.

Where To File.— File this election with the Internal Revenue Service Center listed below.

If the corporation's principal business, office, or agency is located in	Use the following Internal Revenue Service Center address
New Jersey, New York (New York City and counties of Nassau, Rockland, Suffolk, and Westchester)	Holtsville, NY 00501
New York (all other counties), Connecticut, Maine, Massachusetts, New Hampshire, Rhode Island, Vermont	Andover, MA 05501
Florida, Georgia, South Carolina	Atlanta, GA 39901
Indiana, Kentucky, Michigan, Ohio, West Virginia	Cincinnati, OH 45999
Kansas, New Mexico, Oklahoma, Texas	Austin, TX 73301
Alaska, Arizona, California (counties of Alpine, Amador, Butte, Calaveras, Colusa, Contra Costa, Del Norte, El Dorado, Glenn, Humboldt, Lake, Lassen, Marin, Mendocino, Modoc, Napa, Nevada, Placer, Plumas, Sacramento, San Joaquin, Shasta, Sierra, Siskiyou, Solano, Sonoma, Sutter, Tehama, Trinity, Yolo, and Yuba), Colorado, Idaho, Montana, Nebraska, Nevada, North Dakota, Oregon, South Dakota, Utah, Washington, Wyoming	Ogden, UT 84201
California (all other counties), Hawaii	Fresno, CA 93888
Illinois, Iowa, Minnesota, Missouri, Wisconsin	Kansas City, MO 64999
Alabama, Arkansas, Louisiana, Mississippi, North Carolina, Tennessee	Memphis, TN 37501
Delaware, District of Columbia, Maryland, Pennsylvania, Virginia	Philadelphia, PA 19255

When To Make the Election.— Complete and file Form 2553 (a) at any time before the 16th day of the 3rd month of the tax year, if filed during the tax year the election is to take effect, or (b) at any time during the preceding tax year. An election made no later than 2 months and 15 days after the beginning of a tax year that is less than 2½ months long is treated as timely made for that tax year. An election made after the 15th day of the 3rd month but before the end of the tax year is effective for the next year. For example, if a calendar tax year

corporation makes the election in April 1998, it is effective for the corporation's 1999 calendar tax year.

However, an election made after the due date will be accepted as timely filed if the corporation can show that the failure to file on time was due to reasonable cause. To request relief for a late election, the corporation generally must request a private letter ruling and pay a user fee in accordance with Rev. Proc. 97-1, 1997-1 I.R.B. 11 (or its successor). But if the election is filed within 6 months of its due date and the original due date for filing the corporation's initial Form 1120S has not passed, the ruling and user fee requirements do not apply. To request relief in this case, write "FILED PURSUANT TO REV. PROC. 97-40" at the top of page 1 of Form 2553, attach a statement explaining the reason for failing to file the election on time, and file Form 2553 as otherwise instructed. See Rev. Proc. 97-40, 1997-33 I.R.B. 50, for more details.

See Regulations section 1.1362-6(b)(3)(iii) for how to obtain relief for an inadvertent invalid election if the corporation filed a timely election, but one or more shareholders did not file a timely consent.

Acceptance or Nonacceptance of Election.— The service center will notify the corporation if its election is accepted and when it will take effect. The corporation will also be notified if its election is not accepted. The corporation should generally receive a determination on its election within 60 days after it has filed Form 2553. If box Q1 in Part II is checked on page 2, the corporation will receive a ruling letter from the IRS in Washington, DC, that either approves or denies the selected tax year. When box Q1 is checked, it will generally take an additional 90 days for the Form 2553 to be accepted.

Do not file Form 1120S for any tax year before the year the election takes effect. If the corporation is now required to file **Form 1120,** U.S. Corporation Income Tax Return, or any other applicable tax return, continue filing it until the election takes effect.

Care should be exercised to ensure that the IRS receives the election. If the corporation is not notified of acceptance or nonacceptance of its election within 3 months of date of filing (date mailed), or within 6 months if box Q1 is checked, take follow-up action by corresponding with the service center where the corporation filed the election. If the IRS questions whether Form 2553 was filed, an acceptable proof of filing is (a) certified or registered mail receipt (timely filed) from the U.S. Postal Service or its equivalent from a designated private delivery service (see Notice 97-26, 1997-17 I.R.B. 6); (b) Form 2553 with accepted stamp; (c) Form 2553 with stamped IRS received date; or (d) IRS letter stating that Form 2553 has been accepted.

End of Election.— Once the election is made, it stays in effect until it is terminated. If the election is terminated in a tax year beginning after 1996, the corporation (or a successor corporation) can make another election on Form 2553 only with IRS consent for any tax year before the 5th tax year after the first tax year in which the termination took effect. See Regulations section 1.1362-5 for more details.

Cat. No. 49978N

IRS Form 2553 – Election by a Small Business Corporation (continued)

Specific Instructions

Part I

Note: *All corporations must complete Part I.*

Name and Address of Corporation.— Enter the true corporate name as stated in the corporate charter or other legal document creating it. If the corporation's mailing address is the same as someone else's, such as a shareholder's, enter "c/o" and this person's name following the name of the corporation. Include the suite, room, or other unit number after the street address. If the Post Office does not deliver to the street address and the corporation has a P.O. box, show the box number instead of the street address. If the corporation changed its name or address after applying for its employer identification number, be sure to check the box in Item G of Part I.

Item A. Employer Identification Number (EIN).— If the corporation has applied for an EIN but has not received it, enter "applied for." If the corporation does not have an EIN, it should apply for one on **Form SS-4**, Application for Employer Identification Number. You can order Form SS-4 by calling 1-800-TAX-FORM (1-800-829-3676).

Item D. Effective Date of Election.— Enter the beginning effective date (month, day, year) of the tax year requested for the S corporation. Generally, this will be the beginning date of the tax year for which the ending effective date is required to be shown in Item I, Part I. For a new corporation (first year the corporation exists) it will generally be the date required to be shown in Item H, Part I. The tax year of a new corporation starts on the date that it has shareholders, acquires assets, or begins doing business, whichever happens first. If the effective date for item D for a newly formed corporation is later than the date in item H, the corporation should file Form 1120 or Form 1120-A for the tax period between these dates.

Column K. Shareholders' Consent Statement.— Each shareholder who owns (or is deemed to own) stock at the time the election is made must consent to the election. If the election is made during the corporation's tax year for which it first takes effect, any person who held stock at any time during the part of that year that occurs before the election is made, must consent to the election, even though the person may have sold or transferred his or her stock before the election is made.

An election made during the first 2½ months of the tax year is effective for the following tax year if any person who held stock in the corporation during the part of the tax year before the election was made, and who did not hold stock at the time the election was made, did not consent to the election.

Each shareholder consents by signing and dating in column K or signing and dating a separate consent statement described below. The following special rules apply in determining who must sign the consent statement.

- If a husband and wife have a community interest in the stock or in the income from it, both must consent.
- Each tenant in common, joint tenant, and tenant by the entirety must consent.
- A minor's consent is made by the minor, legal representative of the minor, or a natural or adoptive parent of the minor if no legal representative has been appointed.
- The consent of an estate is made by the executor or administrator.

- The consent of an electing small business trust is made by the trustee.
- If the stock is owned by a trust (other than an electing small business trust), the deemed owner of the trust must consent. See section 1361(c)(2) for details regarding trusts that are permitted to be shareholders and rules for determining who is the deemed owner.

*Continuation sheet or separate consent statement.—*If you need a continuation sheet or use a separate consent statement, attach it to Form 2553. The separate consent statement must contain the name, address, and EIN of the corporation and the shareholder information requested in columns J through N of Part I. If you want, you may combine all the shareholders' consents in one statement.

Column L.— Enter the number of shares of stock each shareholder owns and the dates the stock was acquired. If the election is made during the corporation's tax year for which it first takes effect, do not list the shares of stock for those shareholders who sold or transferred all of their stock before the election was made. However, these shareholders must still consent to the election for it to be effective for the tax year.

Column M.— Enter the social security number of each shareholder who is an individual. Enter the EIN of each shareholder that is an estate, a qualified trust, or an exempt organization.

Column N.— Enter the month and day that each shareholder's tax year ends. If a shareholder is changing his or her tax year, enter the tax year the shareholder is changing to, and attach an explanation indicating the present tax year and the basis for the change (e.g., automatic revenue procedure or letter ruling request).

Signature.— Form 2553 must be signed by the president, treasurer, assistant treasurer, chief accounting officer, or other corporate officer (such as tax officer) authorized to sign.

Part II

Complete Part II if you selected a tax year ending on any date other than December 31 (other than a 52-53-week tax year ending with reference to the month of December).

Box P1.— Attach a statement showing separately for each month the amount of gross receipts for the most recent 47 months as required by section 4.03(3) of Rev. Proc. 87-32, 1987-2 C.B. 396. A corporation that does not have a 47-month period of gross receipts cannot establish a natural business year under section 4.01(1).

Box Q1.— For examples of an acceptable business purpose for requesting a fiscal tax year, see Rev. Rul. 87-57, 1987-2 C.B. 117.

In addition to a statement showing the business purpose for the requested fiscal year, you must attach the other information necessary to meet the ruling request requirements of Rev. Proc. 97-1 (or its successor). Also attach a statement that shows separately the amount of gross receipts from sales or services (and inventory costs, if applicable) for each of the 36 months preceding the effective date of the election to be an S corporation. If the corporation has been in existence for fewer than 36 months, submit figures for the period of existence.

If you check box Q1, you will be charged a $250 user fee (subject to change). Do not pay the fee when filing Form 2553. The service center will send Form 2553 to the IRS in

Washington, DC, who, in turn, will notify the corporation that the fee is due.

Box Q2.— If the corporation makes a back-up section 444 election for which it is qualified, then the election will take effect in the event the business purpose request is not approved. In some cases, the tax year requested under the back-up section 444 election may be different than the tax year requested under business purpose. See **Form 8716**, Election To Have a Tax Year Other Than a Required Tax Year, for details on making a back-up section 444 election.

Boxes Q2 and R2.— If the corporation is not qualified to make the section 444 election after making the item Q2 back-up section 444 election or indicating its intention to make the election in item R1, and therefore it later files a calendar year return, it should write "Section 444 Election Not Made" in the top left corner of the first calendar year Form 1120S it files.

Part III

Certain qualified subchapter S trusts (QSSTs) may make the QSST election required by section 1361(d)(2) in Part III. Part III may be used to make the QSST election only if corporate stock has been transferred to the trust on or before the date on which the corporation makes its election to be an S corporation. However, a statement can be used instead of Part III to make the election.

Note: *Use Part III only if you make the election in Part I (i.e., Form 2553 cannot be filed with only Part III completed).*

The deemed owner of the QSST must also consent to the S corporation election in column K, page 1, of Form 2553. See section 1361 (c)(2).

Paperwork Reduction Act Notice.— We ask for the information on this form to carry out the Internal Revenue laws of the United States. You are required to give us the information. We need it to ensure that you are complying with these laws and to allow us to figure and collect the right amount of tax.

You are not required to provide the information requested on a form that is subject to the Paperwork Reduction Act unless the form displays a valid OMB control number. Books or records relating to a form or its instructions must be retained as long as their contents may become material in the administration of any Internal Revenue law. Generally, tax returns and return information are confidential, as required by section 6103.

The time needed to complete and file this form will depend on individual circumstances. The estimated average time is:

Recordkeeping	6 hr., 28 min.
Learning about the law or the form	3 hr., 41 min.
Preparing, copying, assembling, and sending the form to the IRS	3 hr., 56 min.

If you have comments concerning the accuracy of these time estimates or suggestions for making this form simpler, we would be happy to hear from you. You can write to the Tax Forms Committee, Western Area Distribution Center, Rancho Cordova, CA 95743-0001. **DO NOT** send the form to this address. Instead, see **Where To File** on page 1.

compliance. All securities laws contain anti-fraud provisions designed to promote full and fair disclosure of all material information. There are no exemptions from the anti-fraud provisions.

Securities laws compel full and accurate disclosure of all material terms of a proposed securities offering. Information about the persons promoting the offering, the business of the issuer, the proposed use of funds, and detailed financial information is provided so that an investor can make a rational and informed decision about whether or not to invest his or her funds. In practice, many offering circulars amount to little more than a long list of risk factors and reasons why someone shouldn't invest in the security. Nonetheless, securities are bought and sold each day.

What Is a Security?

The term "security" is broadly defined to include notes, stock, treasury stock, preorganization subscriptions, voting trust certificates, certificate of interest or participation in an oil, gas, or mining title; or lease or investment contract. It also includes corporate stock and partnership interests.[9]

Loans are generally excluded from the definition of securities if the loans are documented by a promissory note or loan agreement. The sale or exchange of promissory notes is a sale or exchange of securities. If in doubt, it is probably a security.

What Does Registration of Securities Involve?

Registration is a formal process by which an issuer — the corporation or other entity proposing to sell securities — provides information about itself, its officers and directors to the federal or state securities agency. Information about the business, the use of proceeds to be raised, the marketing plan and detailed financial information is also provided. Much of this information will be contained in a prospectus or offering circular which is included as part of the registration materials. Registration can be a time-consuming and expensive process. You will need a securities attorney to assist you in this process.

Are There Any Exemptions from Registration?

There are exemptions that apply to certain types of securities and certain types of transactions. Common exempt securities include:

- Certain government bonds;
- Securities issued or guaranteed by the U.S. government; and
- Securities listed and traded on public stock exchanges (an exemption from state but not federal securities laws).[10]

Common exempt transactions include:

- Sheriff's sales or other court approved sales;
- Private placements under restrictive federal or state regulations;
- Preincorporation subscriptions not involving more than a limited number of investors, usually 15 to 25;

- Sales to institutional investors, such as banks or insurance companies; or
- Sales pursuant to federal or state securities regulations pertaining to the private placement of securities.[11]

Final Thoughts on Corporate Stock

Like a diamond, corporate stock can have many facets and characteristics. Until you, as owner of the corporation, define the term "stock," it has little meaning. Yet, before you file the articles of incorporation, you must determine what type of stock your corporation will be authorized to issue.

As you have seen, stock can be common or preferred. It can convert from one type to another, and it can be redeemed either at the option of the shareholder or the corporation. Stock can entitle its holder to voting rights or it may be nonvoting. Some states entitle their holders to vote on certain corporate matters.

As an accounting term, the word "stock" implies an amount of cash or property contributed to the capital of the corporation in exchange for the issuance of corporate stock.

Unless restricted, corporate stock is freely transferable, subject, of course, to state and federal securities laws. As a practical matter, there is little market for the stock of closely held corporations, especially where less than 50% of the issued and outstanding capital stock is offered for sale.

Stockholders may be entitled to dividends, distribution of cash, or property made from the earnings and profits of the corporation. If there are no earnings and profits, there can be no dividends. The decision of whether or not to declare a dividend usually rests solely with the board of directors. Board discretion may be affected by the terms of any preferred stock which mandate a payment of a dividend whenever there are sufficient earnings and profits.

S corporations are creatures of the federal tax code which are able to pass through certain items of income, loss, deduction, and credit to shareholders. This approval avoids a tax at the corporate and shareholder level. S corporation rules are technical and must be complied with fully.

As with your articles and bylaws, stock provides an opportunity for flexibility. By creating different classes and preferences for your stock, you can do many things, including the creation of an investment opportunity for outsiders while retaining voting control of the corporation. Your articles must define any differences in classification or preference in your stock. Your bylaws will provide procedural rules though which shareholders can vote for directors or on other corporate business. Your articles, bylaws, and stock certificates should be consistent with each other and prepared with the same goals in mind.

SAMPLE: Stock Subscription Agreement

John Doe, Inc. Stock Subscription Agreement

WHEREAS, it is proposed that a corporation be formed under the laws of the State of _____ under the name John Doe, Inc. or some other name if it is not available for use, and

WHEREAS, the incorporator(s) require that a preincorporation stock subscription be executed by one or more of the anticipated subscribers to the stock of the corporation.

NOW, THEREFORE, in consideration of the promises contained herein and as an inducement to the incorporator(s) to submit the articles of incorporation of John Doe, Inc., the subscribers agree to purchase the number of shares of stock of this corporation and to pay the amount set forth opposite their names, all as designated below. All subscriptions shall be payable at the times and in the manner hereinafter stated, or absent such statement, at the time or times and in the manner designated by the Board of Directors of John Doe, Inc. The subscription shall not be binding on the undersigned unless the aggregate amount of $_____ is subscribed to on or before _____, 1992.

Date	Number of Shares	Amount	Date Subscribed for	Payment
_____	_____	_____	_____	_____

_____
Name

_____
Address

_____

_____
Signature lines

In most states, a preincorporation stock subscription agreement is binding upon and irrevocable by the subscribing shareholder for up to six months. Beware of state and federal securities law issues whenever dealing with stock or other securities.

Chapter 6

Shareholder Agreements

In a literal sense, every time two or more shareholders agree to do something, you have a shareholders' agreement. Shareholders have tremendous flexibility to agree amongst themselves on virtually every conceivable subject matter, though more typically, shareholder agreements are limited to a narrower range of topics. Common shareholder agreement subject matters include:

- Who can be a shareholder of the corporation?
- Who can can serve on the board of directors?
- How will shares be voted in matters presented to shareholders?
- How to you restrict lifetime transfers of corporate stock?
- What happens if a shareholder dies or becomes disabled?
- What occurs if a shareholder files bankruptcy, resigns, retires, or is fired by the corporation?
- How much are your shares worth?
- If the corporation or remaining shareholders are required to buy your shares, when will you be paid?

How do you know what provisions to include in a shareholders' agreement? The answer to this question is complicated. Several factors to consider are:

- How important are the shareholders to the actual conduct of the corporation's business?
- What are the relative ages of the shareholders?
- What are the personalities and relationship of the individual shareholders?
- Are there a number of minority shareholders?

- Do key employees own shares of stock?
- What are the individual needs and desires of each shareholder?

The starting point for any discussion by shareholders of shareholder agreements is deciding what the agreement is intended to do. Each shareholder must express his or her needs. Younger shareholders may be more concerned with making certain that all shareholders are active in the daily operations of the corporation. Older shareholders may be more focused on providing a market to purchase their shares in the event of death, disability, or retirement.

In addition, some shareholders may have spouses or children who are quite capable of running the corporation. Others may lack the necessary skills or interest and would rather be bought out if the shareholder's spouse/father were to die or become disabled.

Minority shareholders may see a shareholders' agreement as a way to maintain an elected representative on the board of directors. Alternatively, a minority shareholder may seek to align himself or herself with a majority shareholder in an agreement. This latter situation might occur where key employees who own small amounts of stock join forces with the majority shareholder in an agreement.

As you can see, what your shareholder agreement contains is largely the result of the people and personalities who own corporate shares of stock. Many individual needs and desires must come together. Be creative, but be responsive to your corporation's shareholders as well.

Types of Shareholder Agreements

There are several different types of shareholder agreements. This chapter will focus on three: the stock purchase or buy-sell agreement; the voting trust; and the voting or pooling agreement. Many hybrids of these three principal forms of agreement exist; however, the following characteristics are common to all shareholder agreements:

- Shareholder agreements are consentual and voluntary;
- The terms and conditions must be reasonable (for example, absolute prohibitions on transfer are not permitted);
- Contract law principles apply to the interpretation and enforcement of shareholder agreements; and
- The agreements must be entered into for a proper purpose. They can't be used to defraud minority shareholders or corporate creditors.

Historically, a stock purchase or buy-sell agreement has been used to control who your fellow shareholders are and to provide a market for your shares in certain circumstances. In the sample stock purchase agreement included in this chapter, the agreement restricts lifetime stock transfers and provides for a buy out of stock upon a shareholder's death, disability, bankruptcy, termination, resignation, or retirement. Your stock purchase or buy-sell agreement could provide for these same situations, or it could be narrower or broader in focus. You make the choice.

Voting trusts and voting or pooling agreements are instruments focused on control of the shareholder voting process. They don't usually regulate who your fellow shareholders are or provide a market for shares. Rather, they are formed to control such things as who can serve as a director of the corporation. For example, assume that John owns 100 shares of stock of John Doe, Inc. and that Jane and Joan each own 50 shares. To increase their clout, Jane and Joan may choose to use a voting trust or a voting or pooling agreement to agree to vote their shares together, most likely to elect a director other than John.

To preserve harmony and promote goodwill among key employees, John may also be willing to enter into this agreement with Jane and Joan. They might not own as much of the corporation, but this agreement, in effect, treats them as equal owners. This is a true benefit for Jane and Joan, but it benefits John Doe and John Doe, Inc. as well.

A word of warning is in order. Shareholder agreements are complicated, involving many legal issues, including tax and securities laws. These agreements should be carefully tailored to fit your situation. Work closely with your business attorney and accountant to put together a shareholders' agreement that will work best for you.

As you move forward in this chapter and review the sample documents, remember that you can be creative and flexible in the documents you use. There are virtually no legally required provisions in any of the sample documents. In fact, the stock purchase which follows is modular by design. If you choose not to deal with lifetime transfers, death, disability, or any other subject matter, delete these provisions.

You should also remember that the title attached to a document, such as stock purchase, voting trust, or pooling agreement, may not accurately reflect the terms and conditions contained in the agreement. There are many hybrids, and you should carefully review any documents to make certain what its terms and conditions are. This is much more important than what the document is called.

A final not of caution is in order. The sample agreements which follow are examples only. As you review them, it is likely that many questions will come to mind. Discuss these questions with your business lawyer or accountant. In the sample agreements, judgments, and assumptions have been made which may not apply to your corporation. A shareholder agreement is a mixture of individual needs and desires, and the contents of a shareholder agreement, will vary widely from agreement to agreement.

Stock Purchase or Buy-Sell Agreement

The most common form of shareholder agreement is the stock purchase or buy-sell agreement. To help illustrate the discussion below, follow the sample stock purchase agreement which is provided on subsequent pages of this chapter. As you do, write your comments and questions on a separate sheet of paper. This will help you prepare your own agreement, and identify issues to discuss with your attorney or fellow shareholders.

Preamble

The first portion of the stock purchase agreement is the preamble, which identifies the parties. The corporation and all of the shareholders are normally considered parties. Shareholders who do not sign the agreement are not bound by it unless the articles or bylaws contain similar restrictions or the shareholder is otherwise aware of the restrictions, though proving knowledge is tricky business in law. Get signatures instead.

Recitals

Use the sample agreements which follow as an example only. They raise issues which may or not be important to you. They will make choices which could cause you some unintended consequences, including tax liability.

Recitals follow the preamble and are simple statements of fact which describe the reasons for entering into the agreement and the goals to be obtained. The recital's goals are to preserve continuity and harmony in the corporation's management and to provide a market for shares upon the death, retirement, disability, etc. of a shareholder. Recitals are a good way to avoid later claims that the agreement is somehow unenforceable because it was formed for an improper purpose.

Events Triggering the Agreement

Following the preamble and recitals are the substantive portions of the agreement. Shareholder agreements will differ widely in this area. Some shareholder agreements seek to accomplish a single objective, such as restrict lifetime transfers of shares. Others, like the sample, seek to achieve multiple goals. You need to choose which goals or objectives your agreement must meet.

Optional Versus Mandatory

In shareholder agreements, pay careful attention to the language used. The word "shall" creates an obligation. Chances are you will want some mandatory provisions and some optional ones.

As you review the enclosed sample agreements and read this chapter, note that certain events require the corporation or the remaining shareholders to purchase shares. Other events merely give rise to an option in favor of the corporation or the shareholders to buy. This distinction is critical, and you must determine in each instance whether or not a purchase requirement should be optional or mandatory. Lifetime transfers are usually optional. Death transfers are more often mandatory, especially where the corporation or remaining shareholders have acquired insurance to fund the purchase. How can you tell the difference? Optional clauses use the terms "may" or "option," while mandatory purchase obligations use the term "shall."

Right of First Refusal for Lifetime Transfers: Can You Control Who Your Fellow Shareholders Are?

Article I restricts lifetime transfers of shares; however, an absolute prohibition against the sale of shares is improper. Such a prohibition would be an unlawful restraint. Article I contains a right of first refusal in favor of the corporation and the remaining shareholders. If a shareholder decides to sell or transfer his or her shares to an outside party, he or she must notify the corporation and the remaining shareholders. This notice must be in writing and contain, among other things, the name and address of the outside party and the terms and conditions of the proposed transfer, including purchase price and conditions of purchase. The corporation and the remaining shareholders have the right to match the offer of the outside party and purchase the shares from the selling shareholder on identical terms.

By using a right of first refusal, the corporation and the remaining shareholders can retain control of the corporation and exclude an outside party who may not be as active or skilled as the selling shareholder or who may have different objectives for the corporation. The selling shareholder is not prejudiced because he or she still receives the payment he or she would have received from the outside party. The corporation and remaining shareholders have an opportunity to look at the outside party to see if he or she is compatible with the other shareholders and the corporation.

Under the sample stock purchase agreement, the corporation or remaining shareholders must purchase all of the shares which the selling shareholder proposes to transfer.

Permitting Lifetime Transfers to Family Members

What if you want to permit transfers to certain family members without triggering the right of first refusal? Under Article I of the sample stock purchase agreement, no provision is made for permitted transfers.

Consider permitting the transfer of a small percentage of stock to immediate family members. This approach can satisfy the transferring shareholder's need to spread his or her largess among family members without giving the family member a significant voice in or control of the business. Keep in mind, however, that the more shareholders your corporation has, the less likely it will be that consent resolutions can be used. Similarly, if your corporation elects S corporation status, you must be careful not to exceed 75 shareholders.

"Solomon's Choice" Clause

Section 1.5 of the sample provides a buy-out mechanism that has been called the "Solomon's Choice" or a "Put up or Shut up" clause. Such a clause is not for every business. Here's how it works: John Doe and Jane Doe are the only shareholders in John Doe, Inc. John decides that he can't stand to work with Jane anymore so he makes a written offer to Jane to acquire all of Jane's stock. When Jane receives this offer, she must do one of two things. She must agree to sell to John upon the terms and conditions presented by John or she can compel John to sell all of his shares to her upon those same terms or conditions. Either way, the status quo is broken.

The Solomon's choice or put up or shut up clause can be effective to deal with a deadlock situation where shareholders or their elected directors are unable to agree. Presumably, a fair price for shares will be offered since the offering shareholder may have to accept that price for his or her shares. These clauses are tricky, and great thought should go into whether or not to include it in your shareholders' agreement. One risk: What if your personal cash flow situation is not good? Can your fellow shareholder take advantage of the situation by offering a ridiculously low price knowing that you can't turn the tables and buy him or her out instead? Perhaps a clause indicating that the price offered can't be lower than the formula price determined elsewhere in the agreement could provide some protection from this situation.

Involuntary Transfers

Return to John Doe, Inc. John, Jane, and Joan are the only shareholders. John has been living a little too far beyond his means, and one of his creditors obtains a judgment against him. As a result of persistent collection efforts, the sheriff obtains John's stock and sells John's stock to Bob at a court ordered sale. Bob's business is the chief competitor of John Doe, Inc. Needless to say, Jane and Joan are horrified.

Article II of the sample stock purchase agreement creates an option in favor of the corporation and the remaining shareholders to purchase shares in the event of an involuntary transfer. Involuntary transfers can include such things as court ordered creditor sales, voluntary or involuntary bankruptcy, or the appointment of a receiver or conservator. If money is paid for the shares on an involuntary transfer, Article II treats the transfer as if it were a lifetime transfer under Article I. The corporation and the remaining shareholders have a first right of refusal to acquire the shares for the same price and on the same terms and conditions. If no money changes hands, the purchase price to be paid is to be determined by using the valuation method described below.

Death

John dies. Under his will, the shares of his stock in John Doe, Inc. are to pass to a trust for the benefit of his spouse and children. Under the trust agreement, the trustee, a local bank, is required to sell all assets which do not currently produce income. John Doe, Inc. has never paid dividends. Its real value is in the long-term potential for gain resulting from a sale of the business. Jane and Joan don't want to sell the business at this time. Jane and Joan are not anxious to run the business with John's wife or children or the bank trustee. They also don't want the bank trustee to sell the shares to an outside buyer. What happens?

Under Article III, the corporation is obligated to purchase the shares of a deceased shareholder, and his or her estate must sell them to the corporation. If the corporation can't purchase the shares (probably because it lacks sufficient funds), the remaining shareholders must purchase the shares. Either the corporation or the remaining shareholders could acquire life insurance on each shareholder so that adequate funds would be available. The corporation could also set aside monies to accomplish the buy out in the event of an uninsurable shareholder. Shareholders may be uninsurable due to prior accident, illness, or disease including alcoholism or drug addiction. Practical uninsurability may exist where the insurance premiums are high due to the age or health of the proposed insured.

In many situations, a buy-out is also preferred by the deceased shareholder. John may not want to burden his wife or children or the bank trustee with involvement in business decisions. He may prefer that they receive cash to invest or use as they choose, including the payment of any estate taxes which might be due. John may also not wish to do business with the spouses or children of Jane or Joan. Not knowing which shareholder will die first, the automatic buy out may be the necessary trade off.

It is not certain how binding such a provision would be on a bankruptcy trustee. If the value is fair and reasonable, the trustee will probably be happy to sell. If not, the trustee will hold onto the shares or sell them to an outside party.

Many different types of insurance policies exist, and the tax consequences to the corporation, the deceased or disabled shareholder and the remaining shareholders may vary. Consult with your legal, accounting and insurance team to consider these issues.

Circumstances will vary widely from business to business. Many spouses and children are active in the business. Other shareholders have no objection to their continuing involvement following the death of the shareholder. If transfers to designated relatives are to be made, this should be expressly stated in the stock purchase agreement. You will need to sit down and discuss this issue candidly and fully with your fellow shareholders.

Disability

What if John becomes disabled and unable to perform his duties on behalf of the corporation? Under Article IV, an option is created in favor of the corporation. Note that in the sample agreement, no option is created in favor of the disabled shareholder or the remaining shareholders. You could provide for such options if that is more consistent with your needs. Once again, disability insurance can provide a source of funds for a buyout.

What is a disability? Section 4.1 defines disability to be the inability to perform the majority of usual duties for a period of 180 days. There are, however, many ways to define disability. Most definitions include a time limitation, but there is no set time period. Your time limit may depend, in part, upon the disability insurance package you have.

Should the time limit be a set number of days during the year without regard to whether or not they are consecutive? For example, assume the agreement defined disability to be the absence from work for 90 consecutive days. John could miss 89 days, crawl into work for one day, and then miss 89 more without being considered disabled. You may wish to combine a short consecutive day limitation such as 60 days with a longer aggregate limitation of 180 days during any calendar or fiscal year.

Retirement

Because many closely held corporations require the active participation of their shareholders, any circumstance which puts a shareholder on the sidelines should be addressed in the stock purchase agreement. The form of withdrawal from active participation is important for purposes of determining what a shareholder will be paid for his or her shares, and whether or not the withdrawing shareholder must sell.

Like disability, each of these events needs to be defined. Without definition, it is impossible to tell whether John has retired or quit. If the benefits to be received are the same, it probably doesn't matter, but if John is to be paid more because he retires, the agreement should make it clear what John must do in order to retire. For example, under Section 4.2 of the sample agreement, a shareholder must be employed by the corporation for at least 10 years before he or she can retire. With less than 10 years of service, the employee can only resign. Here, the corporation is obligated to purchase the shares of a retiring shareholder. Retirement is further defined to be the complete cessation of activities related to the business of the corporation. A shareholder shouldn't be permitted to retire and then resume the same business activities in competition with the corporation.

Care should be taken in defining the term retirement. Many retirees go into teaching or consulting. If these activities are to be permitted, the agreement should so state. Whether or not consulting is permitted may depend in part on whether it is on a paid or volunteer basis such as through the Service Corps of Retired Executives or similar program. Similarly, you may be willing to permit a retiring shareholder to work part-time either for your business or some other. Again, discuss these issues with the other shareholders to see what each of you would like to do in the future.

Resignation or Discharge

A stock purchase agreement may also distinguish between resignation and discharge. Resignation implies a voluntary act undertaken at the initiative of the resigning shareholder. Discharge indicates an action initiated by the corporation. Discharge may be further broken down into discharges with cause and discharges without cause. Check with your business attorney to learn of any state law limitations which might exist. If a distinction is to be made between resignation and discharge, it will be because the amount and timing of payment is different.

Relationship with Employment Agreements

Many corporations will enter into employment agreements with key employees. The reasons for this are many, including treating your key employees more favorably rather than rank and file employees. Added benefits — such as larger salary, increased vacation, performance bonus payments, options to acquire stock, and company cars — are common.

If you have a stock purchase agreement and an employee/shareholder who is a party to an employment agreement, it is important that the stock purchase agreements and employment agreements are consistent with one another. For example, if your stock purchase agreement covers retirement, disability, resignation, and/or discharge, the employment agreement should cover these items as well. Definitions of these terms should be the same in both agreements.

Purchase Price

What happens if an event triggering the stock purchase agreement occurs? If the event requires a mandatory purchase, the purchase price must be determined. If an optional purchase exists, the corporation or remaining shareholders must first indicate their intent to exercise the option. Then, the purchase price must be determined.

One of the best reasons to use a stock purchase agreement is that it creates a market and a buyer for your shares. Without it, you may have a difficult time selling your shares, especially if you own a minority interest of a closely held corporation.

In its simplest form, the purchase price could be the same for any and all types of purchases. This purchase price could be expressed in terms of a certain dollar amount per share or by a formula which must be applied to determine the per share purchase price. Under this approach, no separate definitions for retirement, resignation, or termination would be required. Disability would still require definition.

In the sample stock purchase agreement, lifetime transfers are treated differently than other events requiring purchase. For lifetime transfers, the purchase price to be paid will be the purchase price which the outside party is willing to pay. Although the agreement could provide for a fixed amount upon a lifetime transfer, any fixed amount which was not reasonable in light of the value of the business could be struck down, invalidating all or part of the agreement.

The sample agreement treats involuntary transfers, death transfers, retirement, and disability in the same manner. The purchase price will be the per share value agreed upon by all of the shareholders or the per share value determined according to a formula if no agreement is reached.

Section 6.2 gives the shareholders the ability to set a per share value each year. A unanimous decision on value is required here, although a lesser percentage is acceptable if the shareholders agree to it. The benefit to valuation agreed upon by the shareholders is that the value will more accurately reflect the current value of the business especially in light of intended expenditures in future years. In many instances, this value may be somewhat lower than the value arrived at by the formula.

Formula

If the shareholders can't agree or, as more often happens, fail to agree within a reasonable time, a formula is applied to determine the per share value. (The formula has been omitted from the sample agreement.) Some agreements use a book value formula. Book value is usually easy to compute but fails to take into account the fair market value of assets which may have been depreciated. Book value generally does not include goodwill which the business may have generated including such things as customer lists or name recognition. A formula could be developed to look at fair market value of the assets as well. This would be somewhat more complicated than book value and could require appraisals of assets. Nonetheless, a truer picture of value would be obtained.

Some agreements use a capitalized earnings approach by which net earnings of a business are multiplied by a capitalization rate. Tables showing typical capitalization rates for businesses are available. Check with your accountant or business trade association for this information. This technique is not good for start up operations with no significant earnings history or any business which because of its range of activities makes it difficult to establish a capitalization rate.

Stock purchase agreements must be consistent with the terms of any written employment agreements or personnel policy manual requirements. If employment is terminable only for cause under a policy manual, employment agreement, or state law, it would not make sense to distinguish termination with cause and termination without cause in your stock purchase agreement.

You have many choices and combinations which can set a fair value. Work closely with your accountant to see which formula will provide the most accurate assessment of market value. Remember, you may be the shareholder being bought out, so it is important to achieve fair value.

As noted earlier, some agreements distinguish between retirement, resignation, and termination. The distinction is important primarily in determining what a shareholder is to be paid for his or her shares and when the shareholder will be paid. A retiring shareholder may be entitled to be paid more than one who voluntarily terminates. One reason for the distinction is that retirement is considered a planned event, one that all of the shareholders and the corporation can anticipate. A termination, especially a voluntary one, is an unplanned event which may interrupt some aspect of the corporation's business.

If the agreement further distinguishes between terminations for cause and those without, the difference can be justified on the basis of who initiates the action. If John is terminated from John Doe, Inc. because of a business slow down, John has not directly caused any action leading to his termination without cause. If, on the other hand, John is caught skimming money from corporate bank accounts, John's direct action led to the termination with cause.

How Is the Purchase Price Paid?

Once an event requiring purchase and sale has occurred and the purchase price has been determined, how do you get paid for your shares? Once again, your corporation has a great deal of flexibility in how you can provide for this in your shareholders' agreement. You may choose to keep it simple and get paid immediately in cash. Depending on the size of the purchase price, however, you may wish to defer the purchase price. Some combination of cash and deferred payment may work the best.

In your agreement, you may specify different payment schedules depending on which event triggered the purchase. For example, in the sample agreement, lifetime transfers get paid in the same manner as would have been paid by an outside purchaser. The logic behind this is that is if you are willing to allow an outside buyer to stretch the payment over time, you should extend the same credit to the corporation or the remaining shareholders.

If you use a deferred payment, the stock purchase agreement should provide what the interest rate will be, the term of payment, and that attorneys' fees will be paid by the maker of the note in the event collection efforts are required.

The sample agreement also stipulates that if insurance proceeds are available to cover death or disability, they must be paid over in full. For other situations, the sample requires half payment in cash, with the balance by promissory note that will bear 10 percent interest per year, to be paid in 48 equal monthly installments of principal and interest.

How much you get paid and when requires a realistic assessment of what the corporation or remaining shareholders can pay. You control the timing of payments. Insurance can help the situation a great deal. Without it, however, it makes no sense to obligate the corporation to pay more than it can thereby robbing the business of needed working capital to carry out its day-to-day functions. Keep the purchase price and terms of purchase realistic. Don't shoot yourself and your other shareholders in the foot by setting unreasonable expectations.

Closing and Valuation Date

The closing date answers the question of when you get paid. The valuation date is the date when the formula or other means of valuation is applied. If the agreement uses a fixed rate agreed upon by the shareholders, valuation date is not significant; however, if a formula valuation is required, the concept is important. In the sample agreement, the valuation date is defined to be the last day of the calendar month immediately before the date of death. Using a month end makes the accounting aspects of valuation easier.

As the sample agreement also shows, the closing date is different depending on the event which triggers the sale and purchase. These different dates reflect the corporation's and shareholders' expectations of the amount of time necessary to determine the value and who to pay. For example, if a shareholder dies, it will take time for a trustee to step forward and show his, her, or its authority to act in the deceased shareholder's place or for an administrator to be appointed by the court. Thus, the sample agreement permits 90 days following the appointment of an administrator or the death of the shareholder, whichever should last occur.

Restrictive Endorsement

For restrictions on stock transfers to be effective, the stock certificates must contain language which notifies people of the restriction. Language accomplishing this task is found in Article IX. For example, John, Jane, and Joan are equal shareholders of John Doe, Inc. John, Jane, and Joan have entered into a shareholders' agreement similar to the sample stock purchase agreement. Through clerical error, no restrictive legend was ever typed on the stock certificates. John continues to be hard up for cash. He decides to sell his stock to Bob. Bob is not aware of the restrictions, and finding no restrictions on the certificate, buys the shares from John. Unless Jane and Joan can show that Bob knew or should have known about the restrictions, they will have to get used to running the business with Bob. Joan and Jane are left with a breach of contract claim against John. Had the restrictive language been used, Jane and Joan could have undone the sale to Bob.

How Do You Terminate a Stock Purchase Agreement?

Article X contains several common grounds for termination, including:

- By agreement of all parties to it (this one really doesn't need to be stated);
- When one shareholder acquires all of the stock of the corporation; and
- Upon the dissolution or bankruptcy of the corporation.

Article X also provides that if all of the shareholders should die within 30 days of each other, the agreement will deemed to terminate on the day before the death of the first shareholder to die.

The preamble identifies the corporate parties.

Recitals are simple statements that describe why the agreement is being made and what its goals are.

Article I provides for a right of first refusal in favor of the corporation and the remaining shareholders.

STOCK PURCHASE AGREEMENT

This Agreement is made this February 14, 1992 between John Doe, Jane Doe and Joan Doe (the "Shareholders") and John Doe, Inc., an Oz corporation (the "Corporation").

RECITALS

The Shareholders are the registered owners of all of the issued and outstanding capital stock of the Corporation. The Shareholders and the Corporation believe that it is in their mutual best interests to provide for continuity and harmony in the ownership, management and in the policies of the Corporation.

The Corporation further recognizes that it derives substantial monetary benefit from the continuation of the Shareholders' contribution to the operation of the Corporation and that it would suffer great loss in the event of the death or the termination of interest of any Shareholder.

This Agreement is intended (a) to provide for the purchase by the Corporation of a Shareholder's stock in the event of his or her death, retirement, disability, or termination of employment with the corporation; (b) to provide for the purchase by the Corporation or by the remaining Shareholders of a Shareholder's stock should he or she desire to dispose of any of his or her stock during his or her lifetime; (c) to provide a means of determining the fair market value of the stock of a Shareholder; and (d) in certain instances to provide the funds necessary to carry out such purchase and the procedures whereby such purchases shall be effectuated.

NOW, THEREFORE, in consideration of the recitals and promises contained in this Agreement, and for other good and valuable consideration, the receipt of which is hereby acknowledged, the parties agree as follows:

ARTICLE I. Restricted Lifetime Transfers

Section 1.1. Restricted Transfer. No Shareholder shall during his or her lifetime transfer, encumber, or otherwise dispose of any portion or all of his or her stock interest in the Corporation except as provided herein.

Section 1.2. Option of Corporation. If a Shareholder desires to dispose of any of his or her stock in the Corporation during his or her lifetime, to any person other than the Corporation, he or she shall give the Corporation and all existing Shareholders thirty (30) days written notice (the "Written Notice") of his or her intention to dispose of shares. The Written Notice shall state:

(a) The intention to transfer shares;

(b) The number of shares to be transferred;

(c) The name, business and residence address of the proposed transferee;

(d) The purchase price;

SAMPLE: Stock Purchase Agreement (continued)

(e) The proposed date of transfer; and

(f) All other material terms of the proposed transfer.

The Corporation shall have thirty (30) days after receipt of the Written Notice of such proposed transfer, to exercise an option to purchase all or any portion of the shares proposed to be transferred for the price and upon the terms and conditions provided in the Written Notice.

Section 1.3. Option of Shareholders. If the Corporation does not exercise its option to purchase all or any portion of the shares to be transferred, the remaining Shareholders shall have the option to purchase the shares not purchased by the Corporation within forty-five (45) days of the Corporation's receipt of the Written Notice. Each Shareholder shall have the right to purchase such portion of the remaining stock offered for sale as the number of shares owned by him or her at such date shall bear to the total number of shares owned by all the other Shareholders excluding the selling Shareholder; provided, however, that if any Shareholder does not exercise his or her option to purchase his or her full proportionate share of the stock within forty-five (45) days of the Corporation's receipt of the Written Notice, the balance of the stock may be purchased by the other Shareholders in such proportion as the number of shares owned by each bear to the number of shares owned by all Shareholders then desiring to purchase. If the option to purchase any or all of the stock is not exercised by those remaining Shareholders desiring to purchase within sixty (60) days of the Corporation's receipt of the Written Notice, the Shareholder desiring to sell his or her stock may sell it to the person and in the manner provided in the Written Notice.

Section 1.4. Provisions Applicable to Sections 1.2 and 1.3. The provisions of sections 1.2 and 1.3 are subject to the following:

(a) The Corporation and the remaining Shareholders must in the aggregate exercise their options in such a manner as to purchase all of the shares proposed to be transferred in the Written Notice, and the failure of the Corporation and the remaining Shareholders to purchase in the aggregate all of the shares shall cause the option to purchase to forfeit, and the transferring Shareholder shall be permitted to transfer the shares to the proposed transferee set forth in the Written Notice.

(b) If a Shareholder who proposes to transfer shares dies prior to the closing of the sale and purchase contemplated by sections 1.2 or 1.3, his or her shares shall be subject to sale and purchase under the provisions governing death of a shareholder in Article III, and any action taken under sections 1.1 or 1.2 shall be void.

(c) If any Shareholder shall first deliver a Written Offer (described in Section 1.5) to purchase or sell shares pursuant to Section 1.5, the provisions of sections 1.2 and 1.3 shall be inapplicable and unavailable to all shareholders until the closing of the transfers contemplated by the Section 1.5 Written Offer.

(d) If, during the lifetime of a Shareholder, a transfer is attempted in any manner other than as specifically provided in sections 1.2 or 1.3, or if the transferring Shareholder shall at any time after any transfer reacquire all or any portion of the transferred shares without the express written consent of all other Shareholders, the shares so transferred shall remain subject to this Agreement, as if no transfer had been made.

Section 1.5. Offer to Buy or Sell. If a Shareholder desires to sell all of his or her stock in the Corporation or to acquire by purchase all of the stock of other Shareholders in the Corporation, the Shareholder shall:

Section 1.5 is the Solomon's Choice clause. Any shareholder wishing to use this provision must be prepared to buy or sell shares.

(a) The Shareholder shall set forth in writing and deliver to the Corporation and to all Shareholders a written offer setting forth the purchase price and the terms of purchase upon which he or she is either willing to purchase all of the stock of all other Shareholders or to sell all of his or her own shares of stock in the Corporation (the "Written Offer").

(b) Within thirty (30) days after the receipt of the Written Offer, each other Shareholder shall have the right to purchase from the Shareholder making the Written Offer such portion of the stock offered for sale as the number of shares owned by such other Shareholder on that date shall bear to the total number of shares owned by all other Shareholders excluding the Shareholder submitting the Written Offer. If any Shareholder does not purchase his or her full proportionate share of the stock within thirty (30) days of his or her receipt of the Written Offer, the balance of the stock of the Shareholder making the Written Offer may be purchased by the other remaining Shareholders in such proportion as the number of shares owned by each bears to the number of shares owned by all Shareholders then desiring to purchase. If the election purchase all of the stock is not exercised in full by the remaining Shareholders within forty-five (45) days of the receipt of the Written Offer, the Shareholder making the Written Offer shall have the right and shall be obligated to purchase all of the stock held by all Shareholders including those who initially elected to purchase under the terms of the offer. It is the intent of this provision that the Shareholder making the Written Offer shall either buy or sell all of his or her stock under this provision.

Many sections of this sample document are flexible modules that you can add or delete from your own shareholder agreements as you see fit.

(c) The provisions of Section 1.5 are subject to the following limitations:

(i) The Shareholders must in the aggregate exercise their options in such a manner as to purchase all of the shares proposed to be transferred in the Written Offer or, in the alternative, permit the Shareholder extending the Written Offer to buy and purchase all of the shares held by all other Shareholders in accordance with the terms of the Written Offer.

SAMPLE: Stock Purchase Agreement (continued)

(ii) If a Shareholder who has made a Written Offer dies prior to the closing of the sale and purchase contemplated herein, whether or not the remaining Shareholders have accepted or rejected said offer, the deceased Shareholder's shares shall be the subject of sale and purchase under the provisions governing death in Article III and any action taken under this Section 1.5 shall be void.

(iii) If a Shareholder has first proposed to transfer shares pursuant to Section 1.2 or Section 1.3, the provisions of Section 1.5 shall be inapplicable and shall not be available to any Shareholder until the completion of the options created under sections 1.2 and 1.3.

ARTICLE II. Option Upon Involuntary Transfer

Section 2.1. Involuntary Transfer. If a Shareholder's shares are transferred by operation of law, other than by the death of a Shareholder to a third person other than the Corporation (such as to a bankruptcy trustee, a purchaser at any creditors; or court sale or the guardian or conservator of an incompetent Shareholder), the Corporation within thirty (30) days after receipt of actual notice of the transfer or the remaining Shareholders within ninety (90) days following the Corporation's actual notice, may exercise an option to purchase all, but not less than all, of the shares so transferred from such third party in the same manner as if set forth in sections 1.3 and 1.4. If a purchase price is paid upon the transfer, the price paid shall be deemed to be the purchase price to be paid by the Corporation or remaining shareholders. If no purchase price is paid, the purchase price shall be determined in accordance with Article VI and shall be paid in the manner described in Article VII.

An involuntary transfer can occur in a number of ways: bankruptcy, court-ordered sale, or the appointment of a guardian or conservator.

ARTICLE III. Death of a Shareholder

Section 3.1. Redemption by Corporation. Upon the death of any Shareholder, the Corporation shall purchase, and the estate of the decedent Shareholder shall sell, all of the decedent's shares in the Corporation now owned or hereafter acquired and which were owned by the decedent at the date of his or her death for the purchase price determined in the manner provided in Article VI and upon the terms provided in Article VII.

Section 3.2. Purchase by Surviving Shareholders. To the extent that the Corporation is prevented by law from purchasing all or any portion of the shares owned by the decedent Shareholder or his or her estate, the surviving Shareholders shall purchase all or any portion of such shares from the decedent or the decedent's estate and the latter shall sell them for the purchase price determined in the manner provided in Article VI and upon the terms provided in Article VII.

A death buy-out, funded by insurance, can preserve control of the corporation for the surviving shareholders and also provide a fund of money to the deceased shareholder's relatives for estate taxes.

ARTICLE IV. Disability; Retirement

Section 4.1. Disability; Redemption by Corporation. If any Shareholder

Care should be taken in defining disability and retirement.

shall suffer a permanent disability, that is, the Shareholder's inability, through physical or mental illness to perform the majority of his or her usual duties for a period of 180 days or more, the Corporation may exercise an option to purchase all but not less than all of the shares owned by the disabled Shareholder. Upon exercise of the option, the disabled Shareholder shall be required to sell all of his or her shares to the Corporation. Written notice of exercise of the option shall be provided, if at all, within thirty (30) days following the conclusion of the 180-day period. The purchase price shall be determined in the manner provided in Article IV and upon the terms provided in Article VII.

Section 4.2. Retirement; Redemption by the Corporation. If any shareholder shall retire from employment with the Corporation following the completion of 10 full years of employment with the Corporation, the Corporation shall purchase and the retiring Shareholder shall sell all of the retiring Shareholder's shares in the Corporation now owned or hereafter acquired and which are owned by the Shareholder as of the date of retirement. The purchase price shall be determined in the manner provided in Article VI and upon the terms provided in Article VII. For purposes of this Agreement, the term "retirement" shall mean the complete cessation of employment with the Corporation at any time following the completion of 10 full years of employment by the Shareholder with the Corporation. Any cessation of employment prior to the expiration of 10 years shall be deemed a termination or resignation within the meaning of Article V.

If you choose to include a provision for retirement in your agreement, define what length of service or age qualifies.

ARTICLE V. Termination

Section 5.1. Voluntary Termination; Resignation. In the event any Shareholder voluntarily terminates his or her employment with the Corporation for any reason whatsoever, other than as provided in Section 4.2, the terminating Shareholder shall sell to the Corporation and the Corporation shall purchase from the Shareholder all of the terminating Shareholder's shares in the Corporation now owned or hereafter acquired and which are owned by the terminating Shareholder as of the date of termination for the purchase price determined in the manner provide in Article VI and upon the terms provided in Article VII.

This agreement distinguishes between resignation (a voluntary act), and discharge (an involuntary act).

Section 5.2. Involuntary Termination; Discharge. In the event any Shareholder is discharged from his or her employment with the Corporation for any reason specified in an employment agreement between the Shareholder and the Corporation, the discharged Shareholder shall sell to the Corporation and the Corporation shall purchase from the Shareholder all of the discharged Shareholder's shares in the Corporation now owned or hereafter acquired and which are owned by the discharged Shareholder as of the date of discharge for the purchase price determined in the manner provided in Article VI and upon the terms provided in Article VII.

SAMPLE: Stock Purchase Agreement (continued)

ARTICLE VI. Purchase Price of Stock

Section 6.1. Article I Transfers. For any purchase consummated under the provisions of Article I, the purchase price for the shares and the manner of purchase shall be governed by the provisions of Article I.

Section 6.2. Article II, Article III, and Article IV Transfers. If the purchase is consummated under the provisions of Article II, III, or IV, the purchase price for the shares shall be determined as follows:

(a) Annual Valuation. For the purpose of determining the price to be paid for shares on or before _____, 199__, the value of each share is $_____. The parties agree that the price represents the fair market value of each share of stock including the goodwill of the Corporation. The Shareholders shall redetermine the value of the Corporation on or before _____, 199__, and thereafter within sixty (60) days following the end of each fiscal year. The value agreed upon shall be endorsed on a Schedule attached to this Agreement and made a part of this Agreement in the following form:

> The undersigned mutually agree on this _____, 199__
>
> that for the purpose of this Stock Purchase Agreement, each share
>
> of stock of the Corporation had a value of $_____.

This endorsement shall be signed by each Shareholder and the Corporation. If the Shareholders and the Corporation fail to make a redetermination of value on or before _____, 199__, and thereafter within 12 months immediately preceding the event requiring the sale of the Shareholder's interest, the provisions of subsection (b) shall govern the valuation.

(b) Alternate valuation. If no valuation is made in the manner described above within 12 months prior to an event giving rise to valuation, the per share value of a Shareholder's interest shall be determined by the certified public accountant for the Corporation as of the last day of the calendar month preceding the month of the event giving rise to the sale, and arrived at by the accountant on an accrual basis (whether or not the Corporation is a cash basis taxpayer) in the manner listed below:

> *The description of how the value of the business will be set has been purposely omitted, since there are so many formulas which could be used. Confer with your business lawyer and accountant to determine what will work best for your corporation.*

Section 6.3. Article V Transfers. If the purchase is consummated under Article V, the purchase price of shares shall be determined as follows:

(a) Voluntary termination. If the purchase is consummated under Section 5.1, the purchase price shall be ____ percent of the purchase price determined under Section 6.2.

Section 6.2(a) obligates the shareholders to agree each year as to the value of the corporation's stock. Failing this, the formula Section 6.2(b) would be utilized to fix a value. Work with your accountant to develop a formula which will produce a fair value for the corporation.

SAMPLE: Stock Purchase Agreement (continued)

(b) Discharge. If the purchase is consummated under Section 5.2, the purchase price shall be the purchase price determined under Section 6.2.

ARTICLE VII. Method of Payment

Section 7.1. Purchase or Sale under sections 1.2, 1.3, or 1.5. In the event of a purchase or sale under these provisions, payment of the purchase price shall be in the manner described in the Written Notice or Written Offer, whichever may apply.

Section 7.2. Other Transfers. In the event of a purchase under Articles II, III, IV or V, the purchase price shall be paid in cash, except that at the option of the purchasing party or parties, 50% of the purchase price may be deferred and 50% paid at the closing. The deferred portion of the purchase price shall be evidenced by the promissory note of each purchasing party made payable to the order of the selling party. The promissory note shall bear interest at the rate of 10% per annum from and after the valuation date full amortized in equal monthly payments including interest over a period not to exceed forty-eight (48) months. The first installment shall be due and payable on the first day of the first month following the closing of the purchase. The note can be prepaid at any time without penalty. The note shall provide that in the event that any payment is not made on the due date, the entire balance of the note shall become immediately due and payable at the option of the holder. If the maker of the note is to be the Corporation, the note shall be unsecured, but it shall be personally guaranteed by all surviving Shareholders. The shares of the guarantors shall be pledged as security for the guarantee. If the maker of the note is a Shareholder(s), the note shall be secured by the Shareholder's pledge to the holder of the note of all of the shares purchased. The promissory note shall provide for payment by the maker of the holder's attorneys fees and costs, if permitted under applicable law, in the event that the holder is required to initiate any legal action or proceeding to enforce the obligations of the maker under the promissory note.

If the Corporation or any other purchasing party is the owner and beneficiary of any insurance on the life of a deceased Shareholder from whose estate the Corporation or or other purchasing party is purchasing shares, an amount equal to the death benefits payable to the beneficiary under the policy or policies shall be paid in cash to the estate of the deceased Shareholder on account of the purchase price of the shares, and only the balance, if any, may be deferred. If the insurance proceeds exceed the purchase price of the shares purchased, the excess shall remain the property of the Corporation or other purchasing party. If the Corporation is prohibited by law from using all or any portion of the proceeds of the insurance policy or policies which it may own on the deceased Shareholder's life, this provision shall apply only to insurance proceeds which the Corporation may, by law, use for such purpose.

The method of payment must be fair to the corporation and the paying shareholders. It must also be fair to the receiving shareholder. The amount should not be so large as to create cash flow problems for the corporation. In Section 7.2, a deferred payment plan is described.

SAMPLE: Stock Purchase Agreement (continued)

ARTICLE VIII. Closing Date and Valuation Date

Section 8.1. Valuation Date. The term "Valuation Date" shall mean the last day of the calendar month preceding the month of any event requiring or giving rise to the sale. In the case of the death of a Shareholder, it shall mean the last day of the calendar month immediately preceding the death of the Shareholder.

Section 8.2. Place of Closing. The closing of the sale and purchase of shares shall take place at the general offices of the Corporation unless otherwise agreed by the parties.

Section 8.3. Closing Date. The term "Closing Date" shall mean the following:

(a) If the sale or transfer is effectuated under sections 1.2, 1.3, or 1.5, the closing date shall be the seventy-fifth (75th) day following the Corporation's receipt of the Written Notice or Written Offer; or

(b) If the sale or transfer is effectuated under Section 2.1, the closing date shall be the ninetieth (90th) day following the Corporation's receipt of actual notice of the involuntary transfer; or

(c) If the sale or transfer shall occur under the provisions of Article III, the closing date shall be the thirtieth (30th) day following the appointment of a personal representative of the deceased Shareholder's estate or within ninety (90) days after the date of death of a decedent Shareholder, whichever shall last occur.

(d) If the sale or transfer shall occur under the provisions of Article IV, the closing date shall be within 30 days following the termination of the 180 day disability period for sales or transfers subject to Section 4.1 and within thirty (30) days following the effective date of retirement for sales or transfers subject to Section 4.2.

(e) If the sale or transfer occur under the provisions of Article V, the closing date shall occur immediately upon the close of business on the effective day of termination or discharge.

Section 8.4. Delivery of Documents. Upon the closing of the sale and purchase, the selling and purchasing parties shall execute and deliver to each other the various instruments and documents which shall be required to carry out their agreements hereunder, including the payment of cash, if any, the execution and delivery of promissory notes, and the assignment and delivery of stock certificates, where applicable. Upon the closing, the selling Shareholder shall deliver to the Corporation his or her resignation and that of any nominees as officers, directors, and employees of the Corporation and any of its subsidiaries, and in the event such resignation(s) is not so delivered, each such Shareholder hereby submits his or her resignation from such position(s), such resignation(s) to be effective as of the closing date on which such Shareholder sells his or her stock in accordance with this Agreement.

Date and time periods which appear in this sample are for example only. You can usually shorten or lengthen time frames to fit your own needs.

SAMPLE: Stock Purchase Agreement (continued)

This restrictive legend should appear on the stock certificates to effectively restrict transfer.

Section 8.5. Order of Closing. The order of closing shall be such that the sale and purchase of shares which any surviving or remaining Shareholder is to purchase under this Agreement shall take place immediately prior to the sale and purchase of shares, if any, which the Corporation purchases hereunder.

ARTICLE IX. Endorsement on Stock Certificates

Section 9.1. Form of Endorsement. The shares of the Corporation shall bear the following endorsement:

> Ownership, issuance, and transfer of the shares evidenced by this certificate are specifically restricted by and subject to the provisions of an Agreement executed between the Shareholder whose name appears on the face hereof, the Corporation and the remaining Shareholder(s) of the Corporation. The Agreement provides, in part, for the purchase and sale of the shares of stock evidenced by this certificate and grants certain rights of first refusal and options with regard to the purchase or sale of these shares. By accepting the shares of stock evidenced by this certificate, the holder agrees to be bound by said Agreement, a copy of which is on file in the office of the Corporation at its principal place of business.

ARTICLE X. Termination of Agreement

Section 10.1. Events Causing Termination. This Agreement shall terminate:

(a) Upon the written agreement of the Corporation and all of the Shareholders who then own shares subject to this Agreement; or

(b) Upon the dissolution or bankruptcy of the Corporation; or

(c) Upon acquisition by a single Shareholder of ownership of all the shares of the Corporation which are then subject to this Agreement.

Section 10.2. Disposition of Insurance. In the event of the termination of this Agreement by reason of any of the events set forth in Section 10.1, each Shareholder shall have the right within thirty (30) days after such termination to purchase from the Corporation or from any other Shareholder (including a personal representative of a deceased Shareholder's estate) who owns an insurance policy, or policies on his or her life, such policy or policies, for cash in the amount of the cash surrender value plus the unearned premiums thereon, both amounts to be determined as of the date of termination of the Agreement.

Section 10.3. Death of all Shareholders. This Agreement shall also terminate upon the death of all of the Shareholders of the Corporation within a period of thirty (30) days of one another. If this occurs, the termination shall be effective as of the day before the day of the death of the first Shareholder to die. All shares and any insurance policies owned by the Corporation or any deceased Shareholder's estate shall be owned free of the terms of this Agreement.

SAMPLE: Stock Purchase Agreement (continued)

ARTICLE XI. Miscellaneous General Provisions

Section 11.1. Delivery of Documents. The Corporation and the Shareholders and the executor, administrator, or personal representative of a deceased Shareholder, shall execute and deliver any and all documents or legal instruments necessary or desirable to carry out the provisions of this Agreement.

Section 11.2. Binding on Certain Nonparties. This Agreement shall be binding upon the Shareholders, their heirs, legal representatives, successors or assigns, and upon the Corporation, its successors and assigns.

Section 11.3. Applicable Law. This Agreement shall be governed by the laws of the state of Oz notwithstanding the fact that one or more of the parties to this Agreement is now or may become a resident or citizen of a different state.

Section 11.4. Amendment. This Agreement may be amended at any time, but only by the written agreement of the Corporation and all of its then Shareholders.

Section 11.5. Testamentary Provisions. The Shareholders agree upon request of any party to this Agreement to insert a provision in their wills, or to execute a codicil thereto, directing and authorizing their executors to fulfill and comply with the provisions hereof and to sell and transfer their shares accordingly.

Section 11.6. Notice. Any notice required or permitted hereunder shall be deemed served if personally delivered or mailed by registered or certified mail postage prepaid, and properly addressed to the respective party to whom such notice relates.

Section 11.7. Headings. The headings provided for each Article and Section hereof are for informational purposes only, and shall be disregarded in construing or interpreting this Agreement.

IN WITNESS WHEREOF, the parties have caused this Agreement to be executed as of the day and year set forth above.

John Doe, Inc. by

_____
Authorized Officer

Shareholders:

_____
John Doe

_____
Joan Doe

_____
Jane Doe

As you review these sample agreements, make notes of questions you'll want to discuss with your lawyer regarding your own situation.

Voting Trust Agreements

A second form of shareholder agreement is a voting trust. In this case, shareholders transfer their shares of stock to a trustee. The trustee, who can be one or more individuals, banks, or other entities, holds legal title to the shares and appears as the shareholder of record on the corporation's books. The shareholders retain beneficial ownership and are the beneficiaries under the trust agreement.

Like stock purchase agreements, voting trusts can exist for one or multiple purposes. They are more often used to preserve control of the corporation by requiring the trustees to vote for designated board members and to restrict lifetime share transfers. The trustee can only do what the voting trust agreement says he or she can do. Unlike stock purchase agreements, voting trusts are not valid for more than 10 years, unless they are renewed in writing. Any renewed voting trust is binding only on shareholders who voluntarily agree to renew.

The discussion which follows concerns voting trusts. Much of the discussion concerning stock purchase agreements is equally relevant to voting trusts and agreements and will not be repeated. Each form of shareholder agreement provides opportunities for flexibility and tailoring which you should discuss with your business lawyer and accountant. Remember, your shareholder agreement should do those things you want it to do.

A sample voting trust is included on the following pages. Remember to record your thoughts and questions as you review it. This step will assist you in preparing your agreement.

Preamble and Recitals

Similar to stock purchase agreements, a voting trust must identify the people who are parties to it and should recite the reasons for its existence. The corporation would not be a party to a voting trust agreement involving its own shares.

Trustee Powers

One of the more significant portions of a voting trust defines what a trustee can do. He or she is limited to the powers expressed in the trust. The grant of powers can be broad or specific. Common powers include:

- The right to vote shares;
- The ability to sign consent resolutions;
- The power to appoint proxies to vote shares;
- The power to receive dividends and distributions from the corporation and allocate or pay out the dividends and distributions to trust beneficiaries;
- The power to issue trust certificates to beneficiaries; and
- The power to sell or dispose of shares.

Article IV of the sample voting trust describes the authority and powers of the trustees.

Voting Trust Certificates

When a shareholder transfers shares to a voting trust, he or she should receive a voting trust certificate. This certificate should reflect an interest in the trust consistent with the number of shares transferred to the trust by the shareholder. For example, if you transfer 100 shares of voting common stock to the trust, you should receive a voting trust certificate evidencing 100 trust units. Article II of the sample voting trust agreement describes trust certificates and their manner of transfer, and a sample voting trust certificate is located at the end of this chapter.

Like stock certificates, trust certificates are not mandatory, but they should be used to evidence your ownership interest in the trust. The trust certificates should also contain restrictive language stating the existence of the voting trust and limiting the transfer of the voting trust certificates. Without restrictive language, voting trust certificates may be sold or transferred freely.

Dividends and Distributions

If a trustee receives a cash dividend or distribution from the corporation, the voting trust agreement should provide that amounts received will be paid out to the beneficiaries in accordance with their interest. If you hold 100 trust units which you received in exchange for the transfer of 100 shares, you should receive dividends or distributions attributable to those 100 shares.

Stock dividends may be treated differently, and the language of the voting trust agreement should specify the appropriate treatment. The trustee could convert the stock dividend to additional voting trust certificates and distribute those to the beneficiaries or the trustee could simply keep the shares and make a bookkeeping entry to reflect the percentage ownership of the stock dividend shares. These shares would then be distributed to the beneficiary upon the termination of the trust or withdrawal from the trust by a beneficiary.

What if Your Trustee Resigns or Is Removed?

The voting trust should provide a method for removing a trustee with or without cause and a method to replace a trustee. Ordinarily, if there is more than one trustee, the remaining trustees can select someone to fill the vacancy. If there are no remaining trustees, the beneficiaries could select a successor trustee.

A related issue to consider is what happens if your trustee develops a conflict of interest? For example, what if your trustee becomes a competitor or supplier? You may or may not wish to remove the trustee in such a situation.

How Does the Trust Terminate?

By law, a voting trust can't last longer than 10 years. Any renewal or extension beyond that term must be in writing. Only those shareholders agreeing voluntarily to participate in the renewal are bound by the trust. Like stock purchase agreements, voting trusts should terminate whenever all of the shares of stock are acquired by one person or whenever all of the voting trust beneficiaries should agree to a termination.

You may also want your voting trust to terminate upon a sale, merger, or dissolution of the corporation. You have flexibility in this area. The sample voting trust continues upon sale or merger but not dissolution. The choice is yours. Article V of the sample voting trust describes term and termination of the trust.

Miscellaneous Trustee Duties

A trustee must prepare a list showing the name and address of each beneficial owner of the trust, together with a designation of the number and class of shares transferred to the trust by the shareholder. This list is provided to the corporation, and it must be kept current by the trustee with revisions sent to the corporation. A copy of the voting trust and any amendments must be sent to the corporation as well.

A trustee must act in good faith, exercise due care, and have a duty of loyalty to the trust and its beneficiaries. These duties are similar to those duties imposed on directors and described in Chapter 4. Because the trustee is the legal owner of the shares, the trustee and not the beneficiaries will receive notice of shareholder meetings, proxy solicitations, and similar correspondence from the corporation. You may wish to require the trustee to provide copies of corporation notices to each of the beneficial owners.

Voting Agreements or Pooling Agreements

The final type of shareholder agreement to be considered in this chapter is known as a voting agreement or pooling agreement. A voting agreement can be used alone or in conjunction with a voting trust. A voting agreement is simply an agreement, preferably in writing, among two or more shareholders to vote their shares in a certain manner.

Voting agreements can be used alone or in conjunction with a voting trust. They basically state that two or more shareholders agree to vote in a certain manner.

Unlike a voting trust, the shareholders retain ownership of their shares. No transfer to a trust is required, and there is no trustee. The corporation is not a party to the agreement and need not receive a copy of it. For these reasons, the voting or pooling agreement is easier to prepare and less cumbersome than a voting trust. The voting agreement is used most often to pool voting strength in the election of directors; however, it can extend to any matter requiring the approval of shareholders. For example, shareholders may be asked to approve a plan of merger or dissolution or the sale of substantially all of the assets of the business.

In a voting or pooling agreement, each shareholder votes his or her own shares. If a shareholder refuses to vote in accordance with the voting agreement, the other shareholders recourse is to sue the uncooperative shareholder to specifically enforce the voting agreement or for damages.

Voting agreements can dictate how shares will be voted. Alternatively, the agreement could provide that each shareholder will vote his or her shares according to the majority wishes of the shareholders who are parties to the voting agreement. For example, John, Jane, and Joan each own 100 shares of John Doe, Inc. Their voting agreement obligates each of them to vote all of their shares in favor of John, Jane, and Joan in the election of directors. Or, their voting agreement could provide that each party will vote his or her shares in accordance with the majority wishes.

Using this latter approach, John Doe, Inc. proposes to dissolve. John thinks this is a terrible idea. Jane and Joan support it. Prior to the official shareholder vote, John, Jane, and Joan conduct a prevote. There it is determined that 200 shares favor dissolution and 100 shares oppose it. Because of their shareholders' agreement, John must vote his shares in favor of the dissolution even though he opposes it. If John refuses, Jane and Joan can sue John to specifically enforce the agreement or for damages. Damages in this situation may be difficult to prove, thereby limiting the effectiveness of the voting agreement.

Like other shareholder agreements, voting agreements should contain a preamble identifying parties to the agreement and recitals setting forth the agreement's purpose. The agreement should specify which matters are subject to the agreement, and which are not, and how the agreement can be terminated. These issues have been addressed previously.

Close Corporations and Shareholder Agreements

As noted earlier, close corporations change the rules of the game somewhat. For example, if a close corporation election is made, the close corporation can eliminate the board of directors if its articles so provide. Close corporations also permit shareholders by agreement (similar to a voting agreement) to limit the discretion of the board of directors and otherwise eliminate or modify traditional board functions. Chapter 14 has more information on close corporations.

As a result, shareholder agreements for the sole purpose of electing and retaining seats on the board of directors aren't necessary for some close corporations; however, shareholder agreements for the purpose of limiting transfers of stock, controlling the vote of shareholders, or providing a market for shares continue to exist.

Final Thoughts on Shareholder Agreements

If there is more than one shareholder in your corporation, a shareholder agreement is a virtual necessity. What type of agreement? That's up to you. What provisions should it contain? Once again, that's up to you. Remember, it's not what an agreement is called that's important; it's what the agreement does. Be careful and flexible. Create a shareholder agreement that meets your needs.

Historically, stock purchase or buy-sell agreements have focused on controlling who your fellow shareholders are and providing a market for your shares where a market might not otherwise exist. Control over who your shareholders are is important. Jane Doe, a shareholder, might be a real giant in your industry, but her husband Dinky could be a true horse's behind. You don't want Dinky to become a shareholder in the corporation — at least not one with enough voting strength to affect management and policy making.

Stock purchase or buy-sell agreements come in handy if you die, become disabled, retire, resign, or are discharged from the corporation. If the shares aren't publicly traded, who will buy your shares and at what price? These agreements provide a market for your shares and, presumably, a fair price.

Voting trust agreements or voting or pooling agreements are less commonly used, but they can be used if appropriate. Both of these types of agreement focus on controlling a shareholder's vote, principally the vote for the election of directors. Minority interests may wish to pool their voting strength to elect a representative to the board of directors. Or, a majority owner may wish to reward key employee/shareholders by agreeing to vote with them. In effect, the majority owner is giving the minority interest power beyond the proportional amount of their shareholdings. If the employees are important enough to the business, the majority shareholder may wish to do this to keep them on board.

The sample documents you have seen in this chapter are examples only. Be creative. Use these samples to give you ideas about what your shareholders' agreement should contain. Decide what you want your agreement to do and what areas you would like it to cover. Then, consult with your business lawyer or accountant to bring your ideas to life.

SAMPLE : Voting Trust Agreement

VOTING TRUST AGREEMENT

This Agreement is made this February 14, 1992 between Jane Doe, John Doe, and Joan Doe (the "Shareholders"), Alan Able, Betty Baker and Carmen Coho (the "Trustees") and John Doe, Inc., an Oz corporation (the "Corporation").

RECITALS:

The Shareholders are the registered owners of all of the issued and outstanding capital stock of the Corporation. The Shareholders and the Corporation believe that it is in their mutual best interests to provide for continuity and harmony in the ownership, management, and in the policies of the Corporation.

This Agreement is intended to promote this interest by joining together in this voting trust agreement to promote the election of the Shareholders as directors of the Corporation.

NOW, THEREFORE, in consideration of the recitals and promises contained in this Agreement, and for other good and valuable consideration, the receipt of which is hereby acknowledged, the parties agree as follows:

ARTICLE I. Transfer of Shares to Trustees

Section 1.1. Delivery of Stock. Shareholders shall deliver to the Trustees stock certificates evidencing the ownership by Shareholders of all of their shares in the Corporation. The certificates shall be endorsed in favor of the Trustees to effect the transfer of shares to the Trustees, subject, at all times, to the provisions of this Agreement.

Section 1.2. Registration. Upon surrender of the shares by the Trustee to the Corporation, the Corporation shall issue a new stock certificate representing all of the shares so surrendered to Alan Able, Betty Baker, and Carmen Coho, as Trustees under Voting Trust Agreement dated February 14, 1992. Upon the issuance of this certificate, the Trustees shall hold the stock certificate subject to the terms of this Agreement.

ARTICLE II. Voting Trust Certificates

Section 2.1. Form. The Trustees shall issue and deliver to the Shareholders a voting trust certificate for the shares transferred to the Trustees. The certificate shall be in the form attached hereto as Exhibit A.

Section 2.2. Transfer of Certificates. Voting trust certificates are transferable only on the books of the Trustees by the registered holder of the certificate or by his or her legal representative. To surrender a certificate, the certificate must be presented to the Trustees, properly endorsed, or accompanied by such other instruments of transfer as the Trustees may request. The Trustees shall not be required to recognize any transfer of certificates not made in compliance with this section.

The trustee holds the shares, has voting rights, and receives any dividends payable on the shares.

SAMPLE: Voting Trust Agreement (continued)

Section 2.3. Lost or Misplaced Certificates. If a voting trust certificate is lost, stolen, misplaced or otherwise destroyed or unaccounted for, the Trustees, in their sole discretion, may issue a new voting trust certificate. As a condition to the issuance of a new certificate, the Trustees shall require an affidavit by the holder of the lost or misplaced certificate setting forth the fact that such certificate has been lost or misplaced, and that despite reasonable effort by the holder, the certificate has not been found. The Trustees may require that the holder agree to indemnify the Trustees for any loss, cost or damage sustained by the Trustees as a result of the lost or misplaced certificate.

ARTICLE III. Trustees

In Section 3.1, each shareholder designates a trustee. Care should be taken in selecting a trustee.

Section 3.1. Number; Selection; Removal. During the term of this Agreement, there shall be three trustees. Each shareholder shall have the right to designate one Trustee. Each shareholder shall have the right to remove, with or without cause, any Trustee selected by him or her. In the event a shareholder dies or becomes incapacitated, the power to select and remove that shareholder's trustee shall vest in the personal representative, administrator or conservator appointed or selected to act in the place of the shareholder, whichever may be applicable. If a shareholder refuses to appoint a trustee within sixty (60) days following the resignation or removal of the trustee, the remaining shareholders, acting together, shall have the right to designate a trustee.

Section 3.2. Resignation, Death of the Trustee. A Trustee may resign at any time by giving written notice of resignation to the other Trustees, the Shareholders, and the Corporation. Any such resignation shall be effective thirty (30) days thereafter, unless a successor trustee is appointed prior to the expiration of thirty (30) days. If a Trustee dies, the Shareholder appointing the Trustee shall act promptly to appoint a successor trustee within sixty (60) days following the date of death of the trustee.

Section 3.3. Compensation and Reimbursement of Expenses. The Trustees shall serve without compensation. The Corporation shall reimburse the Trustees for all reasonable expenses incurred by Trustees in conjunction with the performance of Trustees' duties under this Agreement.

ARTICLE IV. Trustees Authority and Powers

Section 4.1. Meetings. Any Trustee may call a meeting of Trustees at any time upon 10 days prior written notice. The written notice shall specify the time, date and place of the meeting and a general statement of the meeting's purpose. Notice may be waived by any Trustee by signed writing or by attendance at the meeting.

Section 4.2. Voting Rights. The affirmative vote of a majority of Trustees shall be sufficient to authorize any action on the part of the Trustees. The

SAMPLE: Voting Trust Agreement (continued)

Trustees shall have the right to exercise in person or by proxy all of the voting rights of the Shareholders with respect to shares subject to this Agreement regardless of the subject matter being voted upon.

Section 4.3. Fiduciary. Trustees are fiduciaries, and as such, must exercise their best good faith judgment in exercising voting rights hereunder. Trustees must act in a manner which Trustees reasonably believe to be in the best interests of the Corporation. Trustees shall not be liable to the holders of certificates for honest mistakes of judgment, or for action or inaction taken in good faith and reasonably believed to be in the best interests of the Corporation, provided, however, that such mistake, action or inaction does not constitute recklessness, fraud, or willful or wanton misconduct.

Trustees must exercise ordinary care, act in good faith, and avoid conflicts of interest.

ARTICLE V. Term and Termination

Section 5.1. Term. Unless terminated sooner in accordance with this Agreement, this Agreement will continue in effect until February 1, 2002.

Section 5.2. Termination. This Agreement shall terminate upon:

(i) The mutual agreement of all parties to this Agreement;

(ii) The death of all Shareholders within a sixty- (60) day period; or

(iii) The Corporation makes an assignment for the benefit of creditors, files a voluntary petition in bankruptcy, is adjudicated a bankrupt or insolvent, files a petition seeking reorganization, liquidation, dissolution or similar relief, or seeks or consents to the appointment of a receiver or trustee with respect to all or substantially all of the Corporation's assets.

A voting trust can't last longer than 10 years, although it may be renewed.

Section 5.3. Effect of Termination. Upon termination of this Agreement, the Trustees shall provide written notice of termination to the Shareholders and the Corporation. The Trustees shall surrender the shares of stock held by it to the Corporation with instructions to issue new stock certificates in the names of the Shareholders for the amounts of stock then held on behalf of each Shareholder. The Shareholders shall surrender to the Trustees voting trust certificates held by them. In exchange, the Corporation or the Trustees shall issue and deliver new stock certificates to the Shareholders.

ARTICLE VI. Dividends and Distributions

Section 6.1. Money and Other Property. Upon a distribution by the Corporation of money or other property (except voting stock of the Corporation described in Section 6.2 below), the Trustees shall distribute the money or other property to the Shareholders in proportion to the interests represented by their voting trust certificates. As an alternative, the Trustees may notify the Corporation in advance of any such distribution of the interests of each Shareholder and request that the Corporation distribute such money or other property directly to the Shareholders.

In Section 6.1, the trustee must pass dividends and distributions along to the shareholders.

SAMPLE: Voting Trust Agreement (continued)

Section 6.2. Voting Stock; Dividends. In the event that the Corporation distributes shares of the Corporation's voting common stock, the Trustees shall receive and hold all stock so distributed and cause the issuance and delivery of additional voting trust certificates to the Shareholders to evidence the Shareholders pro rata portion of any stock dividend or distribution.

ARTICLE VII. Merger, Consolidation, Dissolution

Section 7.1. Merger or Consolidation. In the event the Corporation is merged or consolidated, or all or substantially all of the Corporation's assets transferred to another corporation, this Agreement shall continue in full force and effect subject to the following:

(i) The term "Corporation" shall refer to the surviving corporation to the merger or the corporation to which all or substantially all of the corporate assets have been transferred;

(ii) Any shares received by the Trustees in exchange for the surrender by the Trustees of shares of the Corporation shall be retained by the Trustees, and new voting certificates shall be issued and delivered to the Shareholders; and

(iii) The Shareholders shall deliver to the Trustees voting certificates held by them representing shares in the Corporation.

Section 7.2. Dissolution. In the event the Corporation is dissolved, the Trustees, upon receipt by them, shall distribute to the holders of voting trust certificates all cash, stock, and other property distributed to the Trustees by the Corporation on a pro rata basis. The Trustees may direct the Corporation to make such a distribution directly to the Shareholders.

ARTICLE VIII. Miscellaneous Provisions

Section 8.1. Compliance with Laws. This Agreement shall be governed by the laws of the state of Oz notwithstanding the fact that one or more parties hereto may be residents of different states. The parties agree to comply with all applicable laws and regulations and to perform all acts which may be required to so comply.

Section 8.2. Amendment. This Agreement may be amended only by writing signed by all parties to the Agreement.

Section 8.3. Notice. Any notice required or permitted hereunder shall be deemed served if personally delivered or mailed by registered or certified mail, postage prepaid, and properly addressed to the respective party to whom such notice relates.

Section 8.4. Headings. The headings provided for each Article and Section are for informational purposes only, and shall be disregarded in construing or interpreting this Agreement.

SAMPLE: Voting Trust Agreement (continued)

IN WITNESS WHEREOF, the parties have caused this Agreement to be executed as of the day and year set forth above.

_____

John Doe

_____

Jane Doe

_____

Joan Doe

The Shareholders

_____

Alan Able

_____

Betty Baker

_____

Carmen Coho

The Trustees

John Doe, Inc., an Oz corporation

by _____

President

SAMPLE: Voting Trust Certificate

John Doe, Inc.

Voting Trust Certificate

No. of Shares Represented: 100

Date of Issuance: February 14, 1992

John Doe is entitled to all benefits arising from the deposit of 100 shares of common stock, no par value, of John Doe, Inc., an Oz corporation with the undersigned Trustees pursuant to a Voting Trust Agreement dated February 14, 1992, subject to the terms and conditions of said Agreement.

_____

Alan Able

_____

Betty Baker

_____

Carmen Coho

Trustees

(The information below would appear on the reverse side of this certificate.)

For value received, _____
hereby sells, transfers, assigns and conveys unto _____
this Voting Trust Certificate, and appoints _____
as his or her lawful attorney in fact to transfer this Voting Trust Certificate on the books of the Trustees with full power of substitution.

_____

Signature

_____

Date

A voting trust certificate evidences the ownership by its holder of an interest in a voting trust. Don't buy a voting trust interest without first examining the conditions and terms of the underlying voting trust.

The reverse side of a voting trust certificate will look much like the back of a stock certificate. You should also consider adding language restricting the transferability of the certificate.

Chapter 7

More Paperwork

With articles of incorporation, bylaws, shareholder lists, proxies, shareholder agreements, stock certificates, meeting notices, minutes, and waivers, there's a lot of paperwork involved with your corporation. As this chapter will show, there's even more.

Keep in mind, however, that good recordkeeping and adherence to certain common sense formalities are important parts of every successful business. This is true regardless of whether or not your business is incorporated, a sole proprietorship, or a partnership. Payroll records, inventory lists, billing records are examples of the types of records maintained by most businesses.

How important are good business records? They are of vital importance. As you have seen, certain records are available for inspection by shareholders, while others are available for inspection by auditors, including those working for the Internal Revenue Service, state unemployment divisions, and countless other government agencies. Your records are also subject to inspection by parties to a lawsuit involving your corporation. If an auditor is impressed with the thoroughness and accuracy of your records, the audit will be a much less painful experience.

Good recordkeeping will also facilitate a sale of your business. Prospective purchasers will want to view your records to determine whether or not to purchase it and to determine the purchase price to be offered. Once again, good records are an indication that the business has been well-run. To the prospective purchaser, the risk of hidden liabilities is less when records are complete and logically organized.

Even in the courtroom, good recordkeeping practices pay off. Properly maintained business records can be admitted into evidence if it can be shown that the records were prepared in the ordinary course of business at or near the time of the event shown in the records. The ability to introduce evidence under the business records exception to the hearsay rule can save time and money in litigation.

Good recordkeeping and adherence to corporate formality are largely a function of common sense and developing good business habits. As you read this chapter, you will wonder why such common sense information is included. Yet, as you read Chapter 11, you will learn that many business owners ignore these common sense requirements and end up paying the consequences.

In the following discussion, many unrelated types of paperwork are described. The common thread is that each type could be important in preserving your corporate status and shielding you from personal liability.

Corporate Minutes and Resolutions

In chapters 8 and 9, the need for and importance of shareholder and director meetings will be discussed. Using modern business corporation laws, many smaller corporations have replaced formal meetings with consent resolutions.

A consent resolution is a written corporate resolution which has been signed by a director or shareholder. By signing, the director or shareholder consents to the adoption of the resolution as if the resolution had been formally presented or approved by the board or the shareholders. To be effective, a consent resolution must be signed by all the directors (if a board resolution) or all of the shareholders (if a shareholder resolution). Multiple counterparts of the consent resolution can be used, eliminating the need to have the signatures appear on the same piece of paper.

Whether shareholder or director action is the result of a formal meeting or a consent resolution, the action taken should be evidenced by an appropriate entry in the corporate minute book. Most auditors will begin their review of corporate records with the minute book. If the book is up to date and contains regular records of board and shareholder activity, the auditor will be favorably impressed. This good impression may aid the entire audit process.

What types of activity should be reflected in the minute book? Routine day-to-day business activities don't need to be included. For example, if John Doe, Inc. is engaged in the manufacture and sale of widgets, separate resolutions aren't required to document each sale. The articles or state statute already provide the authority for this activity. However, if John Doe, Inc. does something outside of the scope of its ordinary business, a resolution should be reflected in the corporate minutes. Similarly, a lender or supplier may request a copy of a resolution showing that a particular officer of your corporation has authority to contract with the lender or supplier.

A partial list of activities which require a resolution for the corporate minute book is featured on the opposite page. At a minimum, corporate

List of Activities which Require a Resolution

These are some of the activities which require a resolution for the corporate minute book:

- Opening bank accounts or establishing borrowing authority with a bank (most banks will provide you with a form resolution)
- Written employment agreements
- Shareholder agreements, if the corporation is a party
- Tax elections, such as one to elect S corporation status
- A small business corporation election pursuant to Internal Revenue Code Section 1244 (optional)
- Amendments to the articles or bylaws
- The purchase or sale a business
- The purchase, sale, or lease of property to be used by the business including such things as an office building, computer system, company car or other items outside of the ordinary course of the business
- Loans, financing, bond issuance
- Reorganizations, including mergers
- Dividend declarations
- Approval of plans to merge, liquidate, or dissolve
- Employee benefit plans, including pension and profit-sharing plans, health insurance and others
- Settlement of lawsuits and claims, indemnification of officers and directors
- Stock issuance
- Changes of registered agent or registered office
- Filling vacancies on the board or for officers
- Authority to enter certain contracts
- Establishing committees or appointing members to serve on committees
- Redemption or retirement of corporate shares
- Salary matters pertaining to corporate officers
- Resolutions ratifying prior corporate acts by officers or directors

minutes should reflect organizational activities of the corporation and the results of each annual meeting of directors and shareholders. Organizational minutes of directors should address the:

- Approval of articles of incorporation and bylaws;
- Adoption of stock certificate to be used to evidence ownership of corporate shares;
- Approval of corporate seal, if one is to be used;
- Appointment of corporate officers;
- Authorize the filing of an S corporation election form if that status is desired;
- Issuance of shares (recite the names of the persons who are to receive shares, the number and class of shares they are to receive, and the consideration to be received in exchange for the shares; also recite that when shares are issued and payment made, the shares will be fully paid and nonassessable);
- Designation of bank accounts and borrowing authority specifying the bank and the persons who have check writing and withdrawal authority;
- Approval and authority to execute any lease or purchase of office space or special equipment necessary for the business; and
- Any other matters which appear on the checklist which arise at the time of organization.

If the directors are not named in the articles, the incorporator should designate the initial directors in writing prior to the organizational minutes of the directors. This designation should also appear in the corporate minute book. Alternatively, the shareholders could hold an organizational meeting and elect the initial directors. Thereafter, the directors would conduct the organizational meeting.

If a resolution involves a transaction between the corporation and an officer or director, the resolution should spell out in great detail the terms and conditions of the transaction to show that there has been an arm's length negotiation between the officer and director and the corporation and that the value paid is fair. This process can avoid claims down the road.

Resolutions should clearly state the action authorized and describe by name or office the person or persons authorized to perform acts or sign documents to carry out the action. For example, John Doe, Inc. plans to acquire a new computer system from Computer, Inc. John Doe, company president, has already negotiated the purchase, and the board has authorized it.

A sample resolution would read as follows:

Resolved, that this corporation purchase a System 1000 computer system from Computer, Inc. upon the terms and conditions set forth in the purchase proposal which is attached to this resolution and which incorporated herein as if fully set forth.

Further Resolved, that the President of this corporation be, and he is hereby authorized, to perform any and all acts and execute any and all documents necessary to carry out this resolution.

Further Resolved, that the acts of the corporation's President relating to the negotiations with Computer, Inc. prior to the date of this resolution are hereby ratified and adopted as the acts of the corporation.

This sample resolution has authorized the purchase of the system. Rather than state all of the terms and conditions, the resolution incorporates by reference the "attached" purchase proposal. This is an effective technique especially where the terms and conditions are lengthy. The resolution also gives the company president the authority to finalize the purchase, and the resolution ratifies the activities of the president in negotiating the purchase prior to receiving actual authority.

A sample of organizational meeting minutes using consent resolutions is provided on the following page.

Annual Reports

Each state requires that both domestic and foreign corporations to file an annual report. Some states also require that the corporation pay an annual franchise tax for the privilege of doing business in the state either in conjunction with the annual report or as a separate report.

An annual report generally requires this information:

- The corporation's name and the state or country where it is incorporated;
- The name and address of the registered agent and registered office;
- The address of the principal corporate office;
- The names and business addresses of the president and secretary;
- The code classification of the principal business activity; and
- The federal employer identification number.

Annual reports are required by all states. Failure to file these reports can have serious consequences.

The secretary of state mails the report form to every corporation each year; however, the failure to receive the form from the secretary of state does not excuse the corporation's obligation to file it in a timely manner.

Important dates should be conspicuously marked on the calendars of appropriate corporate officers. The due date for the annual report would be one such date. Tax filing dates, annual meeting dates, and shareholder record dates would also be examples of important dates to mark.

Can a Corporate Charter Be Revoked?

Corporate charters can be revoked or administratively dissolved by the appropriate secretary of state whenever a corporation:

- Fails to file its annual report;
- Fails to pay required fees;
- Fails to appoint and maintain a registered office or agent; or
- Makes a filing containing a materially false statement.

Although most states will notify you of a default and provide 45 days to cure, this is not always true. Efforts should be made to prepare and file reports on a timely basis. Contact your secretary of state to learn the filing requirements and fees which apply to your state.

SAMPLE: Organizational Meeting Minutes Using Consent Resolutions

John Doe, Inc.
Consent by Directors to Resolutions in Lieu of Organizational Meeting
February 14, 1992

The undersigned, being all of the directors of John Doe, Inc., an Oz corporation, acting in accordance with the Oz Business Corporation Act, hereby consent to the adoption of the following recitals and resolutions as if adopted at a duly called meeting of the board of directors of the corporation:

Approve bylaws.

1. RESOLVED, that the bylaws attached hereto be and the same are hereby approved and adopted as the bylaws of the corporation.

Approve stock certificate.

2. RESOLVED, that the specimen stock certificate attached hereto be and the same is approved as the stock certificate to be used by this corporation in conjunction with the issuance of its stock.

Approve corporate seal (if you have one).

3. RESOLVED, that the corporate seal which is affixed to these resolutions be and the same is hereby approved as the official seal of the corporation.

Appoint officers.

4. RESOLVED, that the following persons are hereby appointed to serve in the offices which appear next to their names until their successors shall be duly appointed and shall qualify:

Name	Office
Jane Doe	President
John Doe	Vice-President
Joan Doe	Secretary and Treasurer

Issue stock.

5. RESOLVED, that this corporation shall issue against payment therefore 100 shares of its common stock, no par value, to each of Jane Doe, John Doe, and Joan Doe in exchange for the payment of $1,000 by each, and that when payment is received, the shares shall be issued and shall be considered fully paid and nonassessable;

FURTHER RESOLVED, that upon payment, $100 of each $1,000 payment shall be allocated to the stated capital of the corporation and the remainder shall be allocated to the additional paid in capital of the corporation.

Elect S corporation treatment.

6. RESOLVED, that this corporation elects to be treated as an S corporation, and in that regard shall cause the filing of an appropriate election on Internal Revenue Service *Form 2553.*

SAMPLE: Organizational Meeting Minutes Using Consent Resolutions (cont.)

7. RESOLVED, that the president of the corporation is authorized to establish such depositary accounts for the corporation as she may deem necessary, acting on behalf of the corporation.

Establish bank accounts.

8. RESOLVED, that the actions of the officers and directors of this corporation in support of its incorporation are hereby approved, ratified, adopted, and confirmed.

Approve pre-incorporation acts.

9. RESOLVED, that the officers and directors of this corporation are authorized and directed to perform any and all acts and execute and deliver any and all documents necessary to effectuate the foregoing resolutions.

Authorize officers and directors to carry out these resolutions.

_____

Jane Doe

_____

John Doe

_____

Joan Doe

Being all of the Directors of the Corporation

Note: For consent resolutions, all directors must sign. Directors may sign separate copies of the consent resolutions as long as all directors sign. The same is true for shareholder consent resolutions. All shareholders must sign.

Corporate Recordkeeping

In the Introduction, the importance of good recordkeeping was described. All corporate records and documents should be organized in a logical and orderly manner. Different documents may be required to be produced for different purposes. For example, most business corporation acts describe the types of documents that are available for shareholder inspection. Other documents may be produced in response to investigations by government agencies or by subpoena or a request to produce documents pursuant to litigation. The only limitation on production of documents in a litigation context or pursuant to a government investigation is that the documents be relevant to the matter involved. This is not a difficult standard to satisfy. Keep your records in good order.

The RMBCA and other modern business corporation acts require a corporation to maintain a number of records, including:

Keep thorough and accurate records when incorporated. Many business corporations acts require you to maintain several records.

- All minutes of shareholder and board meetings, and records of all action taken without a meeting by shareholders, directors, or committees formed by directors;
- Appropriate accounting records;
- A list of the shareholders' names and addresses, and the number and class of shares held by each shareholder;
- A current list of the names and business addresses of corporate directors and officers;
- Articles of incorporation and all amendments;
- Bylaws and all amendments;
- Resolutions of the board creating one or more classes of shares and fixing their relative rights, preferences, and limitations; and
- All written communications to shareholders for the last three years.[1]

Records must be maintained in written form or by means capable of conversion into written form. Examples of the latter include information stored on microfiche or in computers. Records should be kept at the principal office of the corporation or at the registered office.

The RMBCA also requires that certain financial information be provided to shareholders, including:

Records should be kept at the corporation's principal or registered office.

- A balance sheet as of the fiscal year end;
- An income statement; and
- A statement of changes in shareholder equity.[2]

Financial reports must include those from any accountant who prepared them as well as a statement by the accountant documenting his or her reasonable belief that the statements were prepared in accordance with generally accepted accounting principles. Financial statements must be mailed to shareholders within 120 days following the close of the fiscal year.

If a corporation has indemnified or advanced expenses to an officer or director during the fiscal year or if the corporation issues or authorizes the issuance of shares in exchange for the promise of future services, the RMBCA requires that this information be disclosed to shareholders in advance of the next shareholders meeting.

Records may be inspected by shareholders. To inspect, a shareholder must:

Shareholders can inspect certain corporate records.

- Make a written demand at least five business days prior to the proposed inspection; and
- Describe with reasonable particularity the business purpose for the inspection and the documents to be inspected.[3]

The records sought must be directly connected with the business purpose stated by the shareholder. Shareholders can't go on fishing expeditions hoping to dredge up evidence of corporate wrong doing. The request must be specific both as to purpose and documents sought.

Employment Agreements and Personnel Policy Manuals

Frequently, corporations will enter into written employment agreements with its employees, especially corporate officers. Written employment agreements, properly drafted, can provide security for the employee, protect the corporation against future competition by the employee, and resolve future disputes. Employment agreements can also contain nondisclosure language limiting an employee's use of corporate trade secrets, customer lists, and similar information.

If a corporation uses a personnel policy manual, the corporation is bound by its terms and conditions regardless of whether or not it uses written employment agreements. Two books, *A Company Personnel and Policy Workbook* and *Developing Company Policies*, published by The Oasis Press®, are good sources of information concerning policy manuals. Policy manuals are a good way to introduce your employees to the company, describe available benefits, explain rules and restrictions, and list appropriate channels of communication and authority.

How Do You Sign Corporate Documents?

Think back to Chapter 4 and the discussion on agency principles, where certain personnel, such as purchasing agents or corporate officers, are clearly designated as agents who are authorized to act on behalf of a corporation. How these corporate agents sign corporate documents is crucial to indicating who or what will be bound to a document's agreement. For example, John Doe is the president of John Doe, Inc. John has been negotiating with Computer, Inc. for the purchase of a new computer system. Computer, Inc. knows nothing about John Doe, Inc. After concluding negotiations, Computer, Inc. presents John with a purchase order. The preamble states that the agreement is between Computer, Inc. and John Doe. Beneath the signature line is typed the name "John Doe." No mention of John Doe, Inc. is found.

If John Doe signs the purchase order as John Doe, without more, John Doe has personally committed to buying the computer system. What should John

How you hold yourself out to the public may determine whether you are personally liable for corporate acts. Whenever you sign any document on behalf of the corporation, from a business contract to a letter, make it clear that your are signing in a corporate and not a personal capacity.

If you convert to a corporation from a partnership or proprietorship, modify your letterhead, business cards, telephone listings, advertisements, and other means of holding yourself out to the public. If you carry over the old letterhead or cards, your customers and suppliers may continue to look to you personally and not the corporation. Take pains to notify your customers, suppliers, and creditors of the change.

have done? First, he should have modified the purchase order to show that the contracting parties were Computer, Inc. and John Doe, Inc. Second, in signing the agreement, John Doe should have revised the signature line to:

John Doe, Inc.
by John Doe, president

These two steps would have made certain that John Doe, Inc. was the purchasing party. Computer, Inc. may not have been willing to sell the computer to John Doe, Inc. without the personal backing of John Doe, individually. In such a case, Computer, Inc. could request a personal guarantee of John Doe, and his spouse, if any. John may not have been willing to guarantee the deal, but that's his choice.

Letterhead and Business Cards

To preserve your corporate integrity, your business cards, letterhead, invoices, and other sources of communication should specify the corporate name. Let your customers and suppliers know that they are dealing with a corporation and not you individually. Don't hold yourself out as John Doe, purveyor of fine widgets; hold yourself out as John Doe, Inc., purveyor of fine widgets — John Doe, president. Sample business cards and letterhead are shown on the opposite page.

If your corporation does business under a fictitious name, you have several choices to consider. First, include both the corporation's legal name and fictitious name. For example, the letterhead could read: "John Doe, Inc. d.b.a. Widget World." Second, the heading could be: "Widget World, a division of John Doe, Inc." Of course, this choice works best if John Doe, Inc. is engaged in different lines of business. A third choice would be to use the heading, "Widget World." If you have properly filed your fictitious name registration, the third choice will suffice. Note that not all states have a fictitious name statute. In these states, use the full corporate name. Fourth, a foreign corporation unable to use its name in another state in which it is qualified might choose, "John Doe, Inc., an Oz corporation doing business in Idaho as Widget World." Regardless of the choice made, all signatures or business cards should show, "John Doe, president." To illustrate these situations regarding fictitious names, review the sample business cards on page 138.

If you are involved in several business activities, each should have a separate letterhead, business card, and similar items. It must be clear to suppliers, customers, and others which hat you are wearing when you are dealing with them on business matters. Confusion over whom you're doing business as could result in several of your business operations being involved in a claim or lawsuit instead of just one.

This same analysis applies to telephone listings and advertisements. Whenever you hold your business out to the public, make it clear that the corporation is the legal entity operating the business.

SAMPLE: Corporate Letterhead and Business Card

John Doe, Inc.
Purveyor of Fine Widgets

February 10, 1993

Mr. William A. Smith
Substantial Industries, Inc.
10 Alcorn Place, Suite 2115
Metropark, NY 02345

Dear Bill,

How is everything at Substantial? Booming as usual, I hope.

Here, we've made a few changes. Our company has recently incorporated and expanded our facilities. Please have your staff use our official new name, John Doe, Inc., on all correspondence, checks, etc. Here's my new business card for your file.

Bill, whenever you are in our part of the country, please come by and take a look at our new wing. We expanded so we could put in three new state-of-the art widget finishing machines. This means we will be delivering your orders in about half the time it used to take. And I think you will be amazed at the dramatically smoother surface we can produce with the new technology.

Thanks for your continuing support. At John Doe, Inc. we are dedicated to producing ever finer, widgets faster to meet your growing needs at Substantial Industries, Inc.

Sincerely,

John Doe
President

12345 West Franklin Avenue
Newtown, OZ 21333
(202) 987-6543
FAX (202) 987-6555

John Doe, Inc.
Purveyor of Fine Widgets

John Doe
President

12345 West Franklin Avenue
Newtown, OZ 21333
(202) 987-6543
FAX (202) 987-6555

SAMPLE: Business Cards with Fictitious Names

This way of expressing the relationship between Widget World and John Doe, Inc. is absolutely clear from a legal standpoint, but lacks the marketing punch a shorter name would give.

John Doe, Inc. d.b.a. Widget World

John Doe
President

12345 West Franklin Avenue
Newtown, OZ 21333
(202) 987-6543
FAX (202) 987-6555

This option works if John Doe, Inc. is involved in several different lines of business, each with its own registered ficticious name, such as Widget World, Toy World, and Builder's World.

Widget World
A Division of John Doe, Inc.

John Doe
President

12345 West Franklin Avenue
Newtown, OZ 21333
(202) 987-6543
FAX (202) 987-6555

If your state has a ficticious name statute, you can just use your registered ficticious name, since anyone curious about Widget World could contact the secretary of state to find out about the company.

Widget World

John Doe
President

12345 West Franklin Avenue
Newtown, OZ 21333
(202) 987-6543
FAX (202) 987-6555

Identification Numbers, Permits, and Licenses

Depending on your business, you will need one or more employer identification numbers. At a minimum, you will need a federal employer identification number. To obtain this federal identification number, file *Form SS-4, Application for Employer Identification Number,* with the Internal Revenue Service. A copy of *Form SS-4* is found at the end of this chapter. You may also need identification numbers, permits, and licenses to deal with such things as unemployment insurance, workers compensation, sales tax, and related matters. Your accountant or business attorney is the best source of information as to which forms you will be required to file. Consider acquiring a copy of *Starting and Operating a Business,* published by The Oasis Press®. A separate volume exists for each state and the District of Columbia.

Insurance

All casualty and liability insurance should be in the name of the corporation. Don't give your insurance carrier an opportunity to avoid paying claims by carrying the policy in your name. Similarly, make certain that corporate property is titled in the corporate name so that claims can be processed if property is stolen or destroyed.

Title to Assets

All property should be titled in the corporate names. From real estate to vehicles, if the corporation owns it, there should be a deed, title, or bill of sale in the corporation's name indicating ownership. If you sell property to the corporation, provide the corporation with a bill of sale. Dates acquired and purchase price paid are important documents to establish ownership and tax basis. If you give property to the corporation, the corporation should acknowledge the gift in a corporate resolution or a letter to you, describing the gift, the date it was made, and a value assigned to the property.

Bank Accounts

You should have a separate bank account for each business you operate. Don't combine business monies with personal monies or monies generated by other businesses. Bills for one business should be paid by checks drawn from the account of that business. If you get in the habit of paying business bills from personal funds, business creditors will come to expect that you will pay all bills personally. Similarly, if you pay the bills of John Doe, Inc. from the account of John Doe Enterprises, Inc., a separate corporation, you create uncertainty as to who is responsible for the payment of bills and debts.

Don't divert corporate monies for personal purposes. Once again, you will cloud the issue of who owns the asset and who is liable for claims resulting from its use. Monies paid from the corporation to you should come to you as salary, repayment of properly documented debt, or dividends.

Chapter 11 discusses the drastic consequences resulting from commingling business and personal funds.

Document Corporate Transactions with Officers and Directors

Keep it simple; use separate accounts for each business and keep these accounts separate from personal accounts.

If your corporation loans money to an officer or director or if it buys, sells, or leases property to or from an officer or director, the transaction should be carefully documented to demonstrate its fairness. Promissory notes providing for repayment terms comparable to those offered by local banks should be used. Security for the loan should be used as well. You must be able to demonstrate to your shareholders and the Internal Revenue Service that these transactions are done on an arm's length basis with no preferential treatment to the officer or director. An arm's length transaction is one which assumes equal bargaining strength. This is not always the case. When you negotiate a loan with your banker, you may feel as if you are at a disadvantage. Presumably your negotiation with the bank will lead to a loan with interest and terms comparable to those in the marketplace. A loan by a corporation or a board member must be on terms and conditions comparable to those the officer or director could have obtained from the bank.

Maintain Adequate Capital

Maintaining adequate capital is not really a part of the paper trail; however, it is an important factor in preserving your corporate status. A corporation should have adequate capital to carry on its business. What is adequate capital? The answer will vary from business to business, but adequate capital presumes that a business will have sufficient funding to meet the reasonably foreseeable needs of the business. This concept probably includes an amount necessary to meet claims. Liability insurance can be used in lieu of having the actual cash to meet claims. Without adequate capital, a person with a claim against a corporation may seek to have liability imposed on the directors, officers, or shareholders. There's more on this topic in Chapter 11.

Final Thoughts on Paperwork

Aargh! With so much paper, why would you want to incorporate in the first place? It's not that bad. Keep in mind that good recordkeeping is an essential part of any successful business, regardless of the form of business. Sole proprietorships, partnerships, limited liability companies, and corporations must all document their activities.

Bad habits sink a lot of businesses. When you incorporate, get started in the right direction. Get in the habit of recording your activities and maintaining required records. Once you're in the habit, the rest is easy. To help you know what to keep track of, the corporate paperwork checklist on the next page partially lists those items you need to include in your corporate recordkeeping.

Corporate Paperwork Checklist

Use this checklist as a guide to conduct your business in the corporate form and monitor your paperwork.

☐ Have you reserved your corporate name with the secretary of state?

☐ Have you prepared and filed your articles of incorporation with the secretary of state?

☐ Have your corporate bylaws been prepared and approved by shareholders and directors?

☐ Do your articles state your corporate purposes?

☐ Do the articles list your registered agent and registered office?

☐ Do the articles provide for preemptive rights and cumulative voting for shareholders? If not, does the applicable business corporation act grant these rights?

☐ Have you registered any fictitious names your corporation will use in its business with the secretary of state?

☐ Will your corporation engage in business in other states? If so, has it qualified to do business as a foreign corporation in a writing kept in the corporate minute book?

☐ Have organizational meeting minutes or consent resolutions been prepared? Do they include such things as:
- approval of articles and bylaws;
- adoption of stock certificates to be used by corporation;
- approval of corporate seal, if any;
- appointment of corporate officers;
- approve tax filings such as S corporation election;
- accept subscription for shares and issue shares;
- designate bank accounts and borrowing authority;
- approval and authority to execute a lease or purchase of office property or equipment;
- approval for any required applications for certificate of authority in other states; and
- approval to obtain required permits, licenses, and identification numbers in the corporate name?

☐ Have minutes or consent resolutions been included for each annual meeting of shareholders and directors?

☐ Have minutes or consent resolutions been included for each regular or special meeting of directors or shareholders?

☐ Has an accurate and current shareholders list been prepared and maintained?

☐ Have meeting notices been provided to each shareholder?

☐ If a special meeting is called, does the meeting notice specify a purpose(s) for the meeting?

☐ If a meeting is convened, are bylaw requirements pertaining to notice satisfied?

☐ Has an agenda been prepared and followed for the meeting?

Corporate Paperwork Checklist (continued)

☐ Are parliamentary procedures to be used at the meeting?

☐ Have you predetermined a method for conducting voting at any meeting of shareholders?

☐ Is there an affidavit of the corporate secretary attesting to the giving of notice?

☐ Are there signed waivers of notice if required?

☐ If consent resolutions are used, are they signed by all directors or shareholders?

☐ Are there meeting minutes or consent resolutions to reflect major activities of the corporation, including:

- opening bank accounts or establishing borrowing authority;
- written employment agreements;
- shareholder agreements, if corporation is a party;
- tax elections;
- amendments to articles or bylaws;
- authorizing the purchase or sale of the business;
- authorizing the purchase, sale or lease of property to be used by the business including such things as office building, computer system, company car or other items outside of the ordinary course of business;
- corporate loans, financing authority or bond issuances;
- reorganizations, including mergers or consolidations;
- dividend declarations;
- plans to dissolve and liquidate;
- approval or authorization of employee benefit plans, including pension and profit-sharing plans, health insurance, and others;
- settlement of lawsuits and claims;
- indemnification of officers and directors;
- issuance of stock;
- changes of registered agent and registered office;
- filling vacancies on the board or for offices;
- authority to enter into certain contracts, including ones for large amounts of money or inventory or contracts outside of the ordinary course of the corporation's business;
- establishing committees or appointing members to serve on committees;
- redemption or retirement of corporate shares;
- salary matters pertaining to corporate officers;
- resolutions ratifying prior corporate acts by officers or directors; and
- resolutions fixing the value of shares pursuant to any stock purchase agreement?

☐ If dividends are declared, do the resolutions authorizing them fix a record date and describe in detail how and when the dividend will be paid or distributed?

Corporate Paperwork Checklist (continued)

☐ If cash dividends are declared, are there sufficient earnings and profits of the corporation to permit the dividends?

☐ If there are preferred shareholders, do their shares provide for cumulative or noncumulative dividend payments?

☐ If a stock dividend is declared, are there a sufficient number of authorized shares to cover the dividend?

☐ If stock is to be issued, do the resolutions:
- state the name of the purchaser;
- recite the consideration to be paid or exchanged;
- describe the timing of payment;
- describe the number and classification of shares to be issued;
- indicate whether the shares are originally issued or treasury stock; and
- state whether the payment is considered full payment?

☐ Do the number of shares proposed to be issued exceed the corporation's authorized number of shares?

☐ Is the stock ledger current and accurate with respect to the names and addresses of shareholders and a listing of the number and classification of shares held by each?

☐ Do the corporate records include:
- articles of incorporation and all amendments;
- bylaws and all amendments;
- all corporate minutes and consent resolutions of directors and officers;
- resolutions of the board creating one or more classes of shares and fixing their relative rights, preferences and limitations;
- all written communication to shareholders for the last three years;
- corporate balance sheet as of the most recent fiscal year end;
- income statement;
- statement of changes in shareholders equity;
- stock purchase agreements;
- voting trusts;
- shareholders list;
- current list of names and addresses of officers and directors;
- federal and state income tax returns for the last six years;
- state franchise tax and annual reports;
- copies of leases, bills of sale pertaining to corporate property;
- insurance policies in corporate name; and
- copies of all contracts or agreements to which corporation is a party?

Form **SS-4** ▶

(Rev. December 1995)

Department of the Treasury
Internal Revenue Service

Application for Employer Identification Number

(For use by employers, corporations, partnerships, trusts, estates, churches, government agencies, certain individuals, and others. See instructions.)

▶ Keep a copy for your records.

EIN

OMB No. 1545-0003

Please type or print clearly.

1   Name of applicant (Legal name) (See instructions.)

2   Trade name of business (if different from name on line 1)

3   Executor, trustee, "care of" name

4a Mailing address (street address) (room, apt., or suite no.)

5a Business address (if different from address on lines 4a and 4b)

4b City, state, and ZIP code

5b City, state, and ZIP code

6   County and state where principal business is located

7   Name of principal officer, general partner, grantor, owner, or trustor—SSN required (See instructions.) ▶

8a Type of entity (Check only one box.) (See instructions.)
☐ Sole proprietor (SSN)
☐ Partnership   ☐ Personal service corp.
☐ REMIC   ☐ Limited liability co.
☐ State/local government   ☐ National Guard
☐ Other nonprofit organization (specify) ▶
☐ Other (specify) ▶

☐ Estate (SSN of decedent)
☐ Plan administrator-SSN
☐ Other corporation (specify) ▶
☐ Trust   ☐ Farmers' cooperative
☐ Federal Government/military ☐ Church or church-controlled organization
(enter GEN if applicable)

8b If a corporation, name the state or foreign country (if applicable) where incorporated | State | Foreign country

9   Reason for applying (Check only one box.)
☐ Started new business (specify) ▶
☐ Hired employees
☐ Created a pension plan (specify type) ▶

☐ Banking purpose (specify) ▶
☐ Changed type of organization (specify) ▶
☐ Purchased going business
☐ Created a trust (specify) ▶
☐ Other (specify) ▶

10 Date business started or acquired (Mo., day, year) (See instructions.)

11 Closing month of accounting year (See instructions.)

12 First date wages or annuities were paid or will be paid (Mo., day, year). **Note:** *If applicant is a withholding agent, enter date income will first be paid to nonresident alien. (Mo., day, year)* . . . . ▶

13 Highest number of employees expected in the next 12 months. **Note:** *If the applicant does not expect to have any employees during the period, enter -0-. (See instructions.)* . . . ▶ | Nonagricultural | Agricultural | Household

14 Principal activity (See instructions.) ▶

15 Is the principal business activity manufacturing? . . . . ☐ Yes ☐ No
If "Yes," principal product and raw material used ▶

16 To whom are most of the products or services sold? Please check the appropriate box.   ☐ Business (wholesale)
☐ Public (retail)   ☐ Other (specify) ▶   ☐ N/A

17a Has the applicant ever applied for an identification number for this or any other business? . . . . ☐ Yes ☐ No
Note: *If "Yes," please complete lines 17b and 17c.*

17b If you checked "Yes" on line 17a, give applicant's legal name and trade name shown on prior application, if different from line 1 or 2 above.
Legal name ▶   Trade name ▶

17c Approximate date when and city and state where the application was filed. Enter previous employer identification number if known.
Approximate date when filed (Mo., day, year) | City and state where filed | Previous EIN

Under penalties of perjury, I declare that I have examined this application, and to the best of my knowledge and belief, it is true, correct, and complete. | Business telephone number (include area code)

Fax telephone number (include area code)

Name and title (Please type or print clearly.) ▶

Signature ▶   Date ▶

Note: *Do not write below this line. For official use only.*

Please leave blank ▶ | Geo. | Ind. | Class | Size | Reason for applying

For Paperwork Reduction Act Notice, see page 4.   Cat. No. 16055N   Form **SS-4** (Rev. 12-95)

SAMPLE: IRS Form SS-4 – Instructions

Form SS-4 (Rev. 12-95)   Page **2**

General Instructions

Section references are to the Internal Revenue Code unless otherwise noted.

Purpose of Form

Use Form SS-4 to apply for an employer identification number (EIN). An EIN is a nine-digit number (for example, 12-3456789) assigned to sole proprietors, corporations, partnerships, estates, trusts, and other entities for filing and reporting purposes. The information you provide on this form will establish your filing and reporting requirements.

Who Must File

You must file this form if you have not obtained an EIN before and:

● You pay wages to one or more employees including household employees.

● You are required to have an EIN to use on any return, statement, or other document, even if you are not an employer.

● You are a withholding agent required to withhold taxes on income, other than wages, paid to a nonresident alien (individual, corporation, partnership, etc.). A withholding agent may be an agent, broker, fiduciary, manager, tenant, or spouse, and is required to file **Form 1042**, Annual Withholding Tax Return for U.S. Source Income of Foreign Persons.

● You file **Schedule C**, Profit or Loss From Business, or **Schedule F**, Profit or Loss From Farming, of **Form 1040**, U.S. Individual Income Tax Return, **and** have a Keogh plan or are required to file excise, employment, information, or alcohol, tobacco, or firearms returns.

The following must use EINs even if they do not have any employees:

● State and local agencies who serve as tax reporting agents for public assistance recipients, under Rev. Proc. 80-4, 1980-1 C.B. 581, should obtain a separate EIN for this reporting. See **Household employer** on page 3.

● Trusts, except the following:

1. Certain grantor-owned revocable trusts. (See the **Instructions for Form 1041**.)

2. Individual Retirement Arrangement (IRA) trusts, unless the trust has to file **Form 990-T**, Exempt Organization Business Income Tax Return. (See the **Instructions for Form 990-T**.)

3. Certain trusts that are considered household employers can use the trust EIN to report and pay the social security and Medicare taxes, Federal unemployment tax (FUTA) and withheld Federal income tax. A separate EIN is not necessary.

● Estates

● Partnerships

● REMICs (real estate mortgage investment conduits) (See the **Instructions for Form 1066**, U.S. Real Estate Mortgage Investment Conduit Income Tax Return.)

● Corporations

● Nonprofit organizations (churches, clubs, etc.)

● Farmers' cooperatives

● Plan administrators (A plan administrator is the person or group of persons specified as the administrator by the instrument under which the plan is operated.)

When To Apply for a New EIN

New Business.—If you become the new owner of an existing business, **do not** use the EIN of the former owner. IF YOU ALREADY HAVE AN EIN, USE THAT NUMBER. If you do not have an EIN, apply for one on this form. If you become the "owner" of a corporation by acquiring its stock, use the corporation's EIN.

Changes in Organization or Ownership.—If you already have an EIN, you may need to get a new one if either the organization or ownership of your business changes. If you incorporate a sole proprietorship or form a partnership, you must get a new EIN. However, **do not** apply for a new EIN if you change only the name of your business.

Note: *If you are electing to be an "S corporation," be sure you file* **Form 2553**, *Election by a Small Business Corporation.*

File Only One Form SS-4.—File only one Form SS-4, regardless of the number of businesses operated or trade names under which a business operates. However, each corporation in an affiliated group must file a separate application.

EIN Applied For, But Not Received.—If you do not have an EIN by the time a return is due, write "Applied for" and the date you applied in the space shown for the number. **Do not** show your social security number as an EIN on returns.

If you do not have an EIN by the time a tax deposit is due, send your payment to the Internal Revenue Service Center for your filing area. (See **Where To Apply** below.) Make your check or money order payable to Internal Revenue Service and show your name (as shown on Form SS-4), address, type of tax, period covered, and date you applied for an EIN. Send an explanation with the deposit.

For more information about EINs, see **Pub. 583**, Starting a Business and Keeping Records, and **Pub. 1635**, Understanding Your EIN.

How To Apply

You can apply for an EIN either by mail or by telephone. You can get an EIN immediately by calling the Tele-TIN phone number for the service center for your state, or you can send the completed Form SS-4 directly to the service center to receive your EIN in the mail.

Application by Tele-TIN.—Under the Tele-TIN program, you can receive your EIN over the telephone and use it immediately to file a return or make a payment. To receive an EIN by phone, complete Form SS-4, then call the Tele-TIN phone number listed for your state under **Where To Apply.** The person making the call must be authorized to sign the form. (See **Signature block** on page 4.)

An IRS representative will use the information from the Form SS-4 to establish your account and assign you an EIN. Write the number you are given on the upper right-hand corner of the form, sign and date it.

Mail or FAX the signed SS-4 **within 24 hours** *to the Tele-TIN Unit at the service center address for your state.* The IRS representative will give you the FAX number. The FAX numbers are also listed in Pub. 1635.

Taxpayer representatives can receive their client's EIN by phone if they first send a facsimile (FAX) of a completed **Form 2848**, Power of Attorney and Declaration of Representative, or **Form 8821**, Tax Information Authorization, to the Tele-TIN unit. The Form 2848 or Form 8821 will be used solely to release the EIN to the representative authorized on the form.

Application by Mail.—Complete Form SS-4 at least 4 to 5 weeks before you will need an EIN. Sign and date the application and mail it to the service center address for your state. You will receive your EIN in the mail in approximately 4 weeks.

Where To Apply

The Tele-TIN phone numbers listed below will involve a long-distance charge to callers outside of the local calling area and can be used only to apply for an EIN. THE NUMBERS MAY CHANGE WITHOUT NOTICE. Use 1-800-829-1040 to verify a number or to ask about an application by mail or other Federal tax matters.

If your principal business, office or agency, or legal residence in the case of an individual, is located in:	Call the Tele-TIN phone number or file with the Internal Revenue Service Center at:
Florida, Georgia, South Carolina	Attn: Entity Control Atlanta, GA 39901 (404) 455-2360
New Jersey, New York City and counties of Nassau, Rockland, Suffolk, and Westchester	Attn: Entity Control Holtsville, NY 00501 (516) 447-4955
New York (all other counties), Connecticut, Maine, Massachusetts, New Hampshire, Rhode Island, Vermont	Attn: Entity Control Andover, MA 05501 (508) 474-9717
Illinois, Iowa, Minnesota, Missouri, Wisconsin	Attn: Entity Control Stop 57A 2306 E. Bannister Rd. Kansas City, MO 64131 (816) 926-5999
Delaware, District of Columbia, Maryland, Pennsylvania, Virginia	Attn: Entity Control Philadelphia, PA 19255 (215) 574-2400
Indiana, Kentucky, Michigan, Ohio, West Virginia	Attn: Entity Control Cincinnati, OH 45999 (606) 292-5467
Kansas, New Mexico, Oklahoma, Texas	Attn: Entity Control Austin, TX 73301 (512) 460-7843

Form SS-4 (Rev. 12-95)   Page **3**

Alaska, Arizona, California
(counties of Alpine, Amador,
Butte, Calaveras, Colusa, Contra
Costa, Del Norte, El Dorado,
Glenn, Humboldt, Lake, Lassen,
Marin, Mendocino, Modoc,   Attn: Entity Control
Napa, Nevada, Placer, Plumas,   Mail Stop 6271-T
Sacramento, San Joaquin,   P.O. Box 9950
Shasta, Sierra, Siskiyou, Solano,   Ogden, UT 84409
Sonoma, Sutter, Tehama, Trinity,   (801) 620-7645
Yolo, and Yuba), Colorado,
Idaho, Montana, Nebraska,
Nevada, North Dakota, Oregon,
South Dakota, Utah,
Washington, Wyoming

California (all other   Attn: Entity Control
counties), Hawaii   Fresno, CA 93888
                                               (209) 452-4010

Alabama, Arkansas,   Attn: Entity Control
Louisiana, Mississippi,   Memphis, TN 37501
North Carolina, Tennessee   (901) 365-5970

If you have no legal residence, principal place of business, or principal office or agency in any state, file your form with the Internal Revenue Service Center, Philadelphia, PA 19255 or call 215-574-2400.

Specific Instructions

The instructions that follow are for those items that are not self-explanatory. Enter N/A (nonapplicable) on the lines that do not apply.

Line 1.—Enter the legal name of the entity applying for the EIN exactly as it appears on the social security card, charter, or other applicable legal document.

Individuals.—Enter the first name, middle initial, and last name. If you are a sole proprietor, enter your individual name, not your business name. Do not use abbreviations or nicknames.

Trusts.—Enter the name of the trust.

Estate of a decedent.—Enter the name of the estate.

Partnerships.—Enter the legal name of the partnership as it appears in the partnership agreement. **Do not** list the names of the partners on line 1. See the specific instructions for line 7.

Corporations.—Enter the corporate name as it appears in the corporation charter or other legal document creating it.

Plan administrators.—Enter the name of the plan administrator. A plan administrator who already has an EIN should use that number.

Line 2.—Enter the trade name of the business if different from the legal name. The trade name is the "doing business as" name.

Note: *Use the full legal name on line 1 on all tax returns filed for the entity. However, if you enter a trade name on line 2 and choose to use the trade name instead of the legal name, enter the trade name on all returns you file. To prevent processing delays and errors, always use either the legal name only or the trade name only on all tax returns.*

Line 3.—Trusts enter the name of the trustee. Estates enter the name of the executor, administrator, or other fiduciary. If the entity applying has a designated person to receive tax information, enter that person's name as the "care of"

person. Print or type the first name, middle initial, and last name.

Line 7.—Enter the first name, middle initial, last name, and social security number (SSN) of a principal officer if the business is a corporation; of a general partner if a partnership; or of a grantor, owner, or trustor if a trust. Do not enter N/A.

Line 8a.—Check the box that best describes the type of entity applying for the EIN. If not specifically mentioned, check the "Other" box and enter the type of entity. Do not enter N/A.

Sole proprietor.—Check this box if you file Schedule C or F (Form 1040) and have a Keogh plan, or are required to file excise, employment, information, or alcohol, tobacco, or firearms returns. Enter your SSN in the space provided.

REMIC.—Check this box if the entity has elected to be treated as a real estate mortgage investment conduit (REMIC). See the **Instructions for Form 1066** for more information.

Other nonprofit organization.—Check this box if the nonprofit organization is other than a church or church-controlled organization and specify the type of nonprofit organization (for example, an educational organization).

If the organization also seeks tax-exempt status, you must file either **Package 1023** or **Package 1024**, Application for Recognition of Exemption. Get **Pub. 557,** Tax-Exempt Status for Your Organization, for more information.

Group exemption number (GEN).—If the organization is covered by a group exemption letter, enter the four-digit GEN. (Do not confuse the GEN with the nine-digit EIN.) If you do not know the GEN, contact the parent organization. Get Pub. 557 for more information about group exemption numbers.

Withholding agent.—If you are a withholding agent required to file Form 1042, check the "Other" box and enter "Withholding agent."

Personal service corporation.—Check this box if the entity is a personal service corporation. An entity is a personal service corporation for a tax year only if:

• The principal activity of the entity during the testing period (prior tax year) for the tax year is the performance of personal services substantially by employee-owners, and

• The employee-owners own 10% of the fair market value of the outstanding stock in the entity on the last day of the testing period.

Personal services include performance of services in such fields as health, law, accounting, or consulting. For more information about personal service corporations, see the **Instructions for Form 1120,** U.S. Corporation Income Tax Return, and **Pub. 542,** Tax Information on Corporations.

Limited liability co.—See the definition of limited liability company in the **Instructions for Form 1065.** If you are classified as a partnership for Federal income tax

purposes, mark the "Limited liability co." checkbox. If you are classified as a corporation for Federal income tax purposes, mark the "Other corporation" checkbox and write "Limited liability co." in the space provided.

Plan administrator.—If the plan administrator is an individual, enter the plan administrator's SSN in the space provided.

Other corporation.—This box is for any corporation other than a personal service corporation. If you check this box, enter the type of corporation (such as insurance company) in the space provided.

Household employer.—If you are an individual, check the "Other" box and enter "Household employer" and your SSN. If you are a state or local agency serving as a tax reporting agent for public assistance recipients who become household employers, check the "Other" box and enter "Household employer agent." If you are a trust that qualifies as a household employer, you do not need a separate EIN for reporting tax information relating to household employees; use the EIN of the trust.

Line 9.—Check only **one** box. Do not enter N/A.

Started new business.—Check this box if you are starting a new business that requires an EIN. If you check this box, enter the type of business being started. **Do not** apply if you already have an EIN and are only adding another place of business.

Hired employees.—Check this box if the existing business is requesting an EIN because it has hired or is hiring employees and is therefore required to file employment tax returns. **Do not** apply if you already have an EIN and are only hiring employees. For information on the applicable employment taxes for family members, see **Circular E,** Employer's Tax Guide (Publication 15).

Created a pension plan.—Check this box if you have created a pension plan and need this number for reporting purposes. Also, enter the type of plan created.

Banking purpose.—Check this box if you are requesting an EIN for banking purposes only, and enter the banking purpose (for example, a bowling league for depositing dues or an investment club for dividend and interest reporting).

Changed type of organization.—Check this box if the business is changing its type of organization, for example, if the business was a sole proprietorship and has been incorporated or has become a partnership. If you check this box, specify in the space provided the type of change made, for example, "from sole proprietorship to partnership."

Purchased going business.—Check this box if you purchased an existing business. **Do not** use the former owner's EIN. **Do not** apply for a new EIN if you already have one. Use your own EIN.

Created a trust.—Check this box if you created a trust, and enter the type of trust created.

SAMPLE: IRS Form SS-4 – Instructions

Note: *Do not file this form if you are the grantor/owner of certain revocable trusts. You must use your SSN for the trust. See the Instructions for Form 1041.*

Other (specify).—Check this box if you are requesting an EIN for any reason other than those for which there are checkboxes, and enter the reason.

Line 10.—If you are starting a new business, enter the starting date of the business. If the business you acquired is already operating, enter the date you acquired the business. Trusts should enter the date the trust was legally created. Estates should enter the date of death of the decedent whose name appears on line 1 or the date when the estate was legally funded.

Line 11.—Enter the last month of your accounting year or tax year. An accounting or tax year is usually 12 consecutive months, either a calendar year or a fiscal year (including a period of 52 or 53 weeks). A calendar year is 12 consecutive months ending on December 31. A fiscal year is either 12 consecutive months ending on the last day of any month other than December or a 52-53 week year. For more information on accounting periods, see **Pub. 538,** Accounting Periods and Methods.

Individuals.—Your tax year generally will be a calendar year.

Partnerships.—Partnerships generally must adopt the tax year of either (a) the majority partners; (b) the principal partners; (c) the tax year that results in the least aggregate (total) deferral of income; or (d) some other tax year. (See the **Instructions for Form 1065,** U.S. Partnership Return of Income, for more information.)

REMIC.—REMICs must have a calendar year as their tax year.

Personal service corporations.—A personal service corporation generally must adopt a calendar year unless:

● It can establish a business purpose for having a different tax year, or

● It elects under section 444 to have a tax year other than a calendar year.

Trusts.—Generally, a trust must adopt a calendar year except for the following:

● Tax-exempt trusts,

● Charitable trusts, and

● Grantor-owned trusts.

Line 12.—If the business has or will have employees, enter the date on which the business began or will begin to pay wages. If the business does not plan to have employees, enter N/A.

Withholding agent.—Enter the date you began or will begin to pay income to a nonresident alien. This also applies to individuals who are required to file Form 1042 to report alimony paid to a nonresident alien.

Line 13.—For a definition of agricultural labor (farmworker), see **Circular A,** Agricultural Employer's Tax Guide (Publication 51).

Line 14.—Generally, enter the exact type of business being operated (for example, advertising agency, farm, food or beverage establishment, labor union, real estate agency, steam laundry, rental of coin-operated vending machine, or investment club). Also state if the business will involve the sale or distribution of alcoholic beverages.

Governmental.—Enter the type of organization (state, county, school district, municipality, etc.).

Nonprofit organization (other than governmental).—Enter whether organized for religious, educational, or humane purposes, and the principal activity (for example, religious organization—hospital, charitable).

Mining and quarrying.—Specify the process and the principal product (for example, mining bituminous coal, contract drilling for oil, or quarrying dimension stone).

Contract construction.—Specify whether general contracting or special trade contracting. Also, show the type of work normally performed (for example, general contractor for residential buildings or electrical subcontractor).

Food or beverage establishments.—Specify the type of establishment and state whether you employ workers who receive tips (for example, lounge—yes).

Trade.—Specify the type of sales and the principal line of goods sold (for example, wholesale dairy products, manufacturer's representative for mining machinery, or retail hardware).

Manufacturing.—Specify the type of establishment operated (for example, sawmill or vegetable cannery).

Signature block.—The application must be signed by (a) the individual, if the applicant is an individual, (b) the president, vice president, or other principal officer, if the applicant is a corporation, (c) a responsible and duly authorized member or officer having knowledge of its affairs, if the applicant is a partnership or other unincorporated organization, or (d) the fiduciary, if the applicant is a trust or estate.

Some Useful Publications

You may get the following publications for additional information on the subjects covered on this form. To get these and other free forms and publications, call 1-800-TAX-FORM (1-800-829-3676). You should receive your order or notification of its status within 7 to 15 workdays of your call.

Use your computer.—If you subscribe to an on-line service, ask if IRS information is available and, if so, how to access it. You can also get information through IRIS, the Internal Revenue Information Services, on FedWorld, a government bulletin board. Tax forms, instructions, publications, and other IRS information, are available through IRIS.

♲ *Printed on recycled paper*

IRIS is accessible directly by calling 703-321-8020. On the Internet, you can telnet to fedworld.gov. or, for file transfer protocol services, connect to ftp.fedworld.gov. If you are using the WorldWide Web, connect to http://www.ustreas.gov

FedWorld's help desk offers technical assistance on accessing IRIS (not tax help) during regular business hours at 703-487-4608. The IRIS menus offer information on available file formats and software needed to read and print files. You must print the forms to use them; the forms are not designed to be filled out on-screen.

Tax forms, instructions, and publications are also available on CD-ROM, including prior-year forms starting with the 1991 tax year. For ordering information and software requirements, contact the Government Printing Office's Superintendent of Documents (202-512-1800) or Federal Bulletin Board (202-512-1387).

Pub. 1635, Understanding Your EIN

Pub. 15, Employer's Tax Guide

Pub. 15-A, Employer's Supplemental Tax Guide

Pub. 538, Accounting Periods and Methods

Pub. 541, Tax Information on Partnerships

Pub. 542, Tax Information on Corporations

Pub. 557, Tax-Exempt Status for Your Organization

Pub. 583, Starting a Business and Keeping Records

Package 1023, Application for Recognition of Exemption

Package 1024, Application for Recognition of Exemption Under Section 501(a) or for Determination Under Section 120

Paperwork Reduction Act Notice

We ask for the information on this form to carry out the Internal Revenue laws of the United States. You are required to give us the information. We need it to ensure that you are complying with these laws and to allow us to figure and collect the right amount of tax.

The time needed to complete and file this form will vary depending on individual circumstances. The estimated average time is:

Recordkeeping . . . . . . 7 min.

Learning about the law or the form . . . . . . 18 min.

Preparing the form . . . . . 45 min.

Copying, assembling, and sending the form to the IRS . 20 min.

If you have comments concerning the accuracy of these time estimates or suggestions for making this form simpler, we would be happy to hear from you. You can write to the Tax Forms Committee, Western Area Distribution Center, Rancho Cordova, CA 95743-0001. **Do not** send this form to this address. Instead, see **Where To Apply** on page 2.

*U.S. Government Printing Office: 1996 - 405-493/40061

Meetings

Chapter 8

Board of Directors' Meetings

As a general rule, directors meet periodically throughout the year at regularly stated intervals. The interval can be expressed in the bylaws or it may develop through custom and usage.

Where directors serve as officers and shareholders, the board may not meet formally except during the annual shareholders' meeting. Of course, in such a situation, they meet informally, perhaps even daily, in the active conduct of the corporate business.

Is It a Regular or Special Meeting?

Board of directors' meetings are described as regular or special. Regular meetings are those which are held at regularly scheduled intervals as set forth in the bylaws or according to custom and usage. An annual meeting is a regularly scheduled meeting, usually designated in the bylaws. For example, the bylaws might provide that the annual meeting is to be held on the second Tuesday in December of each year.

Special meetings are meetings which are held other than at a regularly scheduled interval. A special meeting could consider matters of importance, such as a proposed sale or merger of the business, which arise between scheduled meeting dates. Special meetings could also be scheduled to discuss matters raised at a regular meeting which are of significant importance or require greater time for discussion.

Special meetings can be called by anyone authorized by the bylaws to call such a meeting. Ordinarily, the president or chairperson of the board should have this authority; however, the bylaws may authorize any other number of directors or officers to call a special board meeting.

Is Notice of the Meeting Required?

For regular meetings, no additional notice is needed unless the bylaws require it. It is recommended that some notice of the time, date, and place of the meeting be provided, in any event to make certain that a sufficient number of directors attend.

Although not required, it is good practice to provide written notice for all directors' meetings. Include the time, date, and place. For special meetings, a description of the matters to be considered should also be included.

Special meetings require notice.[1] The bylaws should specify whether or not the notice may be personally delivered or must be delivered by mail. A time limitation must be included. For example, the bylaws could require that written notice of meetings be personally delivered to a director or deposited in the mail no earlier than 14 days before the meeting, and no later than 48 hours before the meeting.

Notice requirements can be waived.[2] Matters might arise which require the immediate attention of the board. By attending the meeting, directors waive any objections to lack of notice unless the director states his or her objection at the beginning of the meeting.

Is There an Agenda?

Neither the business corporation act, articles, nor bylaws require an agenda, though it is a good idea to develop an agenda for each meeting to help keep the meeting moving. Items for the agenda include:

- Call to order by the president or chairperson of the board;
- Approval of minutes from previous meeting;
- Treasurer's report;
- Old business (matters carried over from an earlier meeting, including committee reports);
- New business (matters not yet considered by the board);
- Other new business and matters (items not previously considered and not set forth on the agenda); and
- Adjournment.

A sample agenda is shown on the opposite page.

Are Formal Procedures Required?

Most board of directors' meetings tend to be quite informal, especially for small corporations. Directors openly discuss issues before them trying to reach consensus on matters presented. The presiding officer, usually the president or the chairperson, recognizes individuals to speak and must control the tempo and substance of the discussion. It is important that the same arguments for or against an issue aren't repeated.

Larger boards of directors may require more formal procedures to accommodate its size. Time limits should be used to control the length of the discussion and each speaker's portion of the total time.

SAMPLE: Meeting Agenda

John Doe, Inc.
Board of Directors' Meeting Agenda
February 14, 1992

1. Call to order and president's report.
2. Attendance/establishment of quorum.
3. Minutes of previous meeting.
4. Treasurer's report.
5. Reports (should be in writing and submitted in advance).

   a. Committee

   b. Directors

   c. Legal/accounting

   d. Others
6. Old business (matters previously considered but unresolved)
7. New business
8. Miscellaneous news and announcements.
9. Selection of time, place, and location for next meeting.
10. Adjournment.

An agenda will help corporate meetings flow more smoothly and efficiently.

Board proposals are presented in the form of a resolution. To approve a resolution, a motion is made by a director for the approval of a resolution which is read to the board members present at the meeting. The motion must be seconded by another director. If there is no second, the motion dies.

If the motion is seconded, the presiding officer or secretary should read back the motion. Thereafter, the presiding officer asks if there is any further discussion of the motion presented. Discussions range from little or no comment to a wide ranging free for all. At the conclusion of the discussion, the motion is reread and voted on, often by a show of hands or voice vote. If the bylaws require or the directors agree, a secret written ballot vote could be held, but this is rare.

During a discussion, it may become clear that the motion presented is going to fail. It is equally clear that a similar motion with minor modifications will succeed. The presiding officer can permit discussion to continue on the doomed motion, allowing it to fail, and then entertain a new motion containing the modification. This new motion must be seconded, as well, and discussion concerning it must follow.

If the directors approve, the presiding officer could also ask the director making the initial motion if he or she would consider withdrawing or amending his or her motion. If an amended motion is made, it must be seconded, and thereafter, discussion focuses on the amended motion. The vote would be on the amended motion only. If the motion is withdrawn, the process would begin anew for any later motion.

Keep It Simple

The presiding officer bears the burden of keeping things simple. Occasionally, board members aren't certain which form of resolution they are discussing or voting upon. Therefore, a reading of the motion prior to discussion and a rereading prior to the vote should eliminate confusion.

The board of directors does not have to approve or disapprove all matters presented to it and may defer action to a later meeting; refer it to a committee for further study; or request that additional information be provided. Any committee reports or additional information should be provided in advance of the next meeting to allow the directors the opportunity to study the material prior to the meeting. This approach will save time.

What's a Quorum?

A quorum is the minimum number of directors necessary for the board to conduct business. Unless the articles or bylaws require otherwise, a quorum is a majority of the number of directors.[3] If there are 10 directors, at least 6 are required for the board to transact business. If there are 5 or fewer in attendance, the board can discuss corporate matters generally, but can't authorize or approve any corporate action.

If there is no quorum, the bylaws should authorize a majority of those present to adjourn the meeting and reschedule or reconvene the meeting at a later date. As an alternative, the matter could be submitted to the shareholders for approval. This approach may only be feasible when the directors meeting precedes the annual shareholders' meeting. Otherwise, the corporation will incur the expense of sending out notices to the shareholders.

Are There Any Voting Requirements for the Board?

Each board member has one vote on all matters presented. Board members must contribute his or her independent business judgment and act in a manner which he or she believes to be in the best interests of the corporation and not the board. For these reasons, board members, unlike shareholders, may not vote through proxies.

Unless the articles or bylaws impose a more stringent requirement, the affirmative vote of a majority of the directors present at the meeting is sufficient to authorize the matter presented so long as a quorum exists.[5] For example, if 6 members of a 10-member board are present, the affirmative vote of 4 directors can authorize action. In this example, corporate acts are authorized by only 40% of the directors.

As you prepare your articles and bylaws, consider which board of directors' acts should require a higher percentage or super majority vote. Remember that with any fundamental change — amending corporate articles, sale of business, merger or dissolution — the shareholders will also have a say. For nonfundamental changes, such as executive compensation, purchasing assets of another business, or venturing into an unrelated business opportunity, you may wish to consider a higher quorum or voting requirement.

What If a Director Has a Conflict of Interest?

Directors who have a conflict of interest should not vote on matters involving that conflict. Conflict situations include:

- Executive compensation payable to corporate officers who serve on the board;
- Directors or their family members who own property which the corporation seeks to purchase or lease; or
- Directors or their family members who serve on the board of competitors or suppliers.

If a conflict of interest situation arises, the presiding officer must also determine whether or not the board quorum is preserved. For example, 6 of 10 board members attend a board meeting. One of those directors has a conflict on a matter presented to the board. Does a quorum exist? The answer depends in part on whether or not the bylaws permit the interested director to be counted for quorum purposes. If so, the conflict can be avoided if four disinterested directors vote in favor of the matter presented. If not, the matter must be tabled until a quorum of disinterested directors can be assembled.

Because a board cannot act in the absence of a quorum, directors should be surveyed in advance of the meeting to make certain that a quorum will be present. In addition, modern business corporation laws permit meetings to be conducted by conference telephone call, making it easier to achieve a quorum even though one or more directors are physically absent from the meeting location.[4]

Occasionally, a conflict may disqualify the entire board or at least enough members to prevent board approval. In this situation, consider asking the shareholders to approve the transaction. Shareholder approval would be preferred, but the cost and expense of preparing and distributing notice to shareholders may limit its usefulness.

Can Directors Act as a Board without a Meeting?

An example of consent resolutions is found in Chapter 7, pages 132 and 133.

Modern corporation statutes permit a board to act without having a meeting.[6] Instead, all directors must sign their written consent to the corporate resolutions presented. Once all written consents have been received, the matter authorized is as effective as if it had been approved at a formal meeting of the board of directors.

As noted earlier, directors can participate in meetings via telephone conference call. If a quorum can be established by a conference call, corporate actions can be authorized as well. Any action authorized by conference call should be quickly reduced to corporate minutes and circulated among the board for approval.

With the advent of fax machines, proposed resolutions can be immediately transmitted to directors for approval. A director can sign the resolution or list of resolutions and return it by fax to corporate headquarters. If all directors approve, a unanimous consent resolution could be adopted in minutes. If there is no unanimity, a conference call could then substitute for a meeting, and action can be authorized so long as quorum and voting requirements are met.

Don't Rely on Replacing all Meetings with Consent Resolutions

Using consent resolutions exclusively in lieu of meetings can lead to lazy habits. Consent resolutions signed by each of the directors eliminates the need for a formal face-to-face or teleconferenced meeting. Look in the corporate minute books of many small corporations, and you will find nothing more than consent resolutions. There will be one set for directors and one set for shareholders per year. On the directors' resolutions, there will be one resolution appointing officers for the next year and a second resolution ratifying the acts of the board and corporate officers during the previous year. The forms of resolution are copied from one year to the next with little or no focus on what has actually occurred during the year.

What if, unbeknownst to the board of directors, a corporate officer had been paying bribes or receiving kickbacks? Has the board approved this practice by ratifying all acts in a blanket resolution? Has the board breached its duty of due care by approving such a broad resolution? Consent resolutions can be an effective and efficient means of conducting corporate business, but they tend to reduce the effectiveness of the board while at the same time increasing board members liability exposure.

There's another reason why corporations shouldn't become entirely dependent on consent resolutions. Directors should take time during the year to step away from their daily activities in the business to focus on the current and long-term goals of the corporation. This meeting is also an excellent time to bring your business attorney and accountant into the picture.

By keeping your professional advisers up to date with the business, you will save money in the long run. Your advisers can see problems before they occur and plot a course for you to follow so you avoid headaches in the future. Think of it as preventive law — solving problems before they occur. If your professional advisers are kept reasonably current about your business, they will be able to respond more quickly to you in the event that problems do occur. For more information on selecting and effectively using your business attorney, see the discussion in Chapter 16.

Who Serves on the Board of Directors?

The articles of incorporation indicate the number of directors. The articles may also list the name and address of the initial directors. Thereafter, board members are elected by shareholders at the annual meeting. If a vacancy exists on the board, most bylaws permit the board to appoint a director to fill the unexpired term of the director who has created the vacancy.

For small corporations, directors are often shareholders and officers. Larger corporations will seek a mix of inside directors consisting of corporate officers and outside directors consisting of people associated with other businesses. Outside directors are useful because they bring expertise from other businesses or walks of life and because they are able to look at the corporation's activities with a more objective eye.

Some corporations pay directors a fee for attendance at meetings and most will reimburse expenses incurred while traveling to or participating in the meeting.

Final Thoughts on Directors' Meetings

The board of directors governs the general operation of the corporation, sets goals, issues directives for the officers and employees to carry out, and meets at regularly scheduled intervals during the year. Board meetings must be properly called and the requisite notice provided. For the board to take any action, a quorum must be present.

Directors must exercise due care and be careful to disclose all potential conflicts of interest. If a director has a conflict of interest, he or she may not be eligible to vote on corporate matters involving the conflict.

Modern business corporation acts permit boards to meet by telephone, video conference, or similar means. Modern laws also permit consent resolutions whereby all the directors can authorize certain actions merely by signing a written resolution.

Finally, an annual meeting checklist for board of directors which could assist you in conducting a directors' meeting is found on the following page.

Annual Meeting Checklist for Board of Directors

Use this checklist to be sure you cover and document all essential areas in your annual meetings. If anything is still not taken care of by the end of the meeting, note who will be responsible for completing it and by when.

Basic Information to Document

Name of corporation: _____

Date and state of incorporation: _____

Date of meeting and location: _____

Notification procedures   ☐ Notices mailed   ☐ Waivers in   ☐ Consent resolutions instead of meeting?

Officers at meeting: _____

_____

_____

Attorney at meeting: _____

Accountant at meeting: _____

Insurance adviser at meeting: _____

Others present: _____

_____

Check that Government Reports Have Been Filed

Date of last corporate state and federal tax returns: _____

☐ Have state franchise tax and annual reports been filed? _____

☐ Have annual pension/profit-sharing returns been filed with the IRS? _____

☐ Any other filings to be made? _____

Check General Corporate Operations

Review minute book.

    ☐ Are all minutes properly recorded? _____

    ☐ Any additional minutes needed? _____

    ☐ Mailing affidavits or waivers filed? _____

☐ Officers appointed? _____

☐ Review all employment agreements. _____

☐ Check insurance coverages. _____

Check Stock Records

☐ Is stock ledger current? _____

☐ Has stock been properly issued? _____

☐ Restrictive legend added to stock certificates? _____

☐ Have new shareholders signed stock purchase agreement? _____

Annual Meeting Checklist for Board of Directors (continued)

Review Financial Status

Look at financial statements for prior year-end, current year-to-date, and future budget projections. The corporate treasurer is responsible for gathering these reports, but they can be prepared by others in-house or outside.

Income, expenses and salaries: _____

How much cash available for pension/profit sharing? _____

Net profit: _____

☐ Any dividends to be declared? _____

Review accounts receivable and uncollectible items — Any changes in collection required? _____

Approve how to invest cash reserves. _____

☐ Review status of loans to officers or directors. _____

☐ Other? _____

Review Pension/Profit-Sharing Plan

This information comes from the pension plan administrator. Since it is complicated material, you may want to invite the administrator to come in for that portion of the meeting when this is to be discussed.

☐ Verify that new employees have been properly enrolled. _____

☐ Beneficiary designations filed. _____

☐ Verify proper payment, allocations, and reports made for terminating employees. _____

☐ Verify dates for contributions. _____

☐ Review investment policy. _____

☐ Review of investment gains, income and losses. _____

☐ Review procedures to make certain that plans are being operated properly. _____

☐ Advise principals of amounts vested. _____

☐ Annual reports prepared. _____

☐ Amendments to plans required? _____

Review Other Fringe Benefit Programs

☐ Review and update insurance programs.   ☐ Disability   ☐ Health   ☐ Life

☐ Review status of vacation, holiday and leave, and reimbursement policies. _____

☐ Any bonus payments required? _____

☐ Other? _____

Discuss Any Major Events

☐ Acquisitions or purchases? _____

☐ Sales or leases? _____

☐ Litigation? _____

☐ Changes in banking relationship? _____

☐ Loans or financing? _____

☐ Resignations or removals? _____

☐ Other? _____

Chapter 9

Shareholders' Meetings

Business corporation laws and corporate bylaws spend substantially more time discussing issues involving shareholders' meetings than directors' meetings.[1] The reason for this is largely historical. Shareholders, especially minority shareholders, have traditionally been viewed as requiring more protection from the self-interest of officers and directors.

Shareholders' meetings deal with many of the same issues as directors' meetings. The preceding discussion introduced concepts such as meeting notice, quorum, agenda, and procedures. As you read this chapter, you may wish to refer back to the preceding chapter and the sample bylaws found in Chapter 3.

Is It an Annual or Special Meeting?

For shareholders, meeting terminology varies slightly. An annual shareholders' meeting is required by statute and the bylaws.[2] The bylaws will specify the time and date for the meeting. As you will see, consent meetings have eliminated many annual meetings for smaller corporations.

Annual meetings are usually used for the election of directors; to report to the shareholders about the status of the corporation financially and competitively; and to introduce new products or ideas that the corporation is planning to pursue. Other matters may also be presented by the shareholders.

Any shareholders' meeting other than the annual meeting is a special meeting. They are generally called to discuss matters of great significance to the corporation. Fundamental changes to the corporation, for example, would require a special meeting unless presented at the annual meeting.

Who Can Call a Special Meeting?

The bylaws should answer this question. The board of directors can call a special meeting, and if a fundamental change to the corporation is involved, the board is required to call one. The president or other corporate officers or a director acting alone may be able to call a meeting, and shareholders holding a certain percentage of voting shares can call a meeting.

If corporate officers or individual board members are able to call a meeting, consider requiring that at least two officers or two board members must act together to call the meeting. It can be expensive and time consuming to call and conduct a meeting, so controls must exist to limit the possibility that meetings will be called for frivolous purposes.

Similarly, not every shareholder should be able to call a meeting. Bylaws commonly require that the holders of 10 percent or more of the outstanding voting shares of stock can call a meeting. With this requirement, large shareholders can call a meeting. Smaller shareholders would need to join together to call one. By requiring a certain percentage, you can be reasonably certain that the matter to be presented isn't frivolous.

For anyone other than the board to call a special meeting, the corporation must receive a written request, indicating the time and date of the meeting and a general description of the matters to be discussed. Unless another location is indicated, the meeting will occur at the corporation's headquarters. The request must be made by authorized officers or shareholders owning the requisite percentage of stock. No written request is required if the special meeting is called by the board.

Once a written request is received, the corporate secretary must prepare a notice and have it delivered or mailed according to the bylaws.

Is Notice Required?

Unlike board meetings, notice is required for annual and special meetings of shareholders.[3] Business corporation acts often provide that notice of the meeting be given no more than 60 days nor less than 10 days prior to a meeting. This notice is usually prepared by the corporate secretary or at his or her direction.

Notice may be given personally or by first class mail to all shareholders of record on the record date (defined below). Mailed notices are sent to the shareholder's address shown in the corporate records.

The secretary or person preparing, mailing, or delivering the notices should prepare an affidavit attesting to the mailing or delivery of notices. This affidavit should be retained as a corporate record. A sample form of notice and a sample affidavit attesting to the mailing of the notice are provided on the following pages.

Shareholders can waive notice.[4] This can be done by signing a written waiver of notice or by attending and participating in the shareholders meeting without objection. Two sample forms of waiver of notice are shown on page 165.

SAMPLE: Notice of Annual Meeting of Shareholders

Notice of Annual Meeting of Shareholders

To: The Shareholders of John Doe, Inc.

In accordance with the bylaws of the corporation, please be advised that the annual meeting of shareholders will be held at the principal office of the corporation located at 111 Main Street, Anytown, Oregon at 10:00 A.M., P.S.T., on Monday, December 14, 1992, to consider the following:

1. The election of directors to serve until the next annual meeting of shareholders or until their successors are elected and qualified;

2. [Add any other issues known to be dealt with at the meeting.]; and

3. To transact such other business as may properly be brought before the meeting.

Respectfully submitted,

_____
Corporate Secretary

A similar form may be used for special meetings of the shareholders. The heading should be modified to replace the word annual with the word special. Also, eliminate items 2 and 3. Remember that the notice for special meetings must detail the meeting's purpose.

SAMPLE: Affidavit of Mailing Meeting Notice

Affidavit of Mailing Meeting Notice

State of _____

County of _____

The undersigned, being first duly sworn, states as follows:

1. The undersigned is the duly elected and acting secretary of John Doe, Inc.

2. As secretary, the undersigned caused to be deposited in the United States mail, postage prepaid, the meeting notice attached hereto and by this reference incorporated herein, properly addressed and mailed to the persons and at the addresses set forth in the attached list which is by this reference, incorporated herein.

3. The notices were deposited in the mail on _____, 1992.

Date: _____

_____
Corporate Secretary

Subscribed and sworn to before me this _____, 1992.

My commission expires:

_____

_____
Notary Public

SAMPLE: Waiver of Notice – Directors' Meeting

Waiver of Notice

The undersigned, a director of John Doe, Inc., hereby waives notice of the meeting of the board of directors of John Doe, Inc. to be held on February 14, 1992.

_____

John Doe, Director

_____

Date

If you conduct an actual shareholders or directors meeting, you must comply with the notice provisions of your bylaws or corporation statute. Providing notice can be time-consuming and expensive. Make sure you do it right the first time. If notice provisions are not complied with, you may have to renotice and/or reschedule the meeting. As an alternative, shareholders and directors can waive notice by signing a written waiver like those shown at left.

SAMPLE: Waiver of Notice – Shareholders' Meeting

Waiver of Notice

The undersigned, a shareholder of John Doe, Inc., hereby waives notice of the meeting of shareholders of John Doe, Inc. to be held on February 14, 1992.

_____

John Doe, Shareholder

_____

Date

It is good practice to send a notice of meeting to each shareholder of record whether or not that shareholder has voting rights. Include in the notice a description of all matters which you know will be presented. For special meetings, you are limited to those topics described in the notice, but at annual meetings, additional issues may also be considered. For annual meetings, include in your notice the language, "and such other matters as may be properly presented."

Who Gets the Notice of Meeting?

All shareholders of record as of the record date are entitled to receive notice of the meeting. The record date is that date fixed by the board of directors for determining who receives notice. If the board does not fix a record date, the business corporation act or bylaws may set a record date.[5] For example, the bylaws could declare that the record date for any special meeting of shareholders is that date 70 days prior to the scheduled meeting date. If no record date is designated, as in the case of a special meeting called by shareholders, the record date would be the date the request for special meeting is signed by the requesting shareholders.

A shareholders' list is prepared as of the record date, showing the name and address of each shareholder as of that date. If different classes of stock have been issued, the shareholders' list will also include a description of the class of shares held and whether or not that class has voting rights.

The shareholders list is available for inspection and copying by any shareholder or his or her agent.[6] The list may be used by other shareholders to contact shareholders, solicit proxies, or to simply determine the accuracy of the list. The list should also be available at the shareholders' meeting.

Is a Quorum Required?

Yes, but there's a common misconception about shareholders' meetings and quorum. To illustrate, John Doe, Inc. has three shareholders. John owns 20 shares; Joan owns 25 shares; and Jane owns 55 shares. No other shares are issued and outstanding. John Doe, Inc.'s bylaws define a quorum to be a majority of the issued and outstanding stock. At first glance, one might think that a quorum for John Doe, Inc. would exist if at least two of the three shareholders attend. In fact, a quorum will exist only if Jane is present. Only Jane holds more than half of the issued and outstanding stock of John Doe, Inc. If Jane isn't there in person or by proxy, there is no quorum.

Unless the articles or bylaws require a higher percentage, shareholders owning a majority of the issued and outstanding voting stock must be present at a meeting to constitute a quorum.[7] Shareholders, unlike directors, can be represented by others (a proxy) and need not be personally present at the meeting for quorum and voting purposes.

Who Can Vote at a Shareholders' Meeting?

Any shareholder owning voting shares on the record date can vote.[8] Generally, one vote may be cast for each share held. Shareholders owning nonvoting shares may be entitled to vote on any matters which would affect their class. For example, if a motion was proposed to amend the articles to eliminate nonvoting preferred shares, the holders of those shares would be permitted to vote on this issue. Fundamental changes to the corporation may also require the vote of nonvoting shares.

What is a Proxy?

A proxy is a representative appointed to act in another's place. Shareholders may appoint a proxy to vote their shares at shareholder meetings. To be effective, a proxy must be in writing and must designate the person or persons authorized to vote on behalf of the shareholder.[9] A designation of "my brother" is insufficient. "My brother Robert L. Doe" would be adequate.

Proxies are generally effective for up to 11 months unless earlier revoked. Proxies are easily revoked, and the last proxy in time prevails over any earlier proxy appointments. A proxy can also be revoked if the shareholder shows up at the meeting and decides to vote his or her shares personally.

You may occasionally hear the expression, "coupled with an interest." A proxy coupled with an interest is irrevocable. For example, you own stock in John Doe, Inc. You need to borrow money to pay off some personal loans. Your good friend Bob agrees to loan you the money, but only if you pledge your John Doe, Inc. stock to him as security for repayment of the loan. Bob asks for an irrevocable proxy to allow him to vote your shares until the loan is repaid. This combination of proxy and pledge is a proxy coupled with an interest. The proxy should state conspicuously on its face that it is irrevocable.

Proxies can also be revoked upon the death or incapacity of a shareholder; however, a corporation can honor a proxy until it knows of the shareholder's death or incapacity.

As the number of shareholders grows, the use of proxies becomes more common. A sample proxy is shown on the following page.

Can the Corporation Reject a Proxy or a Shareholder's Vote?

A corporation can reject the vote of a shareholder or his or her proxy if the corporation has a good faith reason for doing so. For example, if the corporation believes that a signature on a proxy has been forged or the person presenting it can't adequately identify himself or herself, it may reject the proxy. Similarly, if the name of the proxy appears to have been altered, the proxy may be rejected. These situations do not commonly occur.

What is Cumulative Voting?

Cumulative voting is a technique used by some corporations in the election of directors. It is designed to protect the interests of minority shareholders by enhancing the ability of minority shareholders to elect at least one director to the board. It's complicated and applies, if at all, only to the election of directors.

Here's how cumulative voting works: The articles of John Doe, Inc. provide for three directors. John, Joan, and Jane are the only shareholders of John Doe, Inc. John owns 25 shares, and Joan and Jane own 30 shares each. There are no other issued and outstanding shares. At the annual meeting,

A proxy is a written authorization which permits an individual or entity so named in the proxy to vote your shares. As a general rule, proxies are always revocable and may easily be revoked.

Before you sign a proxy, check with the corporate secretary to see if it must be notarized. You should also review the bylaws to see if any other proxy requirements exist.

SAMPLE: Proxy

Proxy

KNOW ALL MEN BY THESE PRESENTS, that the undersigned shareholder of John Doe, Inc., an Oregon corporation (the "Corporation"), hereby constitutes and appoints Carl Sniffen, the true and lawful attorney and proxy of the undersigned. The proxy shall be entitled to attend and represent the undersigned at any and all meetings of the shareholders of the Corporation, to be held either by special call or pursuant to other applicable provisions of the bylaws of the Corporation, and for and on behalf of the undersigned to vote on any question, proposition or resolution, or any other matter or adjournments thereof, according to the number of shares of stock of the Corporation which the undersigned is entitled to vote. This power of attorney and proxy shall be revocable upon written notice received by the duly elected secretary of the Corporation.

_____   _____

John Doe   Date

[Add notary lanquage if the corporation requires it.]

three directors are to be elected. If cumulative voting applies, each shareholder has the right to cast three (the number of directors to be elected) times the number of shares owned by each. John would have 75 votes (3 multiplied by 25), and Joan and Jane would each have 90 votes (3 multiplied by 30). The votes could be distributed in any manner the shareholders choose. Presumably, John will cast all 75 votes in his favor to retain his seat on the board.

If cumulative voting doesn't exist, John would have only 25 votes, and his ability to retain a seat on the board would be substantially reduced.

Like preemptive rights, cumulative voting exists automatically in some states unless the articles provide otherwise. In other states, cumulative voting doesn't exist, unless the articles state that it does. Once again, there is an opportunity for flexibility that you won't know about if you simply fill in blanks on form articles of incorporation.

If cumulative voting exists in the election of directors, the meeting notice must conspicuously say so.

For larger boards, you can reduce the impact of cumulative voting by staggering the terms of the board. For example, a nine-member board could serve three-year terms with one-third of directors being elected each year. Such an approach provides continuity and assures a carryover of experienced directors.

What's an Election Inspector?

Election inspectors are individuals designated by the board or shareholders to make certain that shareholder meetings and matters voted on at shareholders meetings are conducted in accordance with law and the bylaws. Election inspectors will:

- Determine the validity and authority of proxies;
- Determine the existence of a quorum;
- Hear challenges to voting rights or proxies; and
- Count ballots and announce results.[10]

Are Secret Ballots Used?

Most matters presented to the shareholders are determined by a show of hands or voice vote, at least with respect to noncontroversial or uncontested matters. If a matter is contested or controversial, a semi-secret ballot system should be used. Checks must be implemented to make certain that no one votes more shares than he or she owns. Because of these checks, the ballot may not be entirely secret. Election inspectors may learn the identity of shareholders casting ballots to make certain that the number of shares voted is consistent with the number of shares owned.

If your corporation has more than four or five shareholders, develop a voting plan for your shareholders' meetings. You may never need to use it, but the system should be in place in advance.

What if There's Unfinished Business or No Quorum?

If this occurs, adjourn the meeting and announce a time and date at which the meeting will reconvene. Your bylaws should permit a meeting to be adjourned until a later date. Statutes usually permit this continuation and will not require that the notice requirements be complied with a second time

By adjourning and later reconvening a meeting, a corporation can save the time and expense associated with formally calling a meeting and providing notice.

if the reconvened meeting is scheduled to take place within a certain time, generally within 120 days of the original meeting date. This process works equally well for situations where no quorum exists or where a quorum exists but not all business is completed.

Your bylaws should provide that if no quorum exists, a majority of those present can adjourn the meeting and schedule a date to reconvene. This is one of the few actions which can be authorized by less than a quorum.

Can Shareholders Act without a Meeting?

Modern business corporation acts permit shareholders to act without a meeting by using consent resolutions.[11] This subject matter has been discussed previously in Chapter 8 with respect to directors. The same issues and caveats are equally applicable.

If the shareholders are all active in the business, consent resolutions may be an expeditious way to handle meetings. After all, each shareholder is likely to be keenly aware of what the corporation is doing anyway.

If shareholders are not active in the business, a formal annual meeting is a good way for shareholders to see and meet with management. Officers and directors can explain what the corporation has done over the past year and what its goals are for the coming year. It is an excellent public relations opportunity.

Consent resolutions are impractical if the number of shareholders is too large or too geographically diverse. Formal meetings will need to be noticed and conducted. The same is true if there are dissident shareholders who tend to disagree with board proposals.

Like board consent resolutions, shareholder consent resolutions often do no more than elect management's slate of directors and ratify acts of the board and officers during the preceding year. A general ratification of acts by the board or officers can be costly. For example, a board acting more in its own self-interest than the corporation's may authorize an action that is not in the best interests of the corporation. Does a general ratification of acts by consent resolution insulate the board from later claims of breach of the duty of loyalty? Although one could argue that the acts of the board aren't protected because the board failed to make a full disclosure, the possibility that the board action has been ratified and approved by the shareholders exists.

Final Thoughts on Shareholders' Meetings

Many closely held corporations avoid formal shareholders' meetings. Shareholders meet periodically without written notice to discuss corporate business, elect directors, and plan for the future. More often than not, someone will write up minutes of the meeting, obtain the signatures of the president and secretary on the minutes, and place the minutes in the corporate minute book.

Today, many business lawyers provide a written form of consent resolutions for their corporate clients. The consent form is circulated among the shareholders for signature. When signed, the resolutions are placed in the corporate minute book. It's easy and convenient. What is lost is the opportunity to carefully reflect on the activities of the corporation and its officers and directors, and to raise questions or offer suggestions about past, present, or future operations.

Unfortunately, where you are dealing with a large group of shareholders or where one or more of the shareholders tends to be disgruntled, formal shareholder meetings are required. In these situations, your corporate bylaws should be close at hand. Your bylaws should describe in detail the requirements to properly notice and conduct a meeting. Many lawsuits have resulted where a corporation has failed to comply with the meetings' requirements of its bylaws.

Your bylaws will address important issues, such as what matters can be raised at a shareholders meeting and what shareholders are eligible to vote on business presented at the meeting. Suffice it to say that attention to detail is a must when preparing for a formal shareholders' meeting.

An annual meeting checklist for shareholders which will assist you in conducting a directors' or shareholders' meeting is presented on the next page.

Annual Meeting Checklist for Shareholders

The shareholders' meeting does not have to examine as many areas as the board of directors' meeting. This checklist shows what the shareholders' meeting should cover. After these matters have been discussed, the shareholders attending may bring up additional issues. You may also wish to include information described in the preceding Annual Meeting Checklist for Board of Directors on page 158.

Basic Information to Document

Name of corporation: _____

Date and state of incorporation: _____

Date of meeting and location: _____

Notification procedures   ☐ Notices mailed   ☐ Waivers in   ☐ Consent resolutions instead of meeting?

Officers at meeting: _____

Attorney at meeting: _____

Accountant at meeting: _____

Insurance adviser at meeting: _____

Shareholders at meeting: _____

Others present: _____

☐ Elect directors.

☐ Any changes required for bylaws or articles?

☐ Review stock purchase agreement.

☐ Any changes required to valuation in stock purchase agreement?

Discuss Any Major Events

☐ Acquisitions or purchases?

☐ Sales or leases?

☐ Litigation?

☐ Resignations or removals?

☐ Other?

Why You Should Care

Chapter 10

Suing and Being Sued as a Corporation

A corporation is a distinct legal entity. As long as requisite formality and mechanics are followed, anyone with a claim against a corporation must look to the corporation for relief. Directors, officers, shareholders, and others are shielded from personal liability by the veil of the corporation. This is true in most instances even though the corporation lacks sufficient assets to pay the claim.

Similarly, when the corporation has a claim against a third party, the corporation, itself, brings the claim. If a supplier fails to deliver promised goods in a timely manner, the corporation can file a claim against the supplier. If a motorist drives his or her car into the corporation's delivery truck, the corporation may seek relief against the motorist.

The Corporation Sues

This part is easy. If a corporation has a claim, it may file a lawsuit in its own name, thus becoming the plaintiff. The complaint must comply with applicable rules of court; the time within which the complaint can be filed; and service of process. The corporation may have to qualify as a foreign corporation in that state prior to filing its complaint.

Of course, a corporation can't act by itself, and therefore, its interests in the complaint must be advanced by an agent. Many states require that corporation's be represented by licensed attorneys in such matters. Corporate directors, officers, or employees may not appear on behalf of the corporation unless such an individual is licensed as an attorney. This principle applies to judicial proceedings and administrative matters as well.

Unlike individuals who may always represent themselves — known as appearing *pro se* — corporations may not represent themselves in many states without an attorney. Check with the local bar association in your state to see if your corporation is required to be represented by an attorney in judicial or administrative proceedings.

The Corporation Is Sued

Because it is a distinct legal entity, corporations can be sued. Complaints can be filed and heard against corporations in courts and in administrative proceedings. These suits and proceedings can be filed in any jurisdiction where the corporation is engaged in business regardless of where the corporation's principal place of business is located.

For example, John Doe, Inc., an Oregon corporation, is engaged in business in Oregon, Washington, Idaho, and Maine. Conceivably, a complaint against the corporation could be filed in any of these states. Local court or administrative rules may be used on occasion to dismiss or transfer actions which are filed in one jurisdiction for the sole apparent purpose of inconveniencing the person or entity against which the claim has been filed.

When a corporation is sued or an administrative claim is filed against it, notice of the law suit and a copy of the complaint are ordinarily served on the corporation's registered agent at the registered office. This means of service of process is not exclusive. Service can often be obtained by serving a corporate officer at the principal place of business or by serving an office manager at this location. Local court rules govern who can be served with the complaint and the manner and sufficiency of the service.

Shareholder Suits

A particular type of lawsuit filed against corporations are suits which are filed by shareholders. These types of actions are generally divided into two classes: individual suits and derivative suits.

Individual Suits

In an individual suit, a shareholder seeks redress against the corporation for a wrong which has occurred to the shareholder. For example, if the corporation breached a contract which it had entered into with the shareholder, the shareholder could file suit against the corporation. If successful, the shareholder would recover damages from the corporation for breach of contract. Similarly, a shareholder injured as a result of the negligence of a corporate employee engaged in corporate business could sue the corporation.

Individual suits are often maintained to compel a corporation to issue a stock certificate, permit inspection of corporate books and records, or to permit the shareholder to vote on corporate matters. With individual suits, the right to sue belongs to the individual shareholder wronged by a corporate action, and any recovery belongs to the shareholder.

Derivative Suits

Derivative suits are claims which are filed on behalf of another. For corporations, derivative suits involve a harm to the corporation which the corporation is unable to redress. For example, assume that the officers and directors of John Doe, Inc. misappropriate funds which belong to the corporation. The corporation has been damaged by this action, but because the officers and directors control the daily operations of the business, the corporation, by itself, is unable to seek relief.

In such a situation, one or more shareholders could bring a derivative action against the offending officers and directors to seek relief. For procedural purposes, the shareholder(s) would file a suit against the directors and officers and the corporation as well. Any recovery would be paid to the corporation. Some states permit successful shareholders to recover attorneys fees in derivative actions.

Derivative actions can also be maintained when an officer or director breaches any of the duties owed by the officer or director to the corporation or otherwise pursues a course of conduct detrimental to the corporation.

The law imposes a number of additional procedural safeguards to deter the filing of derivative lawsuits by disgruntled shareholders. Without these safeguards, many more of these suits would be filed at great expense to the corporation. The safeguards include:

- The shareholder filing the action must have been a shareholder at the time of the alleged harm (unless the shareholder acquired his or her shares by operation of law from a deceased shareholder who was a shareholder at the time of the harm).

- The complaint must allege with particularity that the shareholder has made a demand on the board of directors for relief prior to filing the suit and that the demand was refused.

- If no demand was made, the complaint must state in detail why no demand was made or why the shareholder believes that any such demand would be futile.

- Once filed, the suit may be dismissed or settled only upon approval of the court.

- In some jurisdictions, the shareholder filing the complaint must maintain his or her status as shareholder throughout the proceedings.

Final Thoughts on Lawsuits

Suffice it to say, this is a litigious society. Lots of reasons are offered for this state of affairs. Many blame it on the lawyers; others attribute it to a lottery mentality of a large segment of the population. As with other things in life, there are probably a lot of factors working in combination which cause this situation.

As a lawyer, I often tell my business clients, "Anybody can sue anyone at anytime for anything." This philosophy doesn't bring a smile to many faces.

It does, however, focus my client's attention on prevention. What can a business person do to minimize the risk of costly litigation? From a corporate standpoint, the issues described throughout this book provide many answers. Follow requisite corporate formalities and mechanics, and buy insurance.

Chapter 11

Horror Stories

Introduction

Why be concerned with all of this paperwork and formality? Are there any shortcuts? There are a number of reasons for concern.

- Business corporation laws require articles of incorporation and bylaws and specify other things that must occur.
- Articles of incorporation and bylaws form a contract between the corporation and its shareholders, obligating the corporation to act in accordance with the articles and bylaws.
- Board members and officers owe the corporation and shareholders a fiduciary duty to use good faith, exercise due care, and act in the best interests of the corporation.
- Majority shareholders must act in good faith, in a manner not calculated to oppress the rights of minority shareholders.
- Corporate formality must be respected and observed to preserve the integrity of the corporation and to shield officers, directors, and shareholders or related businesses from personal liability.
- Good recordkeeping habits and paying attention to detail are necessary for any successful business, regardless of whether it is incorporated or not.

Without question, you want to focus on running your business. Yet, paperwork is a part of every business. Like death and taxes, it is unavoidable. Get started on the right foot by building recordkeeping into the routine of your business.

This chapter explores several legal theories which have been used to impose liability on individuals or parent corporations. The term most often used to describe this process is "piercing the corporate veil." Several cases will be used to illustrate this doctrine later in this chapter. After reading these cases, you will be struck by the absolute lack of demonstrated formality and attention to detail.

You may think that it could never happen to you. Hopefully, this is true. Understanding the importance of formality and attention to detail, as well as compliance with applicable statutes, articles, and bylaws will preserve your corporate status and shield you from personal liability. You must develop good recordkeeping habits from the beginning. This is essential.

The cases presented also highlight the variety of contexts in which piercing the veil cases can arise. In effect, any type of claim which can be asserted against a corporation, whether it be contract, tort, government claim or other, can be the subject of an attempt to pierce the corporate veil.

To help you avoid personal liability for corporate acts, a partial checklist of do's and don'ts is provided for your convenience at the end of this chapter.

Disregarding the Corporate Entity

As noted throughout this book, a corporation's separateness must be recognized and acknowledged by the acts of the directors, officers, and shareholders. Courts have long recognized the distinct legal status of the corporation, and courts are reluctant to disregard the corporate status. Although reluctant, courts will pierce the corporate veil in appropriate circumstances.

A number of different legal theories have been used to impose personal liability on individuals or parent corporations in the case of subsidiaries. Some of these theories require that the court disregard the corporate entity or pierce the corporate veil. Not all claims against individuals require that the corporate status be disregarded, however.

Claims can be asserted against directors, officers, and shareholders without disregarding the corporate veil. For example, federal and state tax laws generally impose personal liability on those individuals responsible for preparing and filing income and sales tax returns. The government agency can bring civil and criminal tax claims against the corporation or the responsible individual, or both. There is no reason to examine corporate formality or attempt to disregard the corporate entity.

The same is true for criminal acts and intentional torts. If the officer, director, or shareholder knowingly and voluntarily participated in any aspect of the crime or tort, he or she can be personally liable without piercing the corporate veil. Of course, an aggressive plaintiff's attorney will probably bring claims against the individuals and the corporation using a number of legal theories, including ones which would seek to pierce the veil.

It is also important to note that most piercing the veil cases involve corporations where the shareholders are also the officers and directors. Control is an important concept in these cases. Legal theories commonly used against directors or shareholders who are not shareholders or who only own small amounts of stock involve breach of the duties of due care or loyalty. These duties are described in Chapter 4.

Instrumentality/Alter Ego

The two most common theories used to justify the imposition of personal liability in disregard of the corporate entity are the alter ego theory and the instrumentality rule. Historically, the instrumentality rule applied only to parent/subsidiary situations, but it now seems to apply beyond that context as well.

The alter ego theory says, in effect, that if the shareholders of a corporation disregard the legal separateness of the corporation or proper formality, then the law will also disregard the corporate form if required to protect individual and corporate creditors.[1]

The instrumentality rule has three components, including:

- The shareholder(s) must completely dominate the finances, policy, and business practices of the corporation to the extent that the corporate entity at the time of the transaction had no separate mind, will, or existence of its own. Ownership of all or substantially of the stock of the corporation, alone, is not complete domination.
- The control or domination is used to commit fraud or wrong, to cause the violation of a statute, breach a legal duty, or commit a dishonest or unjust act in violation of the claimant's legal rights.
- The domination and violation of legal rights must have proximately caused the injury to the claimant.[2]

As noted, the instrumentality rule originally developed as a means to impose liability on a parent corporation for the acts of its subsidiary. Often times, subsidiaries were grossly undercapitalized and effectively judgment proof. To remedy this injustice, creditors of the subsidiary were permitted to pierce the veil of the subsidiary and bring claims against the parent corporation.

Courts have blurred the distinctions between the alter ego and instrumentality theories, and many cases use both terms interchangeably. For the purposes of this discussion, the factors examined by the courts in deciding whether to pierce the corporate veil are the same under either theory. In fact, many of the criteria examined are relevant for claims based on breach of fiduciary duty against officers or directors or on criminal law or tort theories.

Before looking at specific cases to illustrate these theories and the criteria used, it is worth recalling that courts are reluctant to pierce the corporate veil. However, courts will strain to permit the piercing whenever its failure to do so could produce an unjust result. If your undercapitalized business seriously injures a bystander, and you have no insurance to cover the injuries, a court will work hard to impose personal liability on you. It is public policy that businesses should be adequately capitalized to meet the reasonable needs of the business including all foreseeable claims.

Contract and Tort Claims

Courts are more apt to pierce the veil in a tort case than they are in a contract case. A tort is any action or failure to act (when there is a duty to act) that causes damage to another. Examples of tort actions include personal injuries, fraud, misrepresentation, negligence, batter, assault, trespass, and invasion of privacy. In a general sense, any claim not based on a contract could be a tort claim.

Once again, a policy decision of the courts comes into play. It is presumed that contract creditors entered a contract voluntarily with an opportunity to find out for themselves about the corporation. If a contract creditor was not diligent in protecting itself at the time of contract, courts are not likely to pierce the corporate veil in the absence of extreme circumstances. Unlike contract creditors, tort claimants rarely volunteer or have an opportunity to find out about the corporation in advance. Of course, many contract claimants will include a claim for fraud and seek recovery directly from the individuals involved in the fraud.

As you review the cases described below, keep in mind that no single criteria is controlling. In almost every instance, the corporation has failed to satisfy a number of criteria. For example, owning all of the stock of the corporation, alone, is not enough to pierce the corporate veil. The same is true where one serves as sole officer and director as well. Look for several factors — such as absence of corporate records or minutes, inadequate capitalization, a serious harm to third parties, commingling of personal and corporate assets, etc. — working in combination.

Taxicab Cases

Every law student studies two or three taxicab cases. Most react with a mixture of horror and amazement that a business could be operated in such a manner. Interestingly, many cab companies still operate in the manner described below.

In *Mull v. Colt*,[3] the plaintiff, Mull, suffered serious injuries when he was struck by a cab driven by Fermaglick. Fermaglick had no assets and was judgment proof, so Mull sued Colt Company, the owner of the cab. At the time of the accident, New York law required that cabs maintain at least $5,000 in liability insurance. The state intended that the $5,000 be a minimum amount, but as might be expected, that's all any cab company carried.

In the course of discovery, Mull learned that Ackerman and Goodman owned all of the stock of Colt Company. Ackerman and Goodman also owned all of the stock of 100 other corporations, each of which owned two cabs and a $5,000 liability insurance policy. All 200 cabs were garaged, maintained, and dispatched from a single location.

If the court did not permit the corporate veil to be pierced, Mull, who spent 209 days in the hospital and endured 20 surgeries, could have only recovered a wrecked cab and $5,000. The court noted that the use of multiple shell corporations each carrying the minimum statutory insurance clearly perverted the legislative intent, and held, "When the statutory privilege of doing business in the corporate form is employed as a cloak for the evasion of obligations, as a mask behind which to do injustice or invoked to subvert equity, the separate personality of the corporation will be disregarded."[4]

Wallace v. Tulsa Yellow Cab Taxi & Baggage Co.[5] also involved a plaintiff who was injured by a taxi. Wallace sued the cab company and recovered a judgment. Unfortunately for Wallace, by the time he tried to collect on the judgment, the cab company had gone out of business. Or did it?

The court permitted Wallace to recover from Tulsa Yellow Cab, a successor corporation. Here are the factors the judge relied upon:

- The taxi business is hazardous by nature (great potential for harm).
- The only asset of the new corporation was $1,000 of paid in stock (inadequate capital).
- The new corporation leased cabs from the old corporation pursuant to a lease which was terminable on 24 hours notice (an unusual provision).
- Although the shareholders of the new corporation were different, the shareholders were former employees of the old corporation and financed the purchase of their stock by money loaned to them by the shareholder of the old company (an unusual procedure with no obvious business purpose).
- The management of the new corporation was the same as the old corporation, so in effect, the corporation's were the same.[6]

In both of these cases, the courts relied upon inadequate capitalization and control as key criteria for piercing the corporate veil. The severity of the harm to the claimants was also a significant factor.

Personal Injury

Of course, all personal injuries aren't the result of taxis. In *Geringer v. Wildhorse Ranch, Inc.*,[7] a widow sued for the wrongful death of her husband and children who were killed in a paddleboat accident at a Colorado ranch. The action was filed against Wildhorse Ranch, Inc. and its principal shareholder. The court pierced the corporate veil noting:

- No corporate stock had been issued in the corporation and no record of the stock existed (absence of records and formality).
- No corporate minutes existed even though the defendant testified that informal board meetings had been conducted (no minutes).
- The principal shareholder operated several corporations out of one office (absence of separation between corporations).
- Debts of one corporation were frequently paid with funds of another corporation or from the principal shareholder's personal funds (commingling; no arm's length dealings).
- The principal shareholder had purchased the paddleboats with funds from another corporation (commingling, related party transaction).

- No record of loans or ledgers existed (no loan documentation).
- Corporate records were so muddled that no clear picture of accountability or organization could be shown (poor recordkeeping).
- Business cards listed the principal shareholder as the "owner" of the corporation (improper way to hold corporation out to public).
- Employees of the corporation believed that the principal shareholder was in control (agency, public perception).
- The principal shareholder knew that the paddleboats leaked and became unstable and overruled employee recommendations that the boats be repaired (active wrongdoing on the part of shareholder).[8]

Contract Creditors

Although a court is more likely to pierce a corporate veil in a tort situation, it will pierce the veil in an appropriate contract situation. The case of *Labadie Coal Co. v. Black*[9] is a good example. There, creditors were able to pierce the veil of a trading corporation and recover against controlling shareholders. The court examined these factors:

- The controlling shareholders owned all of the corporate stock and controlled corporate decisions.
- The corporation failed to maintain corporate minutes or adequate records, including articles of incorporation, bylaws, or a current list of directors.
- No formalities pertaining to the issuance of corporate stock were followed.
- Funds were commingled with funds and assets of other corporations.
- Corporate funds were diverted to the personal use of the shareholders.
- The corporation and the shareholders used the same office for different business activities.
- The corporation was inadequately capitalized.[10]

The court noted that fraud was not required to pierce the corporate veil. All that was required was the presence of an unjust situation. The court also stated:

"Faithfulness to the formalities is the price paid to the corporate fiction, a relatively small price to pay for limited liability. Furthermore, the formalities are themselves an excellent litmus of the extent to which the individuals involved actually view the corporation as a separate being."[11]

Government Claims

Government agencies can pursue many of the same claims as nongovernmental persons and entities. Tort claims and contract claims are not limited to the private sector. For example, in *United States v. Healthwise-Midtown Convalescent Hospital and Rehabilitation Center, Inc.*,[12] the government sought to recover excess payments of Medicare benefits paid to the hospital. The hospital's corporate charter had been revoked for failing to pay required state taxes. The action was pursued against the owner of 50% of the hospital's outstanding stock. The court identified the following factors in ruling in favor of the government:

- The principal shareholder owned 50% of the hospital's stock and 50% of the partnership interests of the partnership which owned the real estate upon which the hospital was built and the furnishings used by the hospital.
- The principal shareholder served as president, a board member, and administrator of the hospital (control).
- Other board members did not attend board meetings. (Note the potential for a claim of breach of duty of care against the non-attending directors.)
- The principal shareholder had check writing authority and controlled the affairs of the corporation.
- The corporation was inadequately capitalized, with liabilities in excess of $150,000 and capital of $10,000.
- Regular board meetings were not conducted (lack of formality).
- Funds were commingled.
- Corporate assets were diverted from the corporation.
- The principal shareholder failed to maintain an arm's length relationship when dealing with the corporation, the partnership and the shareholder. Here, the partnership was paid amounts due and owing to it by the corporation in full, to the detriment of corporate creditors.[13]

The court in *Securities and Exchange Commission v. Elmas Trading Corp.*[14] provided a detailed list of factors to be considered by the court in determining whether or not to pierce the corporate veil. In this case, 16 separate entities consisting of corporations and partnerships were disregarded. The court noted that no one factor was determinative. Rather, all of the facts and circumstances had to be considered in each case. The criteria listed by the court included:

- Failure to observe corporate formalities;
- Nonpayment of dividends;
- Insolvency of the corporation at the time of the transaction;
- Siphoning funds of the corporation by the dominant shareholder;
- Nonfunctioning of other officers or directors;
- Absence of corporate records;
- Use of the same office or business location by the corporation and its individual shareholders;
- Commingling of funds and other assets;
- Unauthorized diversion of corporate assets to other business activities or personal accounts of the shareholders;
- Failure to maintain minutes or adequate corporate records of separate corporate businesses;
- Common ownership of stock between two or more corporations;
- Identical persons serving as officers and/or directors of two or more corporations;

- The absence of corporate assets;
- The use of a corporation as a mere shell, instrumentality, or conduit for a single venture or the business of an individual or another corporation;
- The concealment and misrepresentation of the identity of the responsible ownership, management and financial interest of a corporation or the concealment of personal business activities;
- Failure to maintain an arm's length relationship in transactions between related entities;
- Use of a corporate entity to procure labor, services, or merchandise for another person or entity to the detriment of creditors;
- The manipulation of assets and liabilities between entities so as to concentrate the assets in one and liabilities in another;
- The contracting with another with the intent to avoid performance by the use of a corporation as a subterfuge of illegal transactions; and
- The formation and use of a corporation to transfer to it the existing liability of another person or entity.[15]

Parent as Alter Ego of Subsidiary

When one corporation owns all or substantially all of the voting stock of another corporation, the corporation owning the stock is the parent corporation, and the other corporation is the subsidiary. Historically, the instrumentality rule has been used to impose liability on the parent for activities of the subsidiary. The veil of the parent and subsidiary could potentially be pierced to impose liability on controlling shareholders.

In one case, *Miles v. American Telephone & Telegraph Company,*[16] the court refused to pierce the veil and impose liability on the parent corporation. There, the parent and subsidiary maintained their relationship on an arm's length basis. In another, *Sabine Towing & Transportation Co., Inc. v. Merit Ventures, Inc.,*[17] the subsidiary's veil was pierced.

In *Miles v. American Telephone & Telegraph Company*, the plaintiff, *Miles*, filed a lawsuit against AT&T alleging tortious invasion of plaintiff's privacy by Southwestern Bell, a subsidiary of AT&T. The court granted summary judgment in AT&T's favor, dismissing it from the lawsuit. Listed below are subsidiary activities deemed to be significant by the court not to pierce the corporate veil. The subsidiary:

- Selected its own banks;
- Selected, trained, and supervised its own personnel;
- Set its own rates with the Federal Communications Commission;
- Prepared its own budget;
- Determined its own construction contracts;
- Prepared its own annual report;
- Had its own employee newsletter;
- Paid its own bills;

- Purchased its own property and equipment; and
- Developed its own sales and marketing procedures.[18]

The court in *Miles* also found that:

- The parent and subsidiary were distinct and adequately capitalized financial units;
- Daily operations of the two corporations were separate with formal barriers between the management of the two corporations; and
- Those dealing with the corporations were apprised of their separate identities.[19]

In *Sabine Towing*, the court reached a different result. There, a suit was filed against the parent corporation for breach of shipping agreements. The factors considered by the court in reaching its decision to pierce the corporate veil were:

- Common stock ownership of the parent and subsidiary corporations existed.
- Parent and subsidiary corporations shared the same officers and directors making it impossible for the subsidiary board to act independently.
- The same corporate offices were used by both corporations.
- The subsidiary was inadequately capitalized.
- The subsidiary was financed by the parent whenever the subsidiary ran short of capital.
- The parent existed solely as a holding company with no independent active business of its own.
- The parent used the subsidiary's assets and property as its own.
- No formal documentation of loans between the parent and subsidiary existed.
- Subsidiary decisions were made by the parent.
- There were no records of meetings or other corporate records.
- Subsidiary assets were stripped by the parent to the benefit of the parent and the detriment of the subsidiary.[20]

For parent/subsidiary corporations, the criteria examined in *Miles* provide a better guide for appropriate behavior than the criteria described in *Sabine Towing*. Once again, common sense should point you in the right direction, but it is important that you begin good recordkeeping habits early.

Final Thoughts on Horror Stories

Attention to detail, common sense, good recordkeeping are three characteristics that will go a long way toward preserving your corporation and protecting your personal assets. As many of these cases illustrated, you can't escape personal liability if you don't treat your corporation as a separate legal entity. Don't use your corporation as your personal playground. Use common sense, maintain good records, and pay attention to detail.

Corporate Do's and Don'ts Checklist

Do:

☐ Maintain capital reserves sufficient to meet reasonably foreseeable needs of the corporation, including liability insurance coverage.

☐ Maintain an active and independent board of directors.

☐ If asked to serve on a board of directors, be active and use your best independent business judgment even if that requires you to disagree with management.

☐ Use business cards and letterhead which reflect the corporate name.

☐ Make certain that corporate letters and agreements are signed by the corporation.

☐ Distinguish preincorporation activities by a promoter from post-incorporation activities by officers or directors.

☐ Use formal loan documents, including notes and security agreements, for corporate loans, especially to officers and directors and be sure to have a board resolution authorizing the transaction.

☐ Use written leases, purchase and sale agreements, and bills of sale in transactions involving shareholders, officers, and directors and be sure to have a board resolution authorizing the transaction.

☐ Use separate offices for activities of separate businesses.

☐ Use separate telephone lines for each business.

☐ Use separate employees for each business.

☐ Allow each corporation to own its own assets or equipment or lease them pursuant to written lease agreements.

☐ Apply for all required permits, licenses, and identification numbers in the corporate name.

☐ Obtain necessary business insurance in the corporate name.

Don't:

☐ Commingle personal and corporate assets or assets among related corporations.

☐ Divert corporate assets for personal use.

☐ Engage in any act for an illegal or improper purpose such as to defraud creditors or oppress minority shareholders.

☐ Hold yourself out as the owner of the corporation; you may be a shareholder, officer, or director, but the corporation should be held out as the legal entity for the action.

☐ Engage in transactions between corporations and their shareholders, officers, and directors on any basis other than on an arm's length basis.

☐ If several corporations are involved, don't use the same people as officers and directors of each corporation.

Parent/Subsidiary/Successor Considerations

In addition to the do's and don'ts, parent/subsidiary or successor corporations should be sensitive to the following issues:

Parent/Subsidiary Corporations

To avoid liability by the parent, the subsidiary should be as independent as possible. Answer these questions.

Who makes decisions for the other? _____

Who finances the subsidiary? _____

Does the parent have its own active business or is it merely
a holding company for other businesses?　☐ Yes　☐ No

Who prepares the budget? _____

Is there an identity of officers and directors?　☐ Yes　☐ No

Is there common stock ownership?　　　　　　☐ Yes　☐ No

If a parent corporation controls the decision-making processes of the subsidiary; finances the subsidiary; prepares the subsidiary's budget; shares a complete or partial overlap of officers or directors; and engages in no active business of its own, the parent corporation is more likely to be responsible for the acts of the subsidiary.

Successor Employer or Corporation

If you can answer yes to the first three questions below, the successor corporation may retain liability for acts of its predecessor.

Is there continuity in the work force?　　　　☐ Yes　☐ No

Is there continuity in the management?　　　　☐ Yes　☐ No

Is there continuity in the stock ownership?　　☐ Yes　☐ No

What other items carry over? _____

Related Concepts

Chapter 12

Professional Corporations

When my children were younger, they often visited me at my law office. On several occasions, one or both of them would ask, "What does the P.C. stand for in Stubbs and Mann, P.C.?" Try as I might, I couldn't ever get them to believe that it stood for "pretty cool."

A lot of adults have asked me the same question. People notice the initials "P.C." or "P.A.", especially when they visit their doctor, dentist, or lawyer. These initials indicate that the particular professional they are visiting has incorporated his or her practice.

What Is a Professional Corporation?

Professional corporations are legal entities like any other corporation and are subject to most of the general business corporation laws of the state. They are formed, however, under the professional corporation law of the state. Professional corporations are formed to permit professionals to practice their professions within a corporate environment.

For many years, professionals, such as doctors, lawyers, dentists, accountants, architects and engineers, could not incorporate their businesses. Professional corporation statutes were enacted to enable professionals to enjoy the benefits of incorporation while preserving the personal liability between the professional and his or her client. Today, many of the tax advantages of incorporation have been reduced or eliminated lessening the demand for professional corporations.

How Professional Corporations Differ from Regular Corporations

Generally speaking, professional corporations differ from other corporations in the following ways:

- Professional corporations may engage in only one profession. If John Doe were a licensed architect and lawyer actively engaged in the practice of both professions, he would be required to form separate professional corporations for each profession, if he chose to incorporate his practice.

- A professional corporation must contain in its name a designation that it is a professional corporation, usually by adding the words, "Professional Corporation," "Professional Association," or the abbreviations "P.C." or "P.A."

- Only licensed members of the profession may be shareholders of the professional corporation.

- Professional corporation shareholders may not form a voting trust, though a stock purchase agreement is acceptable.

- Professional shareholders may vote by proxy but only if the holder of the proxy is also a shareholder in the professional corporation.

- Shares of stock in a professional corporation may only be transferred to another member of the same profession. In the event a shareholder dies, most statutes provide that a family member can hold the shares for a short period of time but then must sell them to the professional corporation or to a member of the same profession.

- Shareholders of a professional corporation remain personally liable to their clients. There is no limited liability for acts of professional malpractice. This is true for the negligent or wrongful acts or misconduct of the shareholder and those whose work product he or she supervises or controls.

  In some states, professional corporation shareholders remain jointly and severally liable for the negligent or wrongful acts or misconduct of the other shareholders in the corporation at least in so far as professional malpractice is concerned. For example, assume that John, Jane, and Joan are doctors, and that they have incorporated their medical practice under the name Doe, Doe and Doe, D.O., Inc. If John engages in malpractice, Jane and Joan would be jointly and severally liable with him. If John strikes a parked car as he travels in a corporation vehicle while performing corporation business, Jane and Joan would not be subject to liability.

- Professional corporations can be merged but only with a professional corporation formed to engage in the same professional service.

How Are Professional Corporations Similar?

Except for the areas described above, professional corporations are subject to the same legal requirements as other corporations and are obligated to have articles of incorporation, bylaws, shareholder agreements, director and shareholders meetings, recordkeeping, and registered offices and agents.

Like regular corporations, professional corporations enjoy limited liability to a certain extent. While personal liability remains for professional malpractice, limited liability exists for other claims. For example, if a supplier sues Doe, Doe and Doe, D.O., P.C. for an unpaid bill, only the corporation would be liable and not the individual shareholders. In the preceding example where John struck a parked car, the corporation and possibly John as the driver would have liability, not Jane and Joan.

Who Are Professionals?

The term "professionals" varies from state to state, but it includes lawyers, doctors and dentists and may include accountants, architects, engineers, and others. Check with the professional corporation statute in your state to see which professions are included.

Final Thoughts on Professional Corporations

Professional corporations are like regular corporations with a twist. Much of the general business corporation act is applicable to professional corporations and regular corporations alike. Distinctions are made principally in the areas described above.

If you are a professional considering incorporation under the professional corporation laws of your state, talk to your business lawyer or accountant. Tax law changes over the years have reduced or eliminated many of the tax incentives for incorporating. You should also contact your insurance agent. The premiums for malpractice insurance may vary depending upon whether or not your practice is incorporated.

Chapter 13

Not-for-Profit Corporations and Tax-Exempt Organizations

Just as there are statutes pertaining to business corporations and professional corporations, each state has laws which provide for not-for-profit corporations. This chapter will look briefly at these corporations and a related creature of the Internal Revenue Service known as the tax-exempt organization.

What Is a Not-for-Profit Corporation?

As its name implies, a not-for-profit corporation is a corporation formed under the nonprofit corporation laws of each state. A not-for-profit corporation may make money and many do. Most not-for-profit corporations are formed to promote a goal or purpose deemed socially beneficial. Often, they are formed for charitable, education, religious, or scientific purposes. Other permitted purposes include: civic leagues, labor unions, social clubs, business leagues, trade associations, chambers of commerce, credit unions, fraternal benefit societies, and teacher retirement funds. Net income or profits of not-for-profit corporations are used to promote these beneficial purposes and not to enrich individual members, officers, or directors.

Not-for-profit corporations are created under state law. Tax-exempt status is obtained from the Internal Revenue Service pursuant to federal law.

What Is a Tax-Exempt Organization?

A tax-exempt organization is an organization which has obtained an exemption from federal income tax from the Internal Revenue Service. A tax-exempt organization may or may not be incorporated; not all not-for-profit corporations are tax-exempt. They may not pay tax because they don't generate taxable income. Not-for-profit status is granted by state law, administered by the secretary of state. Tax-exempt status is granted by federal law and administered by the Internal Revenue Service.

Not-for-Profit Corporations Versus Regular Corporations

In many respects, the requirements for not-for-profits are the same as the requirements for regular corporations. Both must file articles of incorporation on forms approved by the secretary of state; retain a registered office and registered agent within the state; and are governed by the provisions of the statutes, articles, and bylaws. Like regular corporations, there is an opportunity for flexibility when forming a not-for-profit organization.

Not-for-profit corporations can and do make money. Profits should be used to promote not-for-profit goals and purposes. Upon dissolution, any remaining assets of a not-for-profit corporation after creditors are paid must be distributed to another not-for-profit corporation.

Not-for-profit corporations have members instead of shareholders. Unlike regular corporations, members are not required. A not-for-profit corporation must have a board, but the board of directors can be self-perpetuating. The articles of incorporation for a not-for-profit corporation will indicate whether or not the organization will have members, and if so, what classes of membership exist and what voting rights the members will have.

The articles will also indicate how the board is elected. If there are members, the board is usually elected by the membership in accordance with the articles and bylaws. If there are no members, the board of directors selects board members and fills vacancies.

Not-for-profit corporation income can't be distributed to its members, officers, or directors. Any income must be applied to the attainment of the not-for-profit purpose. Reasonable salaries can be paid to officers or employees in exchange for services provided. No other distributions or dividends are permitted.

Upon dissolution, any assets of the not-for-profit corporation remaining after the payment of bills and liabilities must be distributed to an organization pursuing similar not-for-profit objectives. Assets can't be distributed to individual members, officers, or directors. Also, if a not-for-profit seeks to merge with another corporation, the merging corporations must both be formed under the not-for-profit corporation laws and be pursuing the same not-for-profit purpose.

In some states, the state's attorney general has jurisdiction over not-for-profit organizations. In these states, not-for-profits must submit an annual report to the attorney general. As you have probably experienced, many not-for-profits serve as fronts for unscrupulous people seeking to enrich themselves at your expense. Annual reporting requirements are designed to help eliminate this problem.

What Is a 501(c)(3) Organization?

Perhaps the most common of tax-exempt organizations, a 501(c)(3) organization, is any organization organized and operated exclusively for religious, charitable, scientific, testing for public safety, literary or educational purposes or to foster national or international amateur sports competition or the prevention of cruelty to children or animals. As a general rule, contributions to 501(c)(3) organizations are tax-deductible, making the status highly desirable for not-for-profit organizations.

How Do You Attain 501(c)(3) Status?

To achieve 501(c)(3) status, you must first attain not-for-profit status under state law. Your articles of incorporation or organization must contain language limiting the purposes of the exempt organization, prohibiting the distribution of net income or earnings to individual members, officers or directors, and providing that upon dissolution, any remaining assets will be distributed to the government or another 501(c)(3) organization.

After you have formed your not-for-profit organization pursuant to state law, you are required to complete the *Application for Recognition of Exemption* on *Internal Revenue Service, Form 1023*. The application is a small booklet which requests information on such things as the activities of the organization, sources of financial support for the organization, whether or not the organization will have members and financial data. Take care when completing this form.

Once completed, submit the form to the Internal Revenue Service (IRS) for its review and comment. In most instances, you will receive a request for additional information or clarification from the IRS. When the IRS approves the application, it will issue a favorable determination letter. If the favorable determination letter is received within 15 months following the formation of the organization, all contributions received by the organization since formation are exempt from income tax by the organization and tax-deductible for the contributor. If more than 15 months have elapsed, the exempt/deductible status is measured from the date of the favorable determination letter.

There are organizational and operational requirements for 501(c)(3) organizations. From an organizational standpoint, the articles of incorporation or articles of organization for not-for-profit corporations or entities seeking this status must contain the limitations described above, and otherwise satisfy the requirements of the appropriate secretary of state.

From an operational standpoint, no part of the net earnings or profits of any exempt organization may be distributed to any individual member, officer or director. A tax-exempt organization can't pay a dividend or make a distribution of funds other than in furtherance of its exempt purpose. Reasonable salaries for services actually rendered are permitted.

Exempt organizations are also prohibited from lobbying as a substantial part of its activities and may not become involved in any political campaign for any office.

If your organization is exempt, it must submit annual reports to the IRS. These reports enable the IRS to monitor the organization's activities and compliance with operational requirements.

It would be beneficial to prepare a rough draft response to Form 1023. From the rough draft, your business lawyer can make any needed modifications to the form. The IRS is particular, and a business lawyer with tax-exempt organization experience can be helpful.

Are There Other Forms of Tax-Exempt Organizations?

There are a number of different forms of tax-exempt organizations, each of which has separate requirements. Presented below is a partial list of 501(c) organizations (exclusive of 501(c)(3)). If you need more information on these, talk to your business attorney or accountant. You may also wish to request the publication described below.

- Instrumentalities of the U.S. government;
- Corporations formed for the exclusive purpose of holding title to property and collecting the income therefrom, if it turns over the entire income less expenses to the exempt organization.
- Civic leagues to promote social welfare;
- Labor, agricultural, or horticultural organizations;
- Business leagues, chambers of commerce, real estate boards, boards of trade, professional sports leagues;
- Social clubs;
- Fraternal benefit societies;
- Voluntary employee benefit associations for the payment of life sickness, accident, or other benefits to association members or their dependents;
- Domestic fraternal societies;
- Teachers retirement funds;
- Benevolent or mutual associations for life insurance, telephone or mutual irrigation;
- Cemetery companies;
- Veterans organizations; or
- Group legal services plans.

Final Thoughts on Not-for-Profit and Tax-Exempt Organizations

Not-for-profit corporations, especially those seeking to become tax-exempt organizations, require special care. At first glance, they would seem to be uncomplicated. Don't interpret not-for-profit to mean "easily accomplished." Your local law library will probably have several volumes devoted to the complexities of tax-exempt organizations. While much of what you have read in this book applies to not-for-profit and tax-exempt organizations, these entities have separate legal and accounting issues which must be addressed.

Fortunately for you, the IRS publishes an informative booklet on tax-exempt organizations. If you would like more information, contact your local IRS office and ask for *Publication 557, Tax-Exempt Status for Your Organization*.

Chapter 14

Close Corporations

Close corporation statutes were first introduced in Chapter 1. Close corporations are a specialized form of corporation, reflecting a modern trend to make law conform to the realities of the marketplace.

What Is a Close Corporation?

A close corporation is a corporation formed pursuant to a close corporation statute. Not all states allow the formation of close corporations. To be a close corporation:

- The state statute must specifically permit one.
- The articles of incorporation must expressly state the corporation's election to be treated as a close corporation.
- The corporation must have no more than 50 shareholders.

Close corporation status is best suited for a business with a small number of shareholders, each of whom is actively involved in the day-to-day business of the corporation. Here, the shareholders could easily function without directors' or formal meetings because of their intimate involvement with corporate activities.

Close Corporation Status Advantages

Close corporations eliminate the need for a lot of the formality often associated with corporations. For example, close corporations can eliminate the board of directors and restrict the ability of shareholders to transfer their shares. Rather than eliminate the board, close corporations can limit the boards' authority and authorize the use of proxies for directors.

Even if your corporation has elected close corporation status, it is a good idea to maintain corporate formality, at least to the extent of using consent resolutions or shareholder meetings. These activities provide a record of what has been done, and who is authorized to perform which acts on behalf of the corporation. This record could be useful in dealing with the IRS and other auditors.

Close Corporation Acts Disadvantages

If a close corporation eliminates or reduces the power of the board, shareholders assume the responsibilities and duties of the board. These responsibilities and duties are described in Chapter 4 and include the duties of ordinary care, good faith, and loyalty to the corporation. Shareholders ordinarily don't owe these duties to the corporation.

Because a close corporation can have up to 50 shareholders, care must be taken if S corporation status is desired. S corporations can have no more than 75 shareholders.

Close corporation statutes do not exist in every state. As a result, questions may arise when a close corporation from one state seeks to qualify to do business in a state without a close corporation statute. This should not be a significant problem, but you may wish to discuss it with the appropriate secretary of state's office prior to filing your application for certificate of authority.

Are Close Corporation Shareholders More Apt to be Personally Liable for Corporate Acts?

The mere fact that a corporation has elected close corporation status should not increase a shareholder's risk of personal liability or the possibility that the corporation's veil will be pierced. Close corporation statutes provide that the failure of the close corporation to observe the usual corporate formalities or requirements relating to the exercise of its corporate powers or the management of its business and affairs is not a basis, by itself, for imposing personal liability on shareholders. While this provision may excuse the need for directors and possibly shareholder meetings, it would not excuse inadequate capitalization of the corporation or operating it for wrongful purposes.

What is the Difference Between a Close Corporation and a Closely Held Corporation?

A closely held corporation's shares are not publicly traded on any stock exchange. Generally, a closely held corporation has a small number of shareholders, although there is no limit on the number.

A close corporation is one which is formed pursuant to a close corporation statute. Close corporations require a statute permitting their formation; not all states have close corporation statutes. The decision to be a close corporation must be stated in the articles of incorporation. A close corporation can have no more than 50 shareholders. While most corporations are closely held, not all closely held corporations are close corporations.

Can Close Corporations Restrict Transfer of their Stock?

A close corporation may choose to restrict the transfer of its shares by its shareholders. Although absolute restrictions are prohibited, the corporation can require that the corporation and the remaining shareholders be granted a right of first refusal in the event of a proposed sale. To protect this right, the certificate should contain the following language:

"The rights of shareholders in a statutory close corporation may differ materially from the rights of shareholders in other corporations. Copies of the articles of incorporation and bylaws, shareholder agreements, and other documents which may restrict transfers and affect voting rights, may be obtained by a shareholder on written request to the corporation."

Final Thoughts on Close Corporations

For many corporations, the same individuals serve as shareholders, officers, and directors. These individuals work side by side, day in and day out. Close corporation statutes reflect this business reality. Why require formal meetings when the principal owners are, in effect, meeting every day?

Corporation statutes have evolved over the years. From very restrictive beginnings, today's business corporation statutes have been liberalized. Close corporation statutes reflect another link in the evolutionary chain.

Chapter 15

Limited Liability Companies

Limited liability companies (LLCs) seek to provide the best of several worlds — the limited liability of corporations, partnership-type taxation, and the opportunity for their members to participate in management. Currently, all 50 states and the District of Columbia have adopted some form of LLC legislation.

However, just because nearly all states have adopted LLC legislation does not mean that their laws are uniform. Always verify your state's specific LLC laws and the laws of states in which you plan to do business. For more state-specific information regarding limited liability companies, consult your state's edition of The Oasis Press' *SmartStart Your Business* series, or The Oasis Press' comprehensive guide to LLCs, *The Essential Limited Liability Company Handbook*.

IRS Requirements for LLC Taxation Benefits

While an LLC is neither a corporation nor a partnership, recent legislation passed by Congress in 1997 establishes the LLC with more than one member as a partnership for tax purposes. Not all states have amended state laws to permit LLCs with fewer than two members. The limited liability company's income is taxed at the members' individual tax rate, rather than at the entity level, eliminating the double taxation of profits that occurs with a C corporation.

In the past, the IRS indicated its intent to tax certain LLCs as corporations. To avoid corporate classification, your LLC was required to avoid at least two of the following three corporate characteristics.

As a hybrid entity combining the benefits of both partnerships and corporations, your LLC must embrace certain corporate characteristics and reject others. The IRS requirements to be taxed as a partnership are among the most important an LLC must fulfill.

- Continuity of Life — Many state LLC acts require that the life of the LLC not exceed 30 years. In order to avoid corporation status, your LLC must have a limited life span.

- Centralization of Management — To have your LLC avoid characterization as a corporation, you should not identify a manager. Rather, you must demonstrate that the company is managed by the members, much as a general partnership is managed by the partners. In addition, you want to avoid the appearance that the company is managed by representation because this is a corporate characteristic.

- Free Transferability of Interests — Most state LLC acts do not allow the free transferability of interests. An LLC member can assign the right to share in profits to an outside person, but not the right to participate in management without the written consent of all the LLC members.

The one corporate characteristic the LLC is designed to keep is limited liability. Most state LLC acts include specific wording that the members of the company cannot be made parties to a lawsuit against the company. Without limited liability, your company is nothing more than a general partnership.

Recently, the IRS indicated its willingness to allow LLCs to designate whether the LLC intended to be taxed as a corporation or a partnership by checking a box. See Treas. Reg. § 301.7701-3. This should greatly simplify planning.

In addition to LLCs, many states have allowed the creation of limited liability partnerships or LLPs. An LLP is akin to a general partnership, open only to designated professionals such as physicians, lawyers, or accountants and used to provide limits on the liability of non-negligent partners. Check the laws in your state to see if an LLP is an option for you.

Other LLC Characteristics

Limited liability companies operate in a manner similar to close corporations. Instead of filing articles of incorporation, a limited liability company files articles of organization. Similarly, limited liability companies use operating agreements instead of bylaws, members rather than shareholders, and managers instead of officers and directors.

Limited liability companies are formed in much the same way as corporations. Statutes detail powers of the limited liability company, mandate the need for registered agents and offices, provide recordkeeping requirements, and require the filing of annual reports.

Unless the articles of organization provide otherwise, management of a limited liability company is vested in the members in accordance with their ownership interests. The articles of organization or operating agreement can vary this requirement in much the same way as articles of incorporation and bylaws can require unanimous or super majority voting requirements. Just as business corporation acts provide opportunity for flexibility, limited liability company laws do the same.

Final Thoughts on Limited Liability Companies

In the past, limited liability was permitted for corporate shareholders and limited partners, groups whose control over the business was indirect at best. Limited liability companies take the evolutionary process one step further — permitting limited liability while at the same time allowing members to participate in control and management.

Limited liability spurs investment. You're more apt to invest your money in an enterprise if you feel secure that your risk is limited to the money you invest. In addition, many non-U.S. businesses recognize the benefits of limited liability companies and may be more inclined to invest in U.S. limited liability companies now that they are recognized in all states plus the District of Columbia. Foreign investment can be a tremendous boon to the growth of your company. With an LLC, you can enjoy limited liability and foreign investment without having to give up direct control of your business, as you might if your business is a corporation.

For years, commentators have suggested that LLCs would become the entity of choice, replacing corporations and partnerships. While that may eventually prove true, current growth and popularity of the LLC remains somewhat limited because little legal precedent for it exists and LLC laws from state to state lack uniformity. In addition, many tax practitioners continue to recommend S corporations over LLCs. A principal reason for this is the possibility for a taxpayer to shield income from self-employment tax by using S corporations dividends. This is a complicated area best left to your tax advisor.

As business owners approach the twenty-first century, these issues will certainly be resolved. When they are, LLCs may replace corporations and partnerships as the entity of choice.

LLCs versus S Corporations

The entity which compares most favorably with an LLC is the S corporation, described in more detail on pages 84 to 86. While both S corporations and LLCs provide limited liability and partnership-like taxation, they do differ in significant ways, as shown in this table. The two entities have other important differences in addition to the ones shown here, and legislation that makes S corporations more attractive to investors was passed by Congress in 1996. You should work closely with your tax advisor in choosing any entity for the conduct of your business.

	S Corporation	LLC
Number of Owners	No more than 75. All shareholders must consent to the election.	No maximum limit. Some states still require at least two members to form.
Nature of Owners	Individuals, U.S. citizens and resident aliens, decedent's estates, bankruptcy estates, and certain trusts, charitable organizations, and certain qualified plan trusts.	All S corporation eligible owners plus corporations, limited or general partnerships, most trusts, nonresident aliens, and pension plans.
Nature of Ownership	Single class of stock.	Different classes and priorities of ownership permitted.
Tax Differences	Shareholders' basis in stock not increased by proportionate share of corporation liabilities. Distribution of appreciated assets by S corporation to shareholders results in realization of gain on distribution. Dividends may not be subject to self-employment tax (consult your tax advisor).	LLC member has basis increase by proportionate share of corporation liabilities. Generally, no current taxable recognition of gain at time of distribution. Earnings may be subject to self-employment tax.

Chapter 16

Using Your Professional Team

Throughout *The Essential Corporation Handbook*, references have been made to your business lawyer, accountant, and insurance agent. These individuals are important to you and your business. To be most effective, you should consider them as your professional team.

Most businesses use lawyers, accountants, and insurance agents; however, surprisingly enough, many business owners never bring these professionals together to work as a team. This is a mistake. Today's business world is complex, and it is rare to find one individual who can handle your legal, accounting, and insurance needs. By bringing these experts together, you have a broader range of experience and ideas to work with, and you can avoid the increased time and expense resulting from duplication of efforts.

What appears in this chapter is one lawyer's approach as to how you can use your business lawyer most effectively. Although written from a lawyer's perspective, this chapter is just as relevant to help you use your accountant and insurance agent.

Here are guidelines to help you select and work with your professional advisers:

Select Good Professionals

A checklist at the end of this chapter provides guidance in selecting a business lawyer. For the most part, substitute the words "accountant" or "insurance agent" for the word "lawyer," and the chart will work just as well for the other professions.

Developing good working relationships with a business lawyer, an accountant, and an insurance agent will save you time and money in the long run.

You need to find experienced professionals who work regularly with business clients. Although direct hands on experience within the same industry as your business is desirable, general business experience is probably sufficient. Word of mouth referrals work best. Talk with others in your industry or community. Contact your accountant to recommend a lawyer or insurance agent and vice versa.

You also need to find a professional who has the time and desire to attend to your business. Many lawyers are good at attracting clients, but the same lawyer may be too busy to adequately service your needs.

Start Early

Too often, you don't contact your professional advisers until a problem has arisen. It's not until you are sued or receive a notice from the Internal Revenue Service that you call your professional. This puts you in a defensive posture, circling your wagons to minimize the damage.

When you start your business, schedule a meeting with your professional team. Tell them what you would like to do, and how you would like to do it. Ask them for their suggestions and ideas to help you fine tune your plan and avoid unknown pitfalls and traps. At this session, you can delegate tasks among your professionals and determine costs.

Getting started on the right foot may cost a little more at the outset, but it will save you time and money in the long run. You may also find that your professional team is willing to discount its usual charges for this type of session in order to get your business.

Learn What You Can Do In-House

Professionals can provide many services; however, you can do some of these services yourself. Talk with your professional team about the types of things you can do in-house and ask your team to instruct your employees so that they can perform the service. For example, lawyers can assist businesses in developing contract and agreement forms; instruct businesses on how to obtain a security interest in goods sold; and set up correct collection practices. If questions come up during these activities, call the professional for advice. By and large, however, you will be able to handle these tasks using your own employees.

Keep Your Professionals Up to Date

Your professionals can't function as a team if they don't know what you're doing. Plan at least one meeting during the year with your team. This meeting could be held in conjunction with an annual shareholders' meeting.

Use the meeting to tell your professionals what the business has done since the last meeting and what you anticipate the business will do over the next year. Include in the discussion financial results and projections, hiring needs, retirement ideas, personnel matters, equipment or real estate needs, and just about anything else that impacts the business. In exchange, your professionals can point out legal or tax issues which could affect your plans.

Don't be alarmed if your professional team members don't always agree. More often than not, you will have to make a decision based upon a range of choices. Your team should tell you what your choices are and the pros and cons of each. Your accountant may feel that a particular choice has greater risk associated with it than your attorney. Ultimately, you must weigh the choices, balance the risks, and make the choice. Your professionals should feel free to challenge one another in a cooperative working environment.

When you meet with your team, spend time talking with them about how to use the team most effectively. Look for new ways to bring professional services in-house. Ask professionals which correspondence or documents they would like to receive for their files. Talk with your professionals about how to reduce professional fees, if possible.

Most importantly, use the session to talk about what you like and don't like about the professional services which you have received. Many smaller businesses find their work being done by a constantly changing mix of lawyers. No business client enjoys being shuffled around. If you're dissatisfied, say so. Like everyone else, professionals want to know if you're unhappy with their service; don't forget to praise your professional when appropriate.

Bring Several Matters Up at One Time

Lawyers and accountants often bill by the hour. Hourly segments are broken down into 6-, 10-, or 15-minute segments depending upon the firm's billing practice. It is often more cost effective for you to make one call on Friday and ask three or four questions than it is to make three or four separate phone calls to ask the same questions.

If it can wait, let it wait until some other matter arises. Don't get carried away with saving fees, however. If the matter is serious or appears to be, make the call.

Ask Questions

Business lawyers spend time immersed in business law matters for many clients. One consequence of this is that the lawyer may take certain things for granted. There is no such thing as a stupid question. If you don't know the answer, ask the question (several at a time, if possible). If you don't understand the answer, that's the professional's problem, not yours. Tell the professional that you still don't understand.

You want to focus your time and energy running your business. You need to understand the legal, accounting, tax, and insurance issues which impact on your business. Ask away.

Question Billing Statements

Clients are often shocked when they get a bill. This generally results from poor communication between professional and client. Know up front how you will be charged. Ask for estimates for projects which you assign to your professionals. If something looks out of line on your bill, ask about it. Mistakes are made. In addition, many professionals will reduce a bill to preserve the relationship with a client. From the professional's perspective, don't nickel and dime every bill. Your professional may fire you.

Remember You Are Important to Your Professional

To the professional, you are a source of income. If the professional serves you well, you are a referral for additional business clients. You also provide the challenge and variety that makes his or her job interesting. Your professional team wants to serve you and your business. Don't let poor communication get in the way.

Final Thoughts on Using Your Professional Team

You will need a business lawyer, accountant, and insurance agent. Too many businesses utilize these experts without allowing them the opportunity to work with you as a team. Each professional brings different skills and perspectives to the table. By bringing your professionals together, you will become better informed and make better decisions for your business.

Checklist for Selecting a Business Lawyer

Use this checklist as a guide to help select a lawyer to be a part of your business team. You can modify the questions to select an accountant or insurance agent as well.

How many years has the lawyer been engaged in practice? _____

Is the lawyer licensed to practice law in your jurisdiction?   ☐ Yes ☐ No

What percentage of time does the lawyer spend in business related matters, including:

Business planning	_____%
Estate planning	_____%
Corporate maintenance	_____%
Personnel and labor matters	_____%
Securities law	_____%
Contract law	_____%
Real estate	_____%
Buying and selling businesses	_____%
Employee benefits	_____%
Tax matters	_____%
Litigation	_____%
Franchise	_____%
Loan documentation	_____%
Bankruptcy	_____%

If the lawyer does not spend significant time in each of these areas, are there other lawyers in the law firm who do?   ☐ Yes ☐ No

Who is your primary lawyer contact? _____

Who will actually do your work? _____

What other lawyers will be involved with your corporation? _____

What is the Martindale-Hubbel rating* of the primary lawyer? _____

What is the Martindale-Hubbel rating of the law firm? _____

How does the firm charge for its services?
☐ Hourly rate? What is it? _____
☐ Project fee?
☐ Contingency fee? What percentage? _____%
☐ Monthly retainer? What is it?

How often does the law firm bill?
☐ Weekly   ☐ Biweekly   ☐ Monthly   ☐ Completion of project   ☐ Other

*Martindale-Hubbel is a national directory of lawyers published by Martindale-Hubbel, Inc. Most lawyers are rated by other practitioners within their geographic area. Ratings range from "cv," "bv," to "av," with "av" being the highest rating. The directory can be found at most city or county law libraries.

Checklist for Selecting a Business Lawyer (continued)

Does the law firm provide estimates of its:

Total fee	☐ Yes	☐ No
Other expenses	☐ Yes	☐ No
Time required	☐ Yes	☐ No
Time of completion	☐ Yes	☐ No

Will the law firm provide business client references? ☐ Yes ☐ No
From the references:

Are they satisfied with the legal service provided?	☐ Yes	☐ No
Is service prompt?	☐ Yes	☐ No
Is billing reasonable	☐ Yes	☐ No
Are estimates accurate?	☐ Yes	☐ No

Who does the work? _____

Other pluses? _____

Other negatives? _____

Will the law firm provide an accountant reference? ☐ Yes ☐ No
From this reference:

Is the law firm easy to work with?	☐ Yes	☐ No
Is the firm competent?	☐ Yes	☐ No
Does the firm respond promptly to requests?	☐ Yes	☐ No

Will the law firm provide an insurance agent reference? ☐ Yes ☐ No
From the reference:

Is the law firm competent?	☐ Yes	☐ No
Does the lawyer understand insurance related issues?	☐ Yes	☐ No

What does the law firm charge for annual maintenance work? _____
(This would include meeting notices, conduct of annual meeting, serving as registered office and agent, and partial completion of required annual report.)

Does the law firm provide periodic updates, newsletters
or other forms of communication about law changes? ☐ Yes ☐ No
Does the law firm charge for this periodic update? ☐ Yes ☐ No

What are the law firm's office hours? _____

Are there any possible conflicts of interest? ☐ Yes ☐ No
If yes, indicate any such conflicts. _____
(This would occur if the firm represented a competitor, major supplier or customer.)

Conclusion

After reading *The Essential Corporation Handbook*, you hopefully have gained some general insight concerning corporate formality and why it is important for your corporation's success. If you come away with a better understanding of the issues discussed in this book, you have made good use of your time. Don't feel you need to memorize all of the specifics, simply use the book as a handy reference tool for future questions or situations.

To help you recall some of the book's important points, a brief "Tip List" is provided below for your review.

- Remember that corporations are distinct legal entities with specific rights, duties, and obligations. If you ignore this fact, you increase your chance of personal liability for corporate acts. Respect the separate identity of your corporation in all aspects of your business.

- Corporations are not rigid entities. On the contrary, they can offer you many opportunities for flexibility through bylaws, articles of incorporation, and shareholder agreements. Make a corporation fit your needs and goals. There is no single model to follow, and what works for you might not work for someone else. Know the range of choices you have and be creative; use this flexibility.

- Develop good habits for your corporation. Observe required corporate formalities and maintain records of corporate activity. Once you've established your routine for maintaining good records, the rest should be easy.

- Choose and use your professional team wisely. Develop good working relationships with your lawyer, accountant, and insurance agent to make the best use of their time and learn what you can do in-house. Work together for the good of your corporation.

- Determine what works best for your corporation by reviewing the book's sample documents, checklists, and forms.

- The business environment is changing. Close corporation statutes and limited liability company laws are two examples of such change. By reading trade journals and utilizing your professional advisers, stay abreast of the changes that may have an impact on your corporation.

- Because business corporation laws vary from state to state, talk with your business lawyer, accountant, and secretary of state before you undertake any action.

If there are other areas which you feel should be covered in later editions of *The Essential Corporation Handbook*, please forward your suggestions, comments, and ideas to: The Oasis Press, Editorial Department, 300 North Valley Drive, Grants Pass, Oregon 97526.

Footnotes

Chapter 1

1. REV. MODEL BUSINESS CORP. ACT (1984).

2. The Model Act has been adopted, in substantial part, in the following states: Arkansas, Florida, Georgia, Indiana, Iowa, Kentucky, Mississippi, North Carolina, Oregon, South Carolina, Tennessee, Virginia, Washington, Wisconsin, and Wyoming.

3. REV. MODEL BUSINESS CORP. ACT. § 1.20 (1984).

4. Id. § 1.23.

5. Id. § 1.29.

6. Id. § 2.02.

7. Id. § 2.06.

8. Id. § 3.01.

9. Id. § 3.02.

10. Id. § 4.01.

11. Id. § 4.02.

12. Id. § 5.01.

13. Id. § 11.02.

14. Id. § 11.07.

15. Id. § 11.05.

16. Id. § 11.04.

17. Id. § 12.01.

18. Id. § 12.02.

19. Id. § 14.02.

20. Id. § 14.03.

21. Id. § 14.05.

22. Id. § 14.06.

23. Id. § 14.07.

24. Id.

25. Id. § 13.01.

26. Id. § 13.02.

27. Id. § 13.20.

28. Id. § 13.28.

29. Id. § 13.30.

30. Id. § 16.01.

31. Id. § 16.20.

32. Id.

33. Id. § 16.21.

34. Id. § 16.02.

35. Id. § 15.01.

36. *National Bellas Hess, Inc. v. Department of Revenue*, 386 U.S. 753, 18 L.Ed.2d 505, 87 S.Ct. 1389 (1967).

37. *DM News*, August 5, 1991, at 1, col. 1.

38. Rev. Model Business Corp. Act § 15.03 (1984).

39. A number of states have adopted close corporation statutes, patterned largely after the Model Statutory Close Corporation Supplement. The Supplement relates to the Model Business Corporation Act adopted by the American Bar Association's Section on Corporation, Banking and Business Law in the 1940's but substantially revised in 1969.

40. Model Stat. Close Corp. Supp. § 3. For additional information concerning corporations, visit your local city or county law library. You will find much more information that is easy to understand and use. You may also wish to look at a multi-volume treatise on corporations. Ask for W. Fletcher, Fletcher Cyclopedia of the Law of Corporations (1990 rev. ed.).

Chapter 2

1. Rev. Model Business Corp. Act § 2.02 (1984).

2. Id.

Chapter 4

1. No minimum age is set forth in the Revised Model Business Corporation Act. Most states have adopted 18 as the minimum age for an incorporator. See, for example, Or. Rev. Stat. § 60.044.

2. Rev. Model Business Corp. Act § 1.29 (1984).

3. Id. § 8.03.

4. Id. § 8.01.

5. Id. § 8.24.

6. Id. § 8.25.

7. See, e.g., Eisenberg, *The Duty of Care of Corporate Directors and Officers*, 51 U. Pa. L. Rev. 945 (1990).

8. Rev. Model Business Corp. Act § 8.31 (1984).

9. Annotation, *What Business Opportunities Are in "Line of Business" of Corporation for Purposes of Determining Whether a Corporate Opportunity Was Presented*, 77 A.L.R. 3d 961 (1977).

10. Kaufman, *Corporate Directorships: Liability Risks and Protective Techniques*, 15 Employee Relations L.J. 21 (1989).

11. Rev. Model Business Corp. Act § 8.40 (1984).

12. Rev. Model Business Corp. Act § 8.40 (1984).

13. Id. § 8.51.

14. Id.

Chapter 5

1. Rev. Model Business Corp. Act § 6.21 (1984).

2. Id. § 6.40.

3. Id. § 8.33.

4. Id.

5. 26 U.S.C. § 1244.

6. Id. § 1361 *et seq.*

7. Id.

8. The Securities Act of 1933, 15 U.S.C. §§ 77a–77aa; Securities Exchange Act of 1934, 15 U.S.C. §§ 78c–78jj. See also, L. D. Soderquist & A. A. Sommer, Jr., Understanding Corporate Law (PLI 1990).

9. 15 U.S.C. §§ 77b(1); 78c(a)(10).

10. 15 U.S.C. § 77c.

11. 15 U.S.C. § 77d.

Chapter 7

1. Rev. Model Business Corp. Act § 16.01 (1984).

2. Id. § 16.20.

3. Id. § 16.02.

Chapter 8

1. REV. MODEL BUSINESS CORP. ACT § 8.22 (1984).

2. Id. § 8.23.

3. Id. § 8.24.

4. Id. § 8.20.

5. Id. § 8.24.

6. Id. § 8.21.

Chapter 9

1. See, for example, REV. MODEL BUSINESS CORP. ACT ch. 7 (1984).

2. Id. § 7.01.

3. Id. § 7.05.

4. Id. § 7.06.

5. Id. § 7.07.

6. Id. § 7.20.

7. Id. § 7.25.

8. Id. § 7.21.

9. Id. § 7.22.

10. The extent of authority of an election inspector varies from state to state. See for example, *Gunzburg v. Gunzburg*, 108 Misc. 2d 896, 422, N.Y. Supp. 2d 577 (1979); *Williams v. Sterling Oil of Oklahoma, Inc.*, 273 A.2d 264 (Del. 1971); *Umatilla Water Users Ass'n v. Irvin*, 56 Or. 414, 108 P. 1016 (1910).

11. REV. MODEL BUSINESS CORP. ACT § 7.04 (1984).

Chapter 11

1. *Mull v. Colt,* 31 F.R.D. 154, 166 (S.D.N.Y. 1962); See also, Annotation, *Disregarding Corporate Existence*, 1 A.L.R. 610 (1919).

2. *Collet v. American National Stores, Inc.*, 708 S.W. 2d 273, 284 (Mo. App. 1986).

3. *Mull v. Colt*, 31 F.R.D. 154 (S.D.N.Y. 1962).

4. Id.

5. *Wallace v. Tulsa Yellow Cab Taxi & Baggage Co.*, 61 P.2d 645 (Ok. 1936).

6. Id.

7. *Geringer v. Wildhorse Ranch, Inc.*, 706 F. Supp. 1442 (D. Colo. 1988).

8. Id.

9. *Labadie Coal Col v. Black*, 672 F.2d 92 (D.C. Cir. 1982).

10. Id. at 97.

11. Id.

12. *United States v. Healthwise-Midtown Convalescent Hospital and Rehabilitation Center,* 511 F. Supp. 416 (C.D. Cal. 1981).

13. Id.

14. *Securities and Exchange Commission v. Elmas Trading Corp.*, 620 F. Supp. 231 (D. Nev. 1985).

15. Id.

16. *Miles v. American Telephone & Telegraph Company*, 703 F.2d 193 (5th Cir. 1983).

17. *Sabine Towing & Transportation Co., Inc. v. Merit Ventures, Inc.*, 575 F. Supp. 1442 (E.D. Tex. 1983).

18 *Miles* at 195.

19. Id.

20. *Sabine Towing & Transportation Co., Inc., v. Merit Ventures, Inc.*, 575 F. Supp. 1442 (E.D. Tex. 1983).

Glossary

Advisory Board of Directors. An advisory board of directors are individuals appointed to advise the elected board of directors. An advisory board is not bound by the duties imposed upon elected board members, and the corporation is not required to follow the recommendations of the advisory board.

Agent. An agent is anyone who is authorized to act on behalf of another. A corporation can only act through its agents; therefore, it is important to define what actions an agent is authorized to perform.

Arm's Length Relationship. An arm's length relationship is a term used to describe a type of business relationship a corporation should have with a close associate to avoid a conflict of interest. For example, when you negotiate with your banker or your supplier, any agreement which results will likely reflect market value and commercially reasonable terms and conditions. When you loan money to your son or daughter, you may be inclined to provide much more favorable terms and conditions. The first example would be considered to be an arm's length relationship, while the second example would not. When your corporation does business with or makes loans to corporate officers and directors, the relationship must be at arm's length to avoid conflicts of interest.

Articles of Incorporation. The articles of incorporation, along with the bylaws and corporate minutes, make up a corporation's charter documents and contain basic information about the corporation. Upon filing the articles with the secretary of state, the corporation comes into existence. Articles are a public record available for inspection by anyone. Commonly, articles will provide the name of the corporation; the number of shares which the corporation is authorized to issue; and the classification of those shares, if any; the name and address of the registered agent; and the name and address of the incorporator. Additional information is also permitted.

Basis. Basis, a tax and accounting term, is the measuring rod against which gain or loss is measured. With stock, basis is what you pay for stock or the fair market value of property you contribute in exchange for the stock.

Board of Directors. The board of directors are in charge of the general supervision and control of the corporation. They appoint officers, and they are elected by the shareholders of the corporation. Board members owe the corporation duties of ordinary care, good faith, and loyalty.

Business Corporation Act. A business corporation act is the collection of laws in each state which pertain to corporations. The Revised Model Business Corporation Act (RMBCA) is used throughout this book as an example of a business corporation act.

Bylaws. The bylaws are the rules and procedures which govern the corporation. Such things as director and shareholder meetings and procedures are described in the bylaws. In the event of a conflict between the articles of incorporation and the bylaws, the articles control. Bylaws can't be inconsistent with the business corporation act as well.

Certificate of Authority. The certificate of authority is a document issued by the secretary of state to a foreign corporation after approving its completed application to do business in the state.

Close Corporation. A close corporation has less than 50 shareholders and elects in its articles of incorporation to be treated as a close corporation. The state in which the close corporation is formed must have a close corporation statute. Close corporations can eliminate or limit the powers of the board of directors, and corporate formality requirements are relaxed.

Closely held Corporation. A closely held corporation is any corporation in which the stock is held by a relatively small group of people or entities. Stock of a closely held corporation is not publicly traded on any stock exchange.

Commingle. Commingling, as used in this book, is the sharing and pooling of personal and corporate assets. For example, rather than maintain separate corporate and personal bank accounts, you choose to use one account for personal and corporate purposes. This is considered commingling and an easy way to become personally liable for corporate acts.

Consent Resolution. A consent resolution is any resolution signed by all of the directors or shareholders, which authorizes a particular action. This act eliminates the need for face-to-face meetings of directors and shareholders.

Contract Creditors. Contract creditors are people or businesses which you owe money or property to because of a written or verbal contractual agreement. If you buy 30 widgets from Widget World, Widget World becomes a contract creditor.

Corporate Charter. See Articles of Incorporation.

Cumulative Voting. Cumulative voting is a voting right which, when applicable, is intended to preserve the voting strength of minority shareholders. For example, if John has 25 voting shares and there are three directors to be elected, John has 75 votes which he may allocate in any manner he chooses. In some states, cumulative voting exists unless the articles reject it. In other states, cumulative voting does not exist unless the articles permit it.

Dissenters' Rights. Dissenters' rights or shareholder appraisal rights are a mechanism designed to protect minority shareholders. Business corporation laws prescribe the procedures by which these rights may be exercised. If a corporation proposes to sell substantially all of its assets or merge with another corporation, minority shareholders may be able to force the corporation to purchase their shares.

Dissolution/Liquidation. Dissolution and liquidation are procedures by which a corporation concludes its activities and prepares to liquidate its assets for the purpose of paying bills and creditors, and if funds remain, make distributions to shareholders. Dissolution can be voluntary, initiated by the corporation, or involuntary, initiated by creditors. When in dissolution, activities of the corporation must be geared to winding up corporate business, not expanding it.

Dividend. A dividend is a distribution of cash or property by a corporation to a shareholder. Dividends are paid out of the corporation's net earnings and profits. If there are no earnings and profits, dividends cannot be paid. Generally, there is no right to have a dividend declared, and the board of directors can decide whether or not to declare a dividend. Certain classes of preferred stock may limit this discretion of the board.

Employment Agreement. An employment agreement is a contract between your corporation and an employee. These agreements can be written or verbal; although all employment agreements should be in writing. Employers are more likely to have employment agreements with key employees. The terms and conditions of an employment agreement should be consistent with statutes, articles, bylaws, and any existing shareholder agreements. Of particular concern to employers is the unintended employment agreement. For example, if your corporation uses a company policy manual, it could rise to the level of an employment agreement. Similarly, if you always require cause prior to terminating an employee, you will be precluded from terminating an employee without cause. These issues are beyond the scope of this book. For additional information on company policies, see *A Company Policy and Personnel Workbook* (The Oasis Press®, 1991), *Developing Company Policies* (The Oasis Press®, 1991), or contact your business attorney.

Fictitious Name. A fictitious name is the trade name under which businesses conduct business. For example, John Doe, Inc. may do business as Widget World. Widget World is a fictitious name. Most states require that businesses using a fictitious name register the name with the secretary of state. This reduces the risk of fraud upon creditors.

Foreign Corporation. A foreign corporation is a corporation formed outside of the state in which it does business. If John Doe, Inc. is formed in Oregon, it is a domestic corporation in Oregon. If it does business in any other state, it is a foreign corporation in that state. Any corporation which does business in another state is required to apply for a certificate of authority to do business in that state.

Incorporator. An incorporator is the person who signs the articles of incorporation. As a general rule, only one incorporator is required, and the incorporator must be at least 18 years of age. Incorporators may have personal liability for false statements contained in the articles of incorporation.

Indemnify. Indemnify means to reimburse or compensate. Many corporate directors and officers will require that they be reimbursed for all cost, expenses, and liability which they incur while acting on behalf of the corporation.

Limited Liability Company. Limited liability companies are intended to provide the limited liability of corporations and the pass-through taxation of partnerships.

Merger/Consolidation. A merger or consolidation occurs when two corporations combine their assets and operations into one corporation. In merger situations, one of the corporations will survive the merger, and it is referred to as the survivor. The other corporation is referred to as the disappearing corporation. The survivor assumes all of the assets and liabilities of the disappearing corporation.

Minutes. The corporate minutes reflect the written record of actions taken or authorized by the board of directors or shareholders. These written records are customarily stored in the corporate minute book.

Not-for-Profit Corporation. A not-for-profit corporation, sometimes referred to as a nonprofit corporation, generally exists for the purpose of carrying out some socially useful objective. Formed under the nonprofit corporation laws of a state, not all of these corporations are tax exempt. And, unlike the name implies, many not-for-profit corporations make money. The money, however, does not get distributed to members, officers, or directors. The money is used to further the socially useful purpose.

Officers. Officers are appointed by the board of directors and serve at the pleasure of the board. The bylaws usually prescribe the titles and duties of each office. Common officers are the president, secretary, and treasurer. Officers direct the daily operations of the corporation.

Par Value. Par value, an accounting term which is rapidly being discarded, is the face value assigned to shares of stock. For example, if shares have a par value of $1 per share, the shares must be sold for at least $1. They may be sold for more, and if so, the first $1 per share is allocated to the paid in capital account of the corporation. If the stock is no par, the board of directors retains the discretion to set a price for the shares and to allocate whatever portion of that price it chooses to the paid in capital account.

Piercing the Corporate Veil. Piercing the corporate veil is a legal theory sometimes used to impose personal liability on shareholders, officers, and directors for corporate acts. This theory permits a court to disregard the separate identity of the corporation.

Preemptive Rights. Preemptive rights, another device intended to protect shareholders, enable shareholders to retain their proportional share ownership. If John owns 10% of the issued and outstanding stock of John Doe, Inc., and if the corporation proposes to issue an additional 100 shares of its stock, John would have the preemptive right to acquire 10 shares of the new issue on the same terms and conditions as the corporation proposed to offer the shares to outsiders. Like cumulative voting, preemptive rights exist in some states unless the articles reject them. In other states, preemptive rights don't exist unless the articles permit them.

Professional Corporation. Professional corporations are formed under the professional corporation laws of the state and are limited to professionals, such as doctors, dentists, lawyers, architects, engineers, and accountants. Professional corporation statutes designate which professionals may incorporate under these statutes. Professional corporation shareholders remain personally liable to their clients for professional malpractice.

Promoter. A promoter, in a corporation context, is one who generates interest and activity in and on behalf of a corporation before its formation. A promoter is usually personally liable for all preincorporation activities.

Proxy. A proxy is a written authorization to vote on behalf of another. Shareholders often vote by proxy, permitting others to vote their shares. Except for close corporations, directors may never vote by proxy. Proxies are usually revocable, but they can be made irrevocable under certain circumstances.

Quorum. A quorum is usually at least half of the directors or the holders of at least half of a corporation's issued and outstanding stock. Before directors or shareholders can authorize any action, a quorum must be present. The bylaws prescribe quorum requirements.

Registered Agent. A registered agent is the person or entity designated in the articles of incorporation to receive service of process and other important notices from the state. A corporation must maintain a registered agent at all times or risk forfeiture of the corporate charter.

Registered Office. The registered office is the place where the registered agent can be found. It may be the corporate office, or it may be the office of the corporation's attorney.

Regulations. Regulations are administrative rules which have the force and effect of laws. Government agencies promulgate rules. If you don't comply, you are subject to the possibility of fines or revocation of the corporate charter.

Revised Model Business Corporation Act (RMBCA). The RMBCA is a model business corporation act which has been adopted in substantial part by a number of states. It is described in Chapter 1 and serves as a guideline to all states considering changes in their business corporation laws. The RMBCA was drafted by the Committee on Corporate Laws of the Corporation, Banking and Business Law Section of The American Bar Association.

Resolutions. A resolution is a formal statement of any decison which has been voted upon. When the board of directors or shareholders authorize a particular action, the authorization most often comes in the form of a corporate resolution. For example, a corporate resolution could read:

"Resolved, that this corporation establish a depositary account with the Slippery Slope Savings and Loan Company."

S Corporation. An S corporation is created under the Internal Revenue Code. A corporation may elect to be treated as an S corporation. Stringent rules exist with respect to how and when the election is made; the number and type of shareholders; and the means by which the election may be terminated. S corporations pay no income tax; rather, all items of income, gain, credit, and loss pass through to the shareholders in proportion to their shareholdings.

Securities. Securities can include notes, stock, treasury stock, preorganization subscriptions, voting trust certificates, partnership interests, investment contracts, and certificates of interest in oil, gas, or mineral rights. Both the offer and sale of securities are regulated by state and federal governments, and care must be taken to comply with applicable laws and regulations.

Shareholders/Stockholders. Shareholders, who own the issued stock of a corporation and are thus its owners, elect directors and vote on fundamental matters, e.g., merger, sale, dissolution. Shareholders do not own specific corporate property; they merely own an interest in the corporation. Some state statutes use the term "shareholder"; others refer to "stockholders."

Statutes. Statutes are laws passed by the the state legislature or U.S. Congress. Business corporation laws are statutes. Statutes often authorize an administrative agency to declare regulations which are used to supplement the statute. In the event of a conflict, statutes control over regulations.

Stock. Stock represents ownership in the corporation and is often evidenced by a stock certificate. Stock can be common or preferred, voting or nonvoting, convertible, redeemable, and so on. The articles of incorporation will determine the designations and classifications of stock.

Stock Purchase Agreement. A stock purchase agreement is an agreement between the shareholders and the corporation. It provides a mechanism to regulate the transfer and sale of corporate stock. Often, a stock purchase agreement will provide a right of first refusal in favor of the corporation or remaining shareholders in the event of a proposed sale of stock by a shareholder. A stock purchase agreement can also provide for a purchase upon the death, disability, retirement, discharge, resignation, or bankruptcy of a shareholder.

Subscription Agreement. A subscription agreement is an agreement between the corporation and a person or entity wishing to acquire stock in the corporation.

Subscription agreements are subject to state and local securities laws.

Tax-Exempt Organization. A tax-exempt organization is any organization which is determined by the Internal Revenue Service to be exempt from federal income taxation. The most common form of tax-exempt organizations are those which are formed pursuant to Internal Revenue Code, Section 501(c)(3), and organized and operated exclusively for religious, charitable, scientific, testing for public safety, literary or educational purposes or to foster national or international amateur sports competition or the prevention of cruelty to children or animals.

Tort. A tort is any act or failure to act (if there was a duty to act) which causes harm or damage. Examples of torts include assault, battery, fraud, misrepresentation, defamation, libel, slander, invasion of privacy, and negligence. If there is a claim against your corporation — other than a claim by the government — it will likely be based in contract or tort.

Voting or Pooling Agreement. A voting or pooling agreement is an agreement, preferably in writing, of two or more shareholders to vote their shares in a certain manner. The most common use of this agreement would be to pool voting strength for the election of directors.

Voting Trust. A voting trust is an agreement among the shareholders of the corporation. Under a voting trust, shareholders transfer their shares of stock to a trustee in exchange for voting trust certificates. The trustee votes the shares in the manner directed in the voting trust agreement. Voting trusts are often used to preserve control of the corporation.

Appendix

Secretaries of State and Corporation Divisions

Secretary of state offices and corporation divisions (or their equivalents) in your state can help you answer questions concerning incorporating. For your convenience, the appropriate office for your state is listed below. The phone numbers and addresses were current at the time of printing, but be aware that this information does change. If a change occurs, check the state government listings in your phone directory. Other helpful offices for obtaining general business information in your state include one-stop business assistance offices (if your state has one), Small Business Development Centers (SBDCs), and state economic development offices. Listings for these offices can also be found in your phone directory. Another helpful resource for listings and basic filing and tax information can be found in the *SmartStart Your Business* guides, an Oasis Press® series that includes a specific edition for each state. This helpful series can be found at your local bookstore or ordered through The Oasis Press® at 1-800-228-2275.

Alabama Secretary of State
Corporations Section
11 South Union Street, Room 207
P.O. Box 5616
Montgomery, AL 36103-5616
(334) 242-5324
http://www.alalinc.net/alsecst/

Alaska Department of Commerce &
 Economic Development
Division of Banking, Securities, and
 Corporations
State Office Building
P.O. Box 110807
Juneau, AK 99811-0807
(907) 465-2530
http://www.commerce.state.ak.us/bsc/bsc.htm

Arizona Corporation Commission
1300 West Washington
Phoenix, AZ 85007-2996
(602) 542-3026
(800) 345-5819 (in Arizona)
http://www.cc.state.az.us

Arkansas Secretary of State
256 State Capitol Building
Little Rock, AR 72201
(501) 682-1010
http://www.sosweb.state.ar.us

California Secretary of State
Corporate Division
1500 11th Street
Sacramento, CA 95814
(916) 657-5448
http://www.ss.ca.gov

Colorado Secretary of State
Corporations Office
1560 Broadway, Suite 200
Denver, CO 80203
(303) 894-2251
http://www.state.co.us/gov_dir/sos

Connecticut Secretary of State
Commercial Recording Division
30 Trinity Street
Hartford, CT 06106
(860) 509-6002
http://www.state.ct.us/sots

Delaware Secretary of State
Division of Corporations
401 Federal Street, Suite 4
P.O. Box 898
Dover, DE 19903
(302) 739-3073
http://www.state.de.us/corp

District of Columbia Department of
** Consumer and Regulatory Affairs**
Corporations Division
614 H Street, NW, Room 407
Washington, DC 20001
(202) 727-7278
http://www.dcra.org

Florida Department of State
Division of Corporations
409 East Gaines Street
P.O. Box 6327
Tallahassee, FL 32314
(904) 488-9000
http://www.dos.state.fl.us

Georgia Secretary of State
Corporations Division
2 Martin Luther King, Jr. Drive, SE
Atlanta, GA 30334
(404) 656-2817
http://www.sos.state.ga.us

Hawaii Department of Commerce and
** Consumer Affairs**
1010 Richards Street
P.O. Box 40
Honolulu, HI 96810
(808) 586-2727
http://www.hawaii.gov/dcca/dcca.html

Idaho Secretary of State
Corporations Division
700 West Jefferson
P.O. Box 83720
Boise, ID 83720-0080
(208) 334-2301
http://www.idsos.state.id.us

Illinois Secretary of State
Business Services
Howlett Building, Room 328
Springfield, IL 62756
(217) 782-7880
http://www.sos.state.il.us

Indiana Secretary of State
Corporations Division
302 West Washington Street, Room E-018
Indianapolis, IN 46204
(317) 232-6576
http://www.ai.org/sos

Iowa Secretary of State
Corporations Division
Hoover State Office Building, Second Floor
Des Moines, IA 50319
(515) 281-5204
http://www.sos.state.ia.us

Kansas Secretary of State
Corporations Division
Capitol Building, Second Floor
300 SW 10th Avenue
Topeka, KS 66612-1594
(785) 296-4564
http://www.state.ks.us/public/sos

Kentucky Secretary of State
Corporation Department
700 Capitol Avenue, Room 154
P.O. Box 718
Frankfort, KY 40602
(502) 564-2848
http://www.sos.state.ky.us

Louisiana Secretary of State
Corporations Division
3851 Essen Lane
P.O. Box 94125
Baton Rouge, LA 70804-9125
(504) 925-4704
http://www.sec.state.la.us

Maine State Department
Bureau of Corporations
State House Station #101
Augusta, ME 04333-0101
(207) 287-4195
http://www.state.me.us/sos/sos.htm

**Maryland State Department of
.Assessments and Taxation
Corporate Charter Division**
301 West Preston Street
Baltimore, MD 21201
(410) 767-1340
http://www.dat.state.md.us

**Massachusetts Secretary of State
Corporations Division**
One Ashburton Place
Boston, MA 02108
(617) 727-2850
http://www.state.ma.us/sec/cor/coridx.htm

**Michigan Department of Consumer and
 Industry Services
Corporation Division**
6546 Mercantile Way
P.O. Box 30054
Lansing, MI 48911
(517) 334-6302
http://www.cis.state.mi.us

Minnesota Secretary of State
180 State Office Building
100 Constitution Avenue
St. Paul, MN 55155-1299
(612) 296-2803
http://www.sos.state.mn.us

**Mississippi Secretary of State
Corporate Division**
P.O. Box 136
Jackson, MS 39205-1350
(601) 359-1633
(800) 256-3494 (Nationwide)
http://www.sos.state.ms.us

Missouri Secretary of State
600 West Main and 208
State Capitol
P.O. Box 778
Jefferson City, MO 65102-0778
(573) 751-4153
http://www.mos1.sos.state.mo.us

**Montana Secretary of State
Corporation Bureau**
State Capitol Building
P.O. Box 202801
Helena, MT 59620-2801
(406) 444-3665
http://www.state.mt.us/sos

Nebraska Secretary of State
State Capitol, Suite 2300
P.O. Box 94608
Lincoln, NE 68509-4608
(402) 471-4079
http://www.no1.org/home/sos

**Nevada Secretary of State
Corporate Division**
101 North Carson Street, Suite 3
Carson City, NV 89701-4786
(702) 687-5203
http://sos.state.nv.us

**New Hampshire Secretary of State
Corporate Division**
State House Annex, Third Floor
Concord, NH 03301-4989
(603) 271-3244
http://www.state.nh.us/sos

**New Jersey Department of State
Division of Commercial Recording**
820 Bear Tavern Road, Second Floor
P.O. Box 308
Trenton, NJ 08625-0308
(609) 530-6400
http://www.state.nj.us/state

**New Mexico Taxation and Revenue
 Department**
1100 South Francis Drive
P.O. Box 630
Santa Fe, NM 87504-0630
(505) 827-0700
http://www.state.nm.us/tax

**New York Department of State
Division of Corporations**
41 State Street
Albany, NY 12231-0001
(518) 473-2492
http://www.dos.state.ny.us

**North Carolina Secretary of State
Corporations Division**
300 North Salisbury Street
Raleigh, NC 27603-5909
(919) 733-4201
http://www.secstate.state.nc.us/secstate

North Dakota Secretary of State
Main Capitol Building
600 East Boulevard Avenue
Bismarck, ND 58505-0500
(701) 328-4284
http://www.state.nd.us/sec

Ohio Secretary of State
State Office Tower, 14th Floor
30 East Broad Street
Columbus, OH 43266-0418
(614) 466-3910
http://www.state.oh.us/sos

Oklahoma Secretary of State
101 State Capitol
2300 North Lincoln Boulevard, Room 101
Oklahoma City, OK 73105-4897
(405) 521-3911
http://www.state.ok.us/~sos/main.htm

Oregon Secretary of State
Corporation Division
255 Capitol Street, NE, Suite 151
Salem, OR 97310-1327
(503) 986-2200
http://www.sos.state.or.us

Pennsylvania Department of State
Corporation Bureau
P.O. Box 8722
Harrisburg, PA 17105-8722
(717) 787-1057
http://www.dos.state.pa.us

Rhode Island Secretary of State
Corporations Division
100 North Main Street
Providence, RI 02903
(401) 222-3040
http://www.state.ri.us/pg1.htm

South Carolina Secretary of State
Edgar Brown Building
P.O. Box 11350
Columbia, SC 29211
(803) 734-2489
http://www.leginfo.state.sc.us./secretary.html

South Dakota Secretary of State
Corporate Division
Capitol Building, Suite 204
500 East Capitol Avenue
Pierre, SD 57501-5070
(605) 773-4845
http://www.state.sd.us/state/executive/sos/sos.htm

Tennessee Secretary of State
Corporate Division
James K. Polk Building, Suite 1800
Nashville, TN 37243-0306
(615) 741-2286
http://www.state.tn.us/sos

Texas Secretary of State
Corporations Division
State Capitol, Room 1.94
1100 Congress
P.O. Box 12697
Austin, TX 78711-3697
(512) 463-5555
http://www.state.tx.us/agency/307.html

Utah Department of Commerce
Division of Corporations and
Commercial Code
160 East 300 South
P.O. Box 45802
Salt Lake City, UT 84145-0802
(801) 530-4849
http://www.commerce.state.ut.us

Vermont Secretary of State
Corporations Division
Heritage I Building
81 River Street
Montpelier, VT 05609-1101
(802) 828-2386
http://www.sec.state.vt.us

Virginia State Corporation Commission
Clerk's Office
Tyler Building, 1300 East Main Street
P.O. Box 1197
Richmond, VA 23218
(804) 371-9733
http://www.state.va.us/scc

Washington Secretary of State
Corporations Division
505 East Union, 2nd Floor
P.O. Box 40234
Olympia, WA 98504-0234
(360) 753-7115
http://www.wa.gov/sec

West Virginia Secretary of State
Corporations Division
1900 Kanawha Boulevard, East, Room 139W
Charleston, WV 25305-0770
(304) 558-8000
http://www.state.wv.us/sos

Wisconsin Secretary of State
Corporations Division
30 West Mittlin, 10th Floor
P.O. Box 7848
Madison, WI 53707-7848
(608) 266-3590
http://badger.state.wi.us/agencies/sos

Wyoming Secretary of State
Corporations Division
State Capitol Building
Cheyenne, WY 82002
(307) 777-5334
http://soswy.state.wy.us

Index

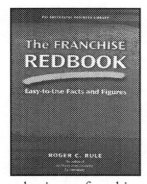

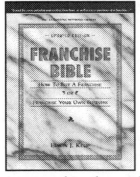

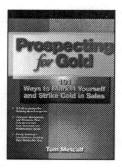

Moonlighting: Earn a Second Income at Home　　　　Pages: 240
Paperback: $15.95　　　　ISBN: 1-55571-406-4

It is projected that half of the homes in America are expected to house some type of business in the next few years. Moonlighting takes the idea of starting your own home-based business a step further. It will show you, in realistic and achievable steps, how you can initially pursue a business dream part-time, instead of quitting your job and being without a financial safety net. This confidence building guide will help motivate you by showing you the best steps toward setting your plan in motion.

Home Business Made Easy　　　　Pages: 233
Paperback: $19.95　　　　ISBN: 1-55571-428-5

An easy-to-follow guide to help you decide if starting a home-based business is right for you. Takes you on a tour of 153 home business options to start your decision process. Author David Hanania also advises potential business owners on the fiscal aspects of small startups, from financing sources to dealing with the IRS.

Which Business?　　　　Pages: 376
Paperback: $18.95　　　　ISBN: 1-55571-390-4

A compendium of real business opportunities, not just "hot" new ventures that often have limited earning potential. Which Business? will help you define your skills and interests by exploring your dreams and how you think about business. Learn from profiles of 24 business areas, reviewing how each got their start and problems and successes that they have experienced.

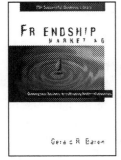

Friendship Marketing　　　　Pages: 187
Paperback: $18.95　　　　ISBN: 1-55571-399-8

If you have every wondered how to combine business success and personal signficance, author Gerald Baron has numerous practical suggestions. After years of working with executives and entrepreneurs, he's found that business success and personal meaning can share common ground. Using dozens of examples, he shows how building relationships is the key to business development and personal fulfillment.

CALL TO PLACE AN ORDER
— or —
TO RECEIVE A FREE CATALOG　**1-800-228-2275**

International Orders (541) 479-9464　　　*Fax Orders* (541) 476-1479
Web site http://www.psi-research.com　　*Email* sales@psi-research.com

PSI Research　P.O. Box 3727　Central Point, Oregon　97502　U.S.A.

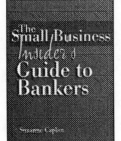

HOW TO ORDER

Mail: Send this completed order form and a check, money order or credit card information to:
PSI Research/The Oasis Press®, P.O. Box 3727, Central Point, Oregon 97502-0032

Fax: Available 24 hours a day, 7 days a week at **1-541-476-1479**

Email: info@psi-research.com (Please include a phone number, should we need to contact you.)

Web: Purchase any of our products online at our Website at **http://www.psi-research.com/oasis/**

Inquiries and International Orders: Please call **1-541-479-9464**

Indicate the quantity and price of the titles you would like:

TITLE	BINDER ISBN	PAPER ISBN	BINDER	PAPERBACK	QTY.	TOTAL
Advertising Without An Agency		1-55571-429-3		☐ 19.95		
Before You Go Into Business Read This		1-55571-481-1		☐ 17.95		
Bottom Line Basics	1-55571-329-7 (B)	1-55571-330-0 (P)	☐ 39.95	☐ 19.95		
BusinessBasics		1-55571-430-7		☐ 16.95		
The Business Environmental Handbook	1-55571-304-1 (B)	1-55571-163-4 (P)	☐ 39.95	☐ 19.95		
Business Owner's Guide to Accounting and Bookkeeping		1-55571-381-5		☐ 19.95		
businessplan.com		1-55571-455-2		☐ 19.95		
Buyer's Guide to Business Insurance	1-55571-310-6 (B)	1-55571-162-6 (P)	☐ 39.95	☐ 19.95		
California Corporation Formation Package		1-55571-464-1 (P)		☐ 29.95		
Collection Techniques for a Small Business	1-55571-312-2 (B)	1-55571-171-5 (P)	☐ 39.95	☐ 19.95		
College Entrepreneur Handbook		1-55571-503-6		☐ 16.95		
A Company Policy & Personnel Workbook	1-55571-364-5 (B)	1-55571-486-2 (P)	☐ 49.95	☐ 29.95		
Company Relocation Handbook	1-55571-091-3 (B)	1-55571-092-1 (P)	☐ 39.95	☐ 19.95		
CompControl	1-55571-356-4 (B)	1-55571-355-6 (P)	☐ 39.95	☐ 19.95		
Complete Book of Business Forms		1-55571-107-3		☐ 19.95		
Connecting Online		1-55571-403-X		☐ 21.95		
Customer Engineering	1-55571-360-2 (B)	1-55571-359-9 (P)	☐ 39.95	☐ 19.95		
Delivering Legendary Customer Service		1-55571-520-6 (P)		☐ 14.95		
Develop and Market Your Creative Ideas		1-55571-383-1		☐ 15.95		
Developing International Markets		1-55571-433-1		☐ 19.95		
Doing Business in Russia		1-55571-375-0		☐ 19.95		
Draw the Line		1-55571-370-X		☐ 17.95		
The Essential Corporation Handbook		1-55571-342-4		☐ 21.95		
Essential Limited Liability Company Handbook	1-55571-362-9 (B)	1-55571-361-0 (P)	☐ 39.95	☐ 21.95		
Export Now	1-55571-192-8 (B)	1-55571-167-7 (P)	☐ 39.95	☐ 24.95		
Financial Decisionmaking		1-55571-435-8		☐ 19.95		
Financial Management Techniques	1-55571-116-2 (B)	1-55571-124-3 (P)	☐ 39.95	☐ 19.95		
Financing Your Small Business		1-55571-160-X		☐ 19.95		
Franchise Bible	1-55571-366-1 (B)	1-55571-526-5 (P)	☐ 39.95	☐ 27.95		
The Franchise Redbook		1-55571-484-6		☐ 34.95		
Friendship Marketing		1-55571-399-8		☐ 18.95		
Funding High-Tech Ventures		1-55571-405-6		☐ 21.95		
Home Business Made Easy		1-55571-428-5		☐ 19.95		
Improving Staff Productivity		1-55571-456-0		☐ 16.95		
Information Breakthrough		1-55571-413-7		☐ 22.95		
Insider's Guide to Small Business Loans		1-55571-488-9		☐ 19.95		
Keeping Score: An Inside Look at Sports Marketing		1-55571-377-7		☐ 18.95		
Kick Ass Success		1-55571-518-4		☐ 18.95		
Know Your Market	1-55571-341-6 (B)	1-55571-333-5 (P)	☐ 39.95	☐ 19.95		
Leader's Guide: 15 Essential Skills		1-55571-434-X		☐ 19.95		
Legal Expense Defense	1-55571-349-1 (B)	1-55571-348-3 (P)	☐ 39.95	☐ 19.95		
A Legal Road Map for Consultants		1-55571-460-9		☐ 18.95		
Location, Location, Location		1-55571-376-9		☐ 19.95		
Mail Order Legal Guide	1-55571-193-6 (B)	1-55571-190-1 (P)	☐ 45.00	☐ 29.95		
Managing People: A Practical Guide		1-55571-380-7		☐ 21.95		
Marketing for the New Millennium		1-55571-432-3		☐ 19.95		
Marketing Mastery	1-55571-358-0 (B)	1-55571-357-2 (P)	☐ 39.95	☐ 19.95		
Money Connection	1-55571-352-1 (B)	1-55571-351-3 (P)	☐ 39.95	☐ 24.95		
Moonlighting: Earning a Second Income at Home		1-55571-406-4		☐ 15.95		
Navigating the Marketplace: Growth Strategies for Small Business		1-55571-458-7		☐ 21.95		
No Money Down Financing for Franchising		1-55571-462-5		☐ 19.95		
Not Another Meeting!		1-55571-480-3		☐ 17.95		
People-Centered Profit Strategies		1-55571-517-6		☐ 18.95		

Sub-total for this side:

TITLE		ISBN	BINDER	PAPERBACK	QTY.	TOTAL
People Investment	1-55571-187-1 (B)	1-55571-161-8 (P)	☐ 39.95	☐ 19.95		
Power Marketing for Small Business		1-55571-524-9 (P)		☐ 19.95		
Proposal Development	1-55571-067-0 (B)	1-55571-431-5 (P)	☐ 39.95	☐ 21.95		
Prospecting for Gold		1-55571-483-8		☐ 14.95		
Public Relations Marketing		1-55571-459-5		☐ 19.95		
Raising Capital	1-55571-306-8 (B)	1-55571-305-X (P)	☐ 39.95	☐ 19.95		
Renaissance 2000		1-55571-412-9		☐ 22.95		
Retail in Detail		1-55571-371-8		☐ 15.95		
The Rule Book of Business Plans for Startups		1-55571-519-2		☐ 18.95		
Secrets of High Ticket Selling		1-55571-436-6		☐ 19.95		
Secrets to Buying and Selling a Business		1-55571-489-7		☐ 24.95		
Secure Your Future		1-55571-335-1		☐ 19.95		
Selling Services		1-55571-461-7		☐ 14.95		
SmartStart Your (State) Business		varies per state		☐ 19.95		
Indicate which state you prefer:						
Small Business Insider's Guide to Bankers		1-55571-400-5		☐ 18.95		
Start Your Business		1-55571-485-4		☐ 10.95		
Strategic Insights		1-55571-505-2		☐ 19.95		
Strategic Management for Small and Growing Firms		1-55571-465-X		☐ 24.95		
Successful Network Marketing		1-55571-350-5		☐ 15.95		
Surviving Success		1-55571-446-3		☐ 19.95		
TargetSmart!		1-55571-384-X		☐ 19.95		
Top Tax Saving Ideas for Today's Small Business		1-55571-463-3		☐ 16.95		
Truth About Teams		1-55571-482-X		☐ 18.95		
Twenty-One Sales in a Sale		1-55571-448-X		☐ 19.95		
WebWise	1-55571-501-X (B)	1-55571-479-X (P)	☐ 29.95	☐ 19.95		
What's It Worth?		1-55571-504-4		☐ 22.95		
Which Business?		1-55571-390-4		☐ 18.95		
Write Your Own Business Contracts	1-55571-196-0 (B)	1-55571-487-0 (P)	☐ 39.95	☐ 24.95		

Success Series	ISBN		PAPERBACK	QTY.	TOTAL
50 Ways to Get Promoted	1-55571-506-0		☐ 10.95		
You Can't Go Wrong By Doing It Right	1-55571-490-0		☐ 14.95		

Oasis Software	FORMAT	BINDER		QTY.	TOTAL
Company Policy Text Files CD-ROM	CD-ROM ☐		☐ 49.95		
Company Policy Text Files Book & CD-ROM Package	CD-ROM ☐	☐ 89.95 (B)	☐ 69.95 (P)		
Winning Business Plans in Color CD-ROM	CD-ROM ☐		☐ 59.95		

Subtotal from other side	
Subtotal from this side	
▶ Shipping	
TOTAL	

Ordered by: *Please give street address*

NAME _____ TITLE _____

COMPANY _____

STREET ADDRESS _____

CITY _____ STATE _____ ZIP _____

DAYTIME PHONE _____ EMAIL _____

Ship to: *If different than above*

NAME _____ TITLE _____

COMPANY _____

STREET ADDRESS _____

CITY _____ STATE _____ ZIP _____

DAYTIME PHONE _____

Shipping:

YOUR ORDER IS:	ADD:
0-25	5.00
25.01-50	6.00
50.01-100	7.00
100.01-175	9.00
175.01-250	13.00
250.01-500	18.00
500.01+	4% of total

PLEASE CALL FOR RUSH SERVICE OPTIONS.
INTERNATIONAL ORDERS, PLEASE CALL FOR A QUOTE ON CURRENT SHIPPING RATES.

Payment Method:
☐ CHECK   ☐ MONEY ORDER
☐ AMERICAN EXPRESS   ☐ DISCOVER
☐ MASTERCARD   ☐ VISA

CREDIT CARD NUMBER

EXPIRATION (MM/YY)   NAME ON CARD (PLEASE PRINT)

SIGNATURE OF CARDHOLDER (REQUIRED)

Fax this order form to: (541) 476-1479 or mail it to: P.O. Box 3727, Central Point, Oregon 97502
For more information about our products or to order online, visit http://www.psi-research.com

OASIS PRESS BOOKS & SOFTWARE

04172000